WILD SPICE

WILD SPICE

120 EXOTIC RECIPES
from Around the World,
Blended to Perfection

ARUN KAPIL

STERLING EPICURE
New York

CONTENTS

INTRODUCTION

I've been around spices all my life. I love them. I love their vibrancy, their huge array of aromas and flavor notes, their provenance, history, cultivation, science; the lot. And I love to cook. Cooking is my dearest passion. I believe any dish can benefit from a touch of spice—just enough to bring out an accent, a nuance, not to cloud or smother. Spices add clarity encouraging tastes to sparkle on your palate. This is food alchemy; the best kind of science there is!

I'd like to show you how I blend and work with spices by introducing you to a new way of cooking with them from a purely flavor and taste perspective. This book's all about how to make the best use of spices in everyday cooking with a whole bunch of well laid-out recipes from snacks and main courses to sides, sauces, and sweet things. It sets out the basic building blocks of spice knowledge using fresh spices, freshly ground to most brilliant effect; a celebration of their natural colors, aromas and flavors.

As a child I was in and out of the kitchen, making rock buns with my Yorkshire Mum, Pam, and spicy dishes with my Dad, Gyan. Where most children had model planes, I had spices! When I moved to London I worked in restaurants to supplement my income in the music business before finally and more recently arriving in Ireland. I came to attend the Ballymaloe Cookery School, fell in love with the country and my beautiful wife, Olive. Nurtured by this generous nation I set up my spice company, Green Saffron, and began trading in whole spices direct with Indian farms, blending fresh flavors at my Irish base. I'm a spice specialist, and very much a home cook.

I create recipes based on my favorite foods, never limited by genre, region or country, simply focused on making delicious food. I've arranged the recipe chapters into food groups and at the beginning of each chapter I introduce the spices that work best with these foods. Some of the recipes may appear lengthy and a little daunting at first, but the instructions are set out in a step-by-step format. They explain exactly what to do, ensure the spotlight is on the spice and the focus clearly on flavor. So, get stuck in, have a go, enjoy your cooking and relish your food!

BUYING FRESH SPICES

Spices should be fresh, vibrant, and zinging with natural flavor. Capturing their essence in the food we eat has to start at the beginning, with the raw spice itself. So how do you know what to look for? We're bombarded with campaigns for organic this, free-range that, local, sustainable, fresh—but they're seldom applied to spices. They should be. Just as with wines, cheeses, coffee, teas, meat, fish, and vegetables, I like to know the provenance of the spices I use, how they're cultivated, and stored, because these things matter to the end product. Spices are parts of plants, and like fruit, vegetables, and grains they are harvested at certain times of year: black pepper in winter, coriander in spring, nutmeg and mace in summer. After harvesting, each spice then needs to be dried, and in some cases cured or matured, before it is ready for sale; this can take from two hours to six months, depending on the spice. In the past, spices took much longer to make their journey from the farm to our tables. Today, there's no reason why we shouldn't be able to buy "farm-fresh" spices—and at greensaffron.com, you can—there's certainly no excuse for dull, sad-looking spices that have been stored too long.

Demand the freshest, best-looking spices from the stores and suppliers you use. The easiest thing to do is simply to use your senses, checking for scent and vibrant color. Asian stores will probably have a good choice of fresh spices because they have a high turnover. When buying online, you may be able to ask more questions about the provenance of your spices; after that, it's a matter of finding a supplier that you trust.

Once you're happy you've hunted down the best, stick to buying spices "little and often," as you need them, instead of a bulk buy that ends up unused at the back of the cupboard. Store spices in airtight containers in a cool, dark place; don't put them in the refrigerator—there's no need.

Most spices are best bought whole, then ground just before you use them. Freshly ground spices are more intense than the whole ones; because the surface area increases, so does volatility and flavor—but the volatile oils, the compounds that give spices their aromas and flavors, are easily lost, which is why I recommend grinding your own spices "to order" for each recipe. Think of the difference between fresh and dried herbs, or between dusty, already ground black pepper and pungent, freshly ground black peppercorns. Now imagine how much more vibrant the flavors of cumin, cinnamon, and coriander will be if you grind them only when you need them. You can use a mortar and pestle, an electric spice mill, a small coffee grinder (preferably not the one you use for coffee)—or just put the whole spices in a strong plastic bag, cover it with a dish towel, and smash with a heavy saucepan or rolling pin until they're ground as coarsely or finely as you want. I know this may seem like "a bit of a grind" at first, but you will notice the flavor difference, your spices will keep better, and you will soon get in the habit and enjoy the sensations of the freshly unlocked fragrance.

8

COOKING WITH SPICES

The food I love revolves around pure flavor, texture, and, particularly, spices. I see spices as flecks of bright, glorious color in a world of monochrome seasoning. To me, fresh, fragrant, raw spices are everyday ingredients. I believe that everyone can cook, and everyone can cook with spices.

Spices add a wealth of beautiful, vibrant flavors; fragrant, subtle aromas. They can create smoky notes, citrus notes, menthol notes, warmth, depth, and a finish that leaves the palate clean yet wanting more. Spices evolved naturally, producing volatile oils as an organic self-defense mechanism. I like to celebrate this "wild" element when I'm blending and cooking with spices. Not opting for regulated, exactly consistent flavors, but creating a flavor for the moment. Spices are the bold ingredients of the food world: left of center, unconventional but a positive influence, with their heart in the right place. Solo or blended, they can be used in any dish. When I'm coming up with spice combinations, I see a cast of characters with different moods and emotions, I see colors, and flood my mind with flavor memories, mixing my Eastern and Western sides. So when it comes to spices, forget conventional wisdom; go with your instincts and think flavor!

To toast or not to toast?

I shudder every time I hear people say, "You should always toast your spices." It really is a bugbear of mine, this willy-nilly toasting, roasting, and frying of spice. WHY? The usual answer is that heat brings out the flavor of the spice. But let's think about that for a minute. A vibrant, volatile "fresh" spice has flavor by its very nature. By heating a spice, you're changing its chemical composition and, therefore, its flavor profile, compressing it all into the toasty midrange but losing any high notes. Now that's wonderful for many dishes, but be aware of how such processes affect the ingredients we use. I may decide to toast some spices at the beginning of a recipe so they are not too dominant, but then add a little more of the same spice near the end of cooking to highlight the flavor. The perfect blend of spices is all about getting the right mixture of notes while maintaining individual flavor integrity.

BUILDING A BLEND

When you host a party, you want to invite guests who will mix well. You need to know their individual characters so you can create a good group. Now this may not necessarily mean they all get on perfectly. Where would be the fun in that? It makes for a more stimulating event when people have different views and want to get them across. Indeed, isn't the phrase "to add a little spice to the mix" meant for just such occasions?

It's a similar situation when using spices. Get to know the characteristics of each spice, then you can use them confidently in every dish, either to add balance or to take the dish's overall flavor in an unexpected direction. Flavor characteristics should mix well together, but they should all be able to hold their own in a dish and bring something wonderful to the party. Happy food mixes with happy spices, such as fennel, coriander, green cardamom; dark, moody food with sultry, exotic spices, such as cloves, star anise, black pepper, black cardamom. Heady, perfumed but astringent rose gets on well with floral, creamy, sweet vanilla. Introduce them to black pepper for its pungent, warming, woody heat, or the perfumed heat of long pepper. Or you might begin with pungent, heavy-hitting asafetida, adding support from characters, such as earthy-sweet turmeric, earthy-citrus cumin, and a zingy, uplifting touch of ginger.

Spice characteristics

The essential character of a spice relates to its volatile oil content, the compounds that give it its fragrance and flavor. Freshness is key, because by definition "volatile" oils are easily lost. Without going too much into chemistry, there are two key groups of compounds: terpenes and benzenes. Terpenes are responsible for the aromatic freshness of a spice, which we describe as floral, piny, or "spicy": the pinenes in pepper, the linalool in coriander, for example. Benzenes provide "sweet," creamy aromas: vanillin in vanilla, eugenol in cloves, cinnamon, cassia, bay leaves, and basil. From these examples, you can begin to see how and why we can all relate to spices in similar ways.

Spice notes

You can tell if a spice blend is right when you simply want to dive into it, when you want the entire fragrance to engulf you and no single spice is too dominant. Without being overly prescriptive, I tend to approach this by thinking in terms of bass, middle, and high notes and achieving a balance. Bass notes, low and lasting, provide depth, and come from turmeric, cumin, as well as black cardamom, ginger, vanilla, tamarind, and star anise. Middle notes means spices that hold their own flavors, such as cassia, coriander, fennel, cloves, pepper, and saffron. High-note spices are top-end, perfumed, cherry-on-the-top types, such as green cardamom, mace, nutmeg, and cinnamon. You can identify these high-note spices by their initial burst of scent and ethereal, volatile nature; they're spices that need to be used sparingly and treated with care—the spice divas.

Colors

I don't want to sound like a crazy warehouse party casualty, but I do relate colors to food types, and from there I make a connection to a spice. Colors reflect moods: think about blue and green and you think calm, serenity; yellow suggests happiness and positivity; reds are full of warmth and energy; black and brown are moody, exotic. I use these natural indicators to steer me in the right flavor direction. For example, the deep golden sphere of an egg yolk suggests the all-pervasive warmth of the sun, and that takes me to the warm golden color of turmeric and the heat of cayenne pepper, which go so well with eggs. When thinking about lamb, I might imagine a green and sunny pasture, and a sweet, serene mood; in terms of spices, I might turn to the uplifting perfume of green cardamom, the bright citrus hit of coriander, or a touch of floral sweetness from cloves.

A–Z of Spices

The following pages describe the spices used in this book; I hope they will encourage you to widen your repertoire. Spices, like herbs, are parts of plants that are rich in flavor compounds. Some leaves are usually considered as spices instead of herbs: curry leaves, for example, or cassia leaves, also known as tejpatta or Indian bay leaves. Barks, such as cassia and cinnamon, are also used as spices. Spices can be fruits, such as black pepper and vanilla; seeds, such as mustard, fenugreek, and nigella (also known as black onion seeds or kalonji); or seed husks or hulls, such as Sichuan pepper. They can be dried gums, or oleoresins, such as asafetida, which is made by tapping the resin from the roots of ferula plants (related to fennel). Ginger and turmeric are rhizomes—rootlike stems—and cloves are dried, unopened flower buds. To me, the most enigmatic spices of all are mace and saffron. Mace, the lacy outer coating to the nutmeg seed, is defined as an aril—an extra seed covering—and saffron is the stigma of a crocus flower.

In this A–Z, I use botanical definitions to describe the part of the plant used as a spice. Botanically, a fruit is simply a seedpod; you may be surprised at how many spices commonly referred to as "seeds" are actually "fruits," albeit generally dried, unripe fruits, including caraway, cumin, and coriander. A fruit is essentially made of two parts: the "housing" or husk, and the seed. The housing may be hard, like the black skin of peppercorns, or soft and fleshy like mace or the red flesh around a pomegranate seed. The housing is generally called "pericarp" when hard and "aril" when soft. White pepper is simply the seed of a peppercorn with the black pericarp removed.

Nature always plays a large part in a spice's flavor. Just as with wine, the soil and climate influence the spice we buy. Even more important are the decisions made by the farmer, such as how and when to harvest and how the spice is processed.

I've included the main volatile oils and other aroma and flavor compounds that contribute to the character of each spice. Each spice also has its "note": bass, mid, or high. These relate to the building blocks I describe on pages 10–11. You will see that certain compounds are common to a number of spices, and this will give you a steer as to which spices work well together in a blend. For example, citrus aromas probably come from limonene, a compound named because it smells like lemons—a "happy" spice characteristic. Anethole gives aniselike aromas and is found in caraway, fennel, star anise, as well as in herbs, such as tarragon and basil. When combining spices to achieve depth and synergy in a dish, I look for characteristics that complement and balance each other.

I have given a little background knowledge about each spice, including where they are mainly cultivated, what to look for when buying fresh spices, and a few ideas on how they are used. Some spices are known by several names, so I've included some of these to help you find them.

AJWAIN (AJOWAN, CAROM)

Botanical name: Trachyspermum ammi
Part used: Fruit ("seeds")
Main flavor and aroma compounds: Thymol,
pinene, cymene, limonene, terpinene
Character: Peppery, anise, bitter
Note: Mid
Buy: Whole

Like caraway, coriander, cumin, and fennel, ajwain is the dried fruit of a flowering plant, and the spice is usually referred to as seeds. The tiny (about 1⁄16 inch/1.5–2mm), egg-shaped gray fruits smell musty and thyme-like; they are sometimes erroneously called lovage or dill seeds. The spice probably originated in Egypt and was introduced to India at the time of Alexander the Great's conquest, around 300 BC. India is the main producer of ajwain, and it is also grown in Pakistan, Afghanistan, Iran, and Egypt.

Ajwain has quite a kick if eaten raw, but when cooked it mellows to something milder and altogether more complex. It imparts its flavor more readily in fat, and in India the seeds are often fried in ghee, which allows the distinctive flavor to permeate the dish. They are used whole, a fabulous addition to lentil and root vegetable dishes, adding peppery notes of anise and thyme. The essential oil thymol gives carom medicinal properties, including digestive and antiflatulent effects.

ALLSPICE

(Jamaican pepper, pimento, English pepper)
Botanical name: Pimenta dioica
Part used: Fruit ("berries")
Main flavor and aroma compounds: Eugenol,
cineol
Character: Heady, complex, exotic, sweet
Note: Mid–high
Buy: Whole or powdered

Native to the Caribbean, Mexico, and Central America, the evergreen allspice tree grows to about 30–65 feet (10–20m) tall. The tiny round fruits are picked while still green, just before they are fully ripe, at which point they begin to lose their aroma. They are then dried and change from green to reddish brown. Allspice "berries" look like large peppercorns with one pronounced freckle.

Jamaica is the largest producer of the spice; it is also cultivated in Barbados, Cuba, and Mexico. I prefer the Jamaican variety to the Mexican because I find it has a sweeter, slightly more complex, flavor.

Christopher Columbus introduced the spice to Europe in the sixteenth century. An Englishman named it "allspice" because he thought it smelled like a mixture of clove, nutmeg, cinnamon, and pepper. This spice is used whole in pickling and ground in cakes, puddings, and pies.

AMCHOOR (MANGO POWDER)

Botanical name: Mangifera indica
Part used: Fruit
Main flavor and aroma compounds: Ocimene,
cubebene, cadinene
Character: Intense astringency, caramel,
sour tang
Note: Mid
Buy: Powdered

Mangoes are native to India and South Asia. Amchoor is a tangy-tart powder made from unripe green mangoes; peeled, sliced, sun-dried, and then ground to a light brown powder. It has a fruity, honeyed caramel aroma and sherbetlike flavor, and in northern India it is dusted over all kinds of cooked and raw foods as a condiment to make dishes really sparkle and come alive. It's a handy way to add fruity flavor and a savory tartness without adding extra moisture, and is used with legumes, vegetable dishes, fish, chutneys, and pickles. Amchoor also contains certain enzymes that make it work as a meat tenderizer, so it's useful in marinades.

ANARDANA (DRIED POMEGRANATE SEEDS)

Botanical name: Punica granatum
Part used: Seeds
Character: tangy sour crunch, fruity sweet end
Note: Mid
Buy: Whole or powdered

Cultivated since ancient times, pomegranates are now grown in many countries around the world. To make anardana, fresh pomegranate seeds are slowly sun-dried, making the flavor deeper and richer and they retain some of the fruit's tannic astringency. The fruity sourness works exceptionally well with poultry and game birds, such as duck, pheasant, quail, or even Cornish game hens, and also with lamb.

Dried pomegranate seeds are great as a snack, much like crunchy raisins. The best hail from the Himalayan wild "daru" variety of pomegranate.

The seeds are also sold powdered, usually roasted first to remove excess moisture. This powder is strewn over snacks in northern India to make a zingy condiment. Anardana is a wonderful ingredient: you'll find yourself reaching for it when something's just a little lackluster and needs to sparkle.

ASAFETIDA

(Hing in Hindi)
Botanical name: Ferula asafoetida
Part used: Resin gum
Main flavor and aroma compounds: Propenyl
disulfide, pinene
Character: Pungent, sulfurous, onion, and
garlic notes
Note: Bass
Buy: Small nuggets

Asafetida is the dried resin gum tapped from the root of the ferula plant; sometimes known as giant fennel, it is native to Iran and Afghanistan, and cultivated in the north of India. There are two main varieties, the milky white Kabuli Sufaid and the deep brown Lal.

It is usually found in powdered form, mixed with gum arabic, rice flour, and turmeric, but I prefer to buy only the pure resin. It is difficult to find in stores, but it can be bought online. Sometimes called "devil's dung," this resin is extremely pungent and must be stored in airtight containers to preserve not only its freshness, but also your sanity. However, when used in cooking, it loses its pungency and adds an almost fruity, intense flavor like fried onions and garlic. Reputed to have antiflatulent properties, it is widely used in lentil-based dishes. I love asafetida and use it to add depth to meat stews, veg dishes, relishes, and chutneys.

CARAWAY

Botanical name: Carum carvi
Part used: Fruit ("seeds")
Main flavor and aroma compounds: Anethole,
limonene, carvone
Character: Delicate smoky anise
Note: Mid
Buy: Whole

Caraway plants are native to Europe, western Asia, and north Africa. The tiny, light brown, ridged, curved fruit (known as "seeds") are about 1⁄8 inch (3–4mm) long and have an anise-citrus flavor. Caraway has been popular in northern Europe and Scandinavia, because it grew locally and unlike other spices it didn't need to be imported. The seeds are usually used whole. They are sometimes added to sauerkraut, but are more often used in baking, from rye breads to festive cookies. In the UK, caraway is traditionally used in "seed cake" and for a Lancashire speciality known as Goosnargh cakes (a type of cookie). In Holland, Germany, and Russia, it flavors the digestif Kümmel. It doesn't often appear in Indian cuisine, but some translated recipes do mistakenly call for it in biryanis and pilafs.

CARDAMOM, BLACK

(Elaichi, or Kali elaichi, in Hindi)
Botanical name: Amomum subulatum
Part used: Fruit (seedpod)
Main flavor and aroma compounds: Cineol,
terpinene, limonene
Character: Smoky, sultry, exotic, camphor,
complex twisted high notes
Note: Bass
Buy: Whole

A member of the ginger family of flowering plants, black cardamom is native to northern India (I get mine from Darjeeling); its dried seedpods are dark brown, wrinkly, and about 1⁄4 inch (2cm) long, packed with dark brown seeds. A species with larger pods is grown in China and Vietnam. In India, we say green cardamom for cooling and black for heat; black cardamom is mainly used in savory dishes, but this is not a rigid rule. Indeed, I use it with mango in my kulfi (ice cream) recipe (see page 244). I love the camphor notes and smokiness that is created as the pods are dried over smoldering embers. This makes them perfect with game and dark meats to accentuate depth of flavor.

CARDAMOM, GREEN

(Elaichi, or Chota elaichi, in Hindi)
Botanical name: Elettaria cardamomum
Part used: Fruit (seedpod)
Main flavor and aroma compounds: Myrcene, limonene, and cineol
Character: Menthol, eucalyptus, heady gingery perfume, uplifting
Note: High
Buy: Whole

Like black cardamom (above), green cardamom is a member of the ginger family and is one of my favorite spices. It is native to southern India (I get mine from Idduki in Kerala) and Sri Lanka and is extensively cultivated in Guatemala. It is the third most expensive spice after saffron and vanilla, largely because each plant only produces 1 pound 2 ounces (500g) of pods a year. The pods are dried in the sun or, commercially, over electric elements, and each pod, about ½ inch (1.5cm) long, is packed with sticky brown-black seeds. Tease them out with your fingers and grind them, or add the whole pods to more robust and savory dishes, and in infusions. The whole pods are not meant to be eaten—the flavor is too intense in one hit—if you find one, just leave it on the side of the plate. Green cardamom has a beautiful, uplifting, citrus, gingery, minty, camphor, hoppy, complex perfume, adding high-end "ping" to both sweet and savory dishes. Try to search out fat, bright green pods instead of the skinny, wizened, pallid offerings all too often on sale.

CASSIA

Botanical name: Cinnamomum tamala
Part used: Bark
Main flavor and aroma compounds: Eugenol, coumarin (trace)
Character: Deep clovelike plus high note sweetness, astringent
Note: Mid
Buy: Whole

Cassia is the dried inner bark of an evergreen tree of the laurel family, native to southern China; it now grows throughout South and Southeast Asia. It is often known as Chinese cinnamon. Indeed, the Hindi for cassia, *dal*

chini, means "Chinese wood." Freshly dried cassia bark has a vibrant, ruddy hue and is highly aromatic, with a slight bitterness. In some countries, cassia and cinnamon are used interchangeably, but cassia has deeper notes than the more delicate, sweeter cinnamon. Cassia's flavor both penetrates and lingers. In India it's considered "warming" and is usually used in savory dishes, especially meat. It's also one of the components of Chinese five-spice powder.

Cassia bark is thicker than that of cinnamon (see below) and is hard to grind. Ideally, process it in an electric spice grinder before you start the recipe. Alternatively, you could use a mortar and pestle—and a lot of elbow grease. Some recipes, especially braises and stews, use whole pieces of cassia; they are not meant to be eaten—you'll soon know if you bite a piece of wood.

CAYENNE PEPPER

Botanical name: Capsicum annuum
Part used: Fruit
Main flavor and aroma compounds: Capsaicinoids
Character: Fruity, pungent heat
Note: Mid
Buy: Powdered or flakes

Cayenne peppers are hot chiles, usually harvested when red and fully ripe, then dried and finely ground to make the bright red spice we know as cayenne pepper. The dried chiles can also be crushed and used in the form of crushed red pepper flakes. Cayenne peppers are also used fresh, or combined with vinegar to make spicy-hot, pungent sauces, much-loved in the southern U.S. states. They take their name from the city of Cayenne in French Guiana, but are grown in many parts of the Americas and Asia. The chile heat rating of cayenne pepper usually ranges between 20,000 and 50,000 Scoville units. If you're not a chile-head, err on the low side, taste your blend, and then add a little more cayenne if you feel it needs more of a kick. I particularly enjoy the spicy heat of cayenne in cooked cheese dishes and with shellfish, as part of the dish or sprinkled on as a final colorful flourish.

CHILES

Botanical name: Capsicum annuum, Capsicum frutescens, *and other species*
Part used: Fruit
Main flavor and aroma compounds: Capsaicinoids
Buy: Fresh or dried, whole or flakes

Although these are not a spice, I use fresh chiles in a similar way to dried ones (cayenne, Kashmiri, paprika), matching them to the dish and balancing them with other flavors: aji (lemon) chiles for their pronounced fruity

notes, fresh Thai chilies for perfumed raw heat, and Scotch bonnets for pure devilment.

Chiles are the fruit of a flowering plant native to Central and South America, and were named "peppers" by Christopher Columbus because he found their spicy heat similar to the black pepper known in Europe. The Portuguese explorer Vasco da Gama is credited with the introduction of chiles to India in 1498. Over time, the chile replaced black pepper as India's preferred method of adding deep and pungent heat to a dish, and India is now the world's biggest producer (and consumer) of chiles. More than 200 varieties of chiles are grown in many countries around the world.

The "heat" of chiles is historically measured in Scoville heat units (SHU). It was devised using a panel of tasters and a dilution of the chile extract, testing when the heat from the capsaicin is no longer detectable; it is, therefore, a subjective scale. Newer chile heat scales are more scientific, but Scoville units are still widely used. For example, jalapeño chiles range from about 2,500 to 4,000 SHU, Thai chiles from 50,000 to 100,000, while Scotch bonnets range from 100,000 to 350,000.

CINNAMON

Botanical name: Cinnamomum zeylanicum
Part used: Bark
Main flavor and aroma compounds: Eugenol, ethyl cinnamate, linalool, coumarin (trace)
Character: Heady, warm, sweet astringency
Note: High
Buy: Whole

True cinnamon is the dried inner bark of a tree native to Sri Lanka; it also grows in India, the Seychelles, and elsewhere. As a spice, it has traveled even more widely. To farm the spice, the tree is coppiced to produce loads of branches; these branches are harvested, the outer bark removed, and the inner bark rolled to form cinnamon's easily recognizable "quills." Once dried, the tan-colored quills are cut into 2¾–4-inch (7–10cm) "sticks." Although it is hard to grind, I recommend buying whole cinnamon sticks and grinding them when you need them; process them in an electric spice grinder or pound them with a mortar and pestle—it's well worth the effort. The flavor of cinnamon quickly deteriorates if it's not sparkling fresh, and the bitterness is more pronounced in the ground spice, especially if overcooked.

In the West, we commonly associate the sweet scent of cinnamon with pastries and desserts, and with mulled wine at Christmas. In South America, it's often paired with chocolate in both sweet and savory dishes. Much more interesting to me is its use in spice blends and savory dishes, where it adds its heady sweetness to meats, such as lamb and chicken.

CLOVE

Botanical name: Eugenia caryophyllus
Part used: Unopened flower bud
Main flavor and aroma compounds: Eugenol, vanillin
Character: Assertive, medicinal, deep, fruity
Note: Mid
Buy: Whole

Cloves come from a large evergreen tree (the leaves are also aromatic) native to the Molucca Islands, the original "Spice Islands" in Indonesia. Each tree produces flower buds for around 80 years—yielding anything from a modest 4½ pounds (2kg) to a bumper 40 pounds (18kg) annually. The unopened flowers are harvested and dried in the sun. The essence of "aromatic sunshine," they are grown in many countries, including Indonesia, Madagascar, Tanzania, India, and Pakistan and are used around the world in both sweet and savory dishes.

The spice is used both whole and ground. In India it finds special favor in meat dishes. In the West, cloves are commonly used with baked ham, stewed fruits, and pickles; an onion studded with a clove adds depth to stocks and sauces. Try always to buy fat-looking cloves. The strong flavor of cloves means they need to be used judiciously. They contain large amounts of the oil eugenol, which accounts for their distinctive flavor. Clove oil acts as an anesthetic.

CORIANDER

(Dhania in Hindi)
Botanical name: Coriandrum sativum
Part used: Fruit ("seeds")
Main flavor and aroma compounds: Linalool, terpinene, pinene
Character: Lemony citrus, muted intensity
Note: Mid
Buy: Whole

The flowering plant whose dried fruits are known as coriander seeds is native to a large area around the Mediterranean, but has been established much farther afield for thousands of years, and two distinct varieties have developed. In Europe and North Africa, the fruits, ⅛ inch (3–4mm) in diameter, are spherical, brownish, and have a woody, peppery, orange aroma. Far superior, to my mind, are the slightly larger, football-shape greeny yellow fruits of the Indian coriander; you may think you know coriander, but when you experience it in its freshest form, nothing can prepare you for the intense citrus hit of this lemon bomb.

The aroma fades fast, so—as with most spice—I recommend grinding as and when you need it. The "seeds" are brittle, so coriander is one of the easiest spices to grind. In Indian cooking, coriander "seeds" are used in generous quantities and accurate measurements are not so crucial when using this amiable spice. They're used whole or

ground, generally in savory dishes. Around the Mediterranean and in northern Europe, coriander is used in meat dishes, sausages, and as a pickling spice; it's the traditional spice in Irish corned beef.

Fresh coriander leaves—aka cilantro—are a popular herb in many parts of Asia and Central and South America; their distinctive, strong, grassy-citrus flavor derives from an essential oil that is not present in the dried fruit ("seeds").

CUMIN

(Zeera or jeera in Hindi)
Botanical name: Cuminum cyminum
Part used: Fruit ("seeds")
Main flavor and aroma compounds: Cuminaldehyde, pinene, cymene
Character: Earthy citrus, peppery, gentle anise
Note: Bass
Buy: Whole

Cumin is the fruit (usually called "seeds") of a flowering annual plant that grows well in any country with a long, hot summer. The "seeds"—just under ¼ inch (5mm) long and ridged—are harvested when they turn yellow-brown and are then dried. Native to Egypt and the Eastern Mediterranean region, the largest producer and consumer of cumin today is India; Turkey, Iran, Syria, Egypt, Mexico, and China are other major producers. The Romans introduced it to much of Europe, and Spanish and Portuguese colonists introduced it to the Americas.

A glorious spice with zingy lemon and anise flavors in equal parts, rounded out with a down-to-earth comforting warmth and almost astringent notes of fresh black pepper. It gives savory, earthy depth to a dish, a kind of "bedrock" flavor for lighter aromatics, typically coriander, to dance upon. The seeds can be dry-roasted or fried in ghee to maximize their intensely savory flavor. Cumin is important in much Indian cooking, and is essential in Garam Masala and Panch Phoran (see pages 266–67). It is highly reputed for its digestive properties—indeed, the Hindi for cumin, *jeera*, is derived from a Sanskrit word meaning "digestive."

CUMIN, BLACK

Botanical name: Bunium bulbocastanum
Part used: Fruit ("seeds")
Main flavor and aroma compounds: Cuminaldehyde, terpinene, cymene
Character: Earthy anise
Note: Bass
Buy: Whole

Black cumin grows wild in Kashmir, Afghanistan, and Iran and is sometimes considered superior to "ordinary" cumin; the flavor is "darker," sweeter, and almost smoky. Each plant yields about ¼ ounce (5–8g) of

seed, making it a pricy spice. In Hindi it is called *shahi* ("royal") or *kala* ("black") cumin.

The thin black "seeds" are about ⅛ inch (3mm) long, and have an earthy, nutty, savory, and somewhat herby, floral flavor. The seeds are usually used whole, not ground, and are often toasted before use, which brings out the nutty qualities. Black cumin is confined mainly to the cuisines of northern India, Iran, and Afghanistan, particularly in breads, garlic-onion-ginger pastes, and steamed rice dishes.

FENNEL

Botanical name: Foeniculum vulgare
Part used: Fruit ("seeds")
Main flavor and aroma compounds: Anethole
Character: Sweet middle, muted anise
Note: Mid
Buy: Whole

Fennel seeds are the fruit of a plant with yellow flowers and feathery leaves that grows wild in the Mediterranean region, and that has long been established across Asia and in North America. The "seeds" vary in size and shape; I prefer the slightly smaller, more delicate type, about ⅛ inch (3–4mm) long, but whichever type you come across, they should always be bright, vibrant green.

Fennel is popular in French and Italian kitchens, often used with fish and in pork dishes and salami. The ground spice is an essential constituent of Chinese five-spice powder, while, used whole, the seeds make up one-fifth of the quintessential Bengali spice mixture Panch Phoran (see page 266). Fennel is equally popular in other parts of India: as a pickling spice, in southern Indian garam masala and paired with ginger in Kashmiri cuisine, where it's also used to flavor baked goods. Toasting mutes the spice's sweetness, and it tends to be treated this way when it is used in bread and cheese recipes. Imparting its anise flavor to all it touches, the seeds are often chewed as a breath freshener. The Indian classic Mishri and Soonf, a mixture of crystal sugar and fennel seeds commonly known as *paan*, not only acts as a palate cleanser, but is also a natural digestif.

FENUGREEK

Botanical name: Trigonella foenum graecum
Part used: Seeds
Main flavor and aroma compounds: Beta-pinene, camphor, beta-caryophyllene
Character: Bitter, sweet pea flavors
Note: Mid
Buy: Whole

This annual plant, a member of the bean family, flourishes in warm, dry conditions and is cultivated worldwide, especially throughout the Indian subcontinent, the Near East, and North Africa. The little sandy yellow, jagged, cube-shape seeds aren't used often in Western cuisine. Some find the spice's bitterness off-putting, but it's possible to temper the bitterness somewhat with toasting. Most recipes advise against letting the seeds darken, but in both Gujarati and Nepalese cuisine they are allowed to almost blacken in oil to add a smoky, roasty, almost meaty flavor to both the oil and the entire dish. I use this technique for the potato part of my Bacon Chop recipe (see pages 34–35). Whole fenugreek seeds form one-fifth of the Bengali spice blend Panch Phoran (see page 266). The ground spice is a common component of curry powder, and it is often used in south Indian vegetable and legume dishes, as well as in the wonderfully hot Ethiopian spice mix *berbere*. It has recently been discovered to have blood sugar regulating properties to the extent that is it now a spice suggested to many people who have type-2 diabetes.

GINGER
Botanical name: Zingiber officinale
Part used: Rhizome ("root")
Main flavor and aroma compounds: Pinenes, camphene, cineole, linalool, borneol, turpineol, nerol, geraniol, zingiberene
Character: Citrus, piny, soft heat
Note: Bass
Buy: Fresh or powdered

Ginger is the rootlike fleshy stem of a flowering plant native to southern China and tropical Asia. Its use in Asian cooking dates back some 4,000 years; it goes well with both savory and sweet foods, and was one of the earliest spices to be traded around the Mediterranean; it became one of the most popular spices in Europe. Later traders introduced it to Africa and the Americas.

Ginger is available in a whole host of forms, each with a slightly different expression of ginger's lively, citrusy warmth. When buying the fresh "root," it should be firm, with smooth, taut, light brown skin (which is usually peeled off before use); if you can see a slice of the flesh, it should be light yellow and not too fibrous. Avoid wizened, flabby pieces. Dried ginger is ground to a fine, dark beige powder, preferably with visible tiny fibers. Whole pieces of dried ginger are sometimes used as a flavoring. Chunks of ginger may be preserved in syrup, sometimes known as "preserved ginger," or cooked in syrup and then coated in sugar (crystallized ginger). Mild young ginger can be pickled; paper-thin slices are often served with Japanese food.

"Gingerbread" was first recorded in Europe in AD 992, and in India, ginger increased in popularity from the thirteenth century, with the rise of Muslim rule. Today, a paste of fresh ginger and garlic is the basis for many savory dishes in India, Thailand, and other Southeast Asian countries.

Sweetly spicy ginger is also well known for its medicinal properties, often brewed up as a tea. The Hindi word for ginger, *adrak*, means "fire in the belly," and it is known to aid digestion and can help relieve nausea, especially motion sickness and morning sickness in pregnancy.

INDIAN BAY LEAF
(Tejpatta, Malabar leaf, cassia leaf)
Botanical name: Cinnamomum tamala
Part used: Leaf
Main flavor and aroma compounds: Eugenol and linalool
Character: Delicate, citrus, top note cinnamon
Note: High
Buy: Whole

Indian bay are the leaves of the cassia tree, which is also grown for its bark in India, China, and Bhutan. They are different from the "traditional" Mediterranean bay leaves (*Laurus nobilis*), being light green and about three times as long, with a delicate, orangy citrus, cinnamon-like fragrance that's perfect for Asian stocks and broths. I use them in an ice cream (see page 234) for their gentle perfume and lightly twisted cassia flavor.

JUNIPER
Botanical name: Juniperus communis
Part used: Fruit ("berries")
Main flavor and aroma compounds: Pinenes, sabinene, limonene
Character: Pine high note, deep berry perfume
Note: High
Buy: Whole

This spice is the key flavoring in modern gin and its ancestor, genever—the Dutch word for juniper. It's the unripe green berries that provide the characteristic flavor in your fing and tonic, whereas the ripe purple-black berries are the ones you'll use in the kitchen. When buying, be sure they're plump, round, and taut-skinned. To use juniper berries, lightly crush them to release the complex fragrant flavors and aromas.

Juniper "berries" are the fruit of a prickly evergreen shrub that grows wild throughout Europe and North America. The ancient Greeks and Romans used juniper, and it has been found in Egyptian tombs. These days it is most associated with northern Europe and Scandinavia, often found in fish preparations, such as rollmop herrings. Juniper is also perfect paired with cabbage—both braised and pickled—and game, loved for its clean, sharp qualities.

KASHMIRI CHILES
Botanical name: Capsicum annuum
Part used: Fruit
Main flavor and aroma compounds: Capsaicinoids
Character: Smoky, fruity perfume, gentle heat, glorious red color
Note: Mid
Buy: Whole or flakes

True Kashmiri chiles are grown in the Kashmir and Jammu region. As the peppers ripen, they turn deep red and the flavors become sweeter and more rounded—and their heat increasingly searing. Kashmiri chiles are usually sold dried; they have a wonderful deep red sheen, and as well as color and spicy heat from the capsaicin content, they impart a pronounced fruity, slightly smoky flavor. You can buy whole chiles and chop them as required, or as flakes. Always (carefully) taste a few flakes before adding to a recip—the heat level can vary wildly from batch to batch, but you're looking at around 6,000 to 11,000 Scoville heat units.

MACE
Botanical name: Myristica fragrans
Part used: Aril
Main flavor and aroma compounds: Myristicin, pinene, limonene, borneol, terpineol, geraniol, safrol
Character: Intense floral perfume, clean-cut astringent warmth
Note: High
Buy: Whole

Mace is one of my favorite spices. It has a finer aroma than nutmeg, with a slight hint of anise. Mace and nutmeg are both derived from an evergreen tree, native to the Moluccas, the "Spice Islands" of Indonesia, and now cultivated in Grenada in the West Indies, Malaysia, and southern India. The nutmeg fruit looks like a pale apricot; when ripe it splits to reveal its horse chestnutlike seed (nutmeg) in a lacy coat, or aril (mace). The two parts are separated after harvesting; the mace is dried and (usually) flattened. Traditionally and somewhat romantically referred to as a "blade" of mace, but because the arils are often broken into two or three pieces, a blade may mean different things to different cooks. Fresh mace is a bright, pinky red, highly aromatic, with astringent, almost numbing characteristics; as it dries it fades to an orange color and loses some of the intensity of the aroma.

You need a light touch; with mace, less is more, because it's a powerful flavor that can easily overwhelm other spices. It's wonderful with seafood and meaty dishes of beef and lamb, and it's also a wonderful flavoring for dairy-base desserts and sauces, such as béchamel (a white sauce), to which it imparts a warm orange color. I love the way this spice can add perfume and sweetness yet also cut through richness and add a "clean finish" to define flavors on the tongue.

Always buy whole mace instead of ground; however, mace can be hard to grind, so I suggest that before adding it to a spice blend, you process it in an electric spice grinder, or use a mortar and pestle—and elbow grease.

MUSTARD SEEDS, BLACK

Botanical name: Brassica nigra
Part used: Seeds
Main flavor and aroma compounds:
Isothiocyanates
Character: Nutty, pungent heat
Note: Bass
Buy: Whole

Mustard plants are part of the Brassica family, like cabbages. Black mustard is native to southern Europe and western Asia, and is one of the oldest spices in the world; it is mentioned in Sumerian texts dating to around 3000 BC. I prefer the nutty, more pungent flavor of black mustard to the brown mustard (*Brassica juncea*) that originated in northern India, although the two are more or less interchangeable. Brown mustard is easier to cultivate and is now commonly grown in Europe, while both are now grown in India. The black variety is slightly larger than the brown and has a blueish black hue.

Mustard's heat is different from chile heat, traveling up the nose and dissipating quickly. When ground and mixed with cold liquid, the "heat" is the result of a chemical reaction between two natural compounds found in mustard: sinigrin and the enzyme myrosin. Interestingly, this reaction does not happen when hot liquids are used, because heat (or acidity or alcohol) destroys some of the enzyme. So if you are mixing mustard from scratch, let the intrinsic heat build before adding vinegar, which stops the reaction.

The flavor of mustard seeds is different when they are cooked whole. They can be dry-roasted but are more commonly dropped into hot oil, and when they make an audible "pop," they become slightly grayish and develop a rounded, nutty flavor that complements savory dishes, especially fish and legumes. Black mustard seeds are a crucial part of the Bengali spice blend Panch Phoran (see page 266).

Mustard seeds are also pressed to make a cooking oil that is used in many parts of the Indian subcontinent.

NIGELLA SEEDS (BLACK ONION SEEDS, KALONJI)

Botanical name: Nigella sativa
Part used: Seeds
Main flavor and aroma compounds: Nigellone, thymoquinone, allyl propyl disulphide
Character: Floral pepper notes, muted bitterness
Note: Mid
Buy: Whole

Nigella seeds come from a flowering plant native to South and Southwest Asia; it's not related to the onion, although the spice is commonly called black onion seeds. The tiny black seeds are approximately cuboid and have little odor; when ground or chewed, they develop a vaguely oregano-like scent. The taste is aromatic and slightly bitter, pungent, smoky, even peppery.

You'll see them sprinkled over Indian naan and breads from Turkey; in fact, the Turkish name translates as "bun's herb." In north India, Punjabi and Bengali cooks use nigella to flavor cooked vegetables. The spice forms one-fifth of the Bengali spice blend Panch Phoran (see page 266). Dry-toasting or frying in oil makes the complex flavor of nigella more rounded and a little nuttier.

NUTMEG

Botanical name: Myristica fragrans
Part used: Seed kernel
Main flavor and aroma compounds:
Myristicin, pinene, limonene, borneol, terpineol, geraniol, safrol
Character: Bittersweet heady perfume, astringent
Note: High
Buy: Whole

Nutmeg is the hard, brown, egg-shaped seed (about $\frac{1}{10}$ inch/2.5mm long) of the tree that also gives us mace (see above). The tree is native to parts of Indonesia and is cultivated in Malaysia, the Caribbean, and southern India. Early traders prized it for its medicinal and aphrodisiac properties, and in large quantities it is a hallucinogen, but not a good one; it makes you feel queasy and uneasy.

With its uplifting, "full-on" fragrance, it's a spice that must whisper, not shout, with a tendency to overpower and render a dish unpalatably bitter if overused: "a grating of nutmeg" means a single rub along a grater. Its slight astringency cuts through richness in both sweet and savory dishes. Béchamel sauce is lifted by a touch of nutmeg, while the French spice blend Quatre Épices (see page 266) includes nutmeg and is used in sausages and pâtés. The British often use nutmeg in sweet dishes, mulled wine, and hot milk drinks. It's widely used in Dutch cooking and in the Caribbean. It also perks up pumpkin—in Italian pasta fillings and in American pumpkin pie. It's often grated over cooked spinach in Italy, and I'd always recommend a generous grating in mashed potatoes to give it a subtle lift, but to me nutmeg is best when used with chocolate to enhance the nuances and notes of cacao.

PAPRIKA

Botanical name: Capsicum annuum
Part used: Fruit
Main flavor and aroma compounds:
Capsaicinoids
Character: Soft, peppery, fruity
Note: Mid
Buy: Powdered

I tend to associate paprika with Hungary (and goulash) and Spain (and chorizo). But the spice is appreciated elsewhere, too, for example, in the Arabic spice blend *baharat*.

Paprika is a powder made from ground dried red chile peppers; it is the proportion of fruit, membrane, and seeds used that dictates the strength of the final product, not the pungency of the pepper variety itself. Paprika can be broadly divided into hot, sweet and smoked. Until the 1920s, when a sweet pepper plant was identified and cultivated, all paprika in Central Europe was the hot type. Today, the product labeled simply "paprika" is the sweet, mild type.

In Hungary, you'll find salt and paprika, not salt and pepper, as table condiments. Different types of paprika are commonly used within a single dish to create the perfect blend of flavors, much like the use of multiple chile varieties in Mexican cooking.

Spanish paprika, *pimentón*, comes in mild or "sweet," medium spicy, and piquant versions. Pimentón de la Vera, from La Vera in western Spain, has a smoky character because the peppers are dried over oak wood. Typically, Spanish paprika is sweeter and milder than its Hungarian counterpart. The sugar content means paprika readily burns and turns bitter, so be careful at the stove when working with it.

PEPPERCORNS, BLACK

Botanical name: Piper nigrum
Part used: Fruit ("berry")
Main flavor and aroma compounds: Piperine, chavicine, pinenes, careen, limonene, cubenol, asaricin, 2-ethyl-3,5 dimethylpyrazine (also found in cacao)
Character: Pungent, fruity, Parma violet, fresh leather
Note: Mid
Buy: Whole

So well-known and distinctive that the term "peppery" is widely used when describing other aromas, it is pungent with a sharp, yet warming, woody, fresh leather, Parma violet, almost vanilla note. Pungent-hot-pungent.

Peppercorns are the fruits of a perennial climbing vine; picked while unripe, they shrivel and darken as they dry. Green peppercorns are picked even earlier, "brined" to halt maturation, and can then be dried. Native to southwest India and now widely cultivated in tropical regions, although the best pepper is grown in India. Pepper's popularity largely stems from its ability to transform a dish in an instant, bringing food to life without overpowering it. In India, pepper was the original way to add heat, millenia before the arrival of chiles in the sixteenth century.

When freshly ground, black pepper is both pungent and headily aromatic. Add ground black pepper toward the end of the cooking process so that the flavor is not "cooked out." Whole peppercorns are often included in marinades and slow-cooked dishes.

Widely acknowledged as the king of spices, pepper has also been called "black gold," and it accounts for more than one-quarter of global spice trade. It should be stored in an airtight and opaque container, because light reduces its spiciness.

PEPPER, CUBEB

(Cubebs, Javanese pepper)
Botanical name: Piper cubeba
Part used: Fruit
Main flavor and aroma compounds: Cubebene
Character: Intense twist, rounded peppery, rose
Note: Mid–high
Buy: Whole

The dried, unripe fruits of a member of the pepper family, cubebs resemble common black peppercorns, but with a little spiky stem protruding from each. Native to Java, Indonesia, cubebs were popular in Europe until the seventeenth century and were used interchangeably with black pepper. Cubeb has a pronounced bitterness, which may well have contributed to its fall from favor, although the flavor mellows with cooking; in the Middle Ages cubebs were candied and eaten whole. Commonly used to flavor liquor, such as gin, this spice reputedly has aphrodisiac and medicinal properties, such as treating respiratory complaints.

I like to use cubebs in place of allspice, except when the more complex sweetness of allspice (Jamaican pepper) is required. In North Africa, particularly Tunisia and Morocco, cubebs appear in some recipes for *ras el hanout*—a blend of around 20 superior spices, often including rose petals, that translates as "top of the shop."

PEPPER, LONG

(Indian long pepper, *pippali* in Tamil)
Botanical name: Piper longum *Part or type: Flower spike*
Main flavor and aroma compounds: Piperine
Character: Intense pepper, clove mid-notes, nutmeg, pine
Note: High
Buy: Whole

Indian long pepper is the flower spike of a vine that grows wild throughout India. It is hotter and more pungent than the closely related black pepper. Each peppercorn resembles a diminutive grayish black catkin about 1 inch (2.5cm) long and contains many poppy seed-size fruits within, much like a pinecone and its nuts. Look for it in the Indian grocery store under the name *pippali*.

The Romans valued long pepper more highly than black, and today it is used in Indian pickles, a number of Indonesian and Malaysian dishes, as well as North African spice blends. The incenselike flavor is hard to pinpoint; it tastes somewhat "ancient," with a hint of clove, nutmeg, and top-note ginger. I like to use it to help define flavors, particularly, and probably not surprisingly, peppery notes. To use, simply rub the spike along a grater.

PEPPER, SICHUAN

Botanical name: Zanthoxylum piperitum
Part used: Pericarp (seed husk)
Main flavor and aroma compounds: Linalool, limonene, cineole, pinene, citronellal, turpineol
Character: Citrus, pepper, high-note perfume, mouth-numbing
Note: High
Buy: Whole

Sichuan, or Szechuan, pepper is not related to either black pepper or chile; it was given this name by Westerners because it produces a perception of "heat," but it lacks the pungency of other pepper types. The dried seed husk of the shrublike prickly ash tree, Sichuan pepper can be used either whole or ground. It is usually added at the last stages of cooking to preserve the fragrant aromatic quality. Finely ground, it's part of Chinese five-spice powder. The uniquely citrus, hot-and-numbing sensation this spice offers is much prized in Sichuan cuisine and in many a spice blend I create. I love the tingling, numbing, buzzing sensation experienced when biting down on a husk, similar to a cross between licking a battery and drinking a carbonated beverage.

The variety called Timur is an important ingredient in Nepal, particularly in pickles and meat dishes, while in India, the *tephal* variety is used predominantly along the Konkan Coast of west India. The Chinese also flavor oil with the spice, or roast it and blend it with salt as a table condiment.

PEPPER, WHITE

Botanical name: Piper nigrum
Part used: Seeds
Main flavor and aroma compounds: Piperine
Character: Sweet, pungent, peppery
Note: Mid
Buy: Whole

The same fruits that become black pepper also give us white pepper. White pepper comes from skinned, fully ripe peppercorns. Skinning the corns means that some volatile aromas are lost, but white pepper retains the full pungency of its black counterpart.

The spice is mainly used in the West, often where a "peppery" flavor is called for but the visibility of black pepper would spoil the appearance of a dish. It will provide pungent heat but not the highly fragrant quality of black pepper. In Japan, it's sometimes used as an alternative to Sichuan pepper.

Once ground, the spice becomes earthier with time, even occasionally described as "moldy." This "farmyard" taint can actually more commonly be attributed to a fault in outdated processing methods.

ROSE PETALS

Botanical name: Rosa centifolia, Rosa damascena, *and other species*
Part used: Flower petal
Main flavor and aroma compounds: Citronellol, geraniol, nerol, linalool, farnesol, pinenes, terpinene, limonene, camphene, neral, eugenol
Character: Heady floral sweetness, deep perfume, soft astringency
Note: Mid
Buy: Dried petals

Roses may be a quintessential feature of an English country garden, but the fragrant petals also have a long history of use in a host of culinary applications. Edible species include the cabbage, damask, and musk roses largely used in Persian and Middle Eastern cooking and the Indian rose, a fragrant variety. When buying them dried, look for a deep purple-red color and strong fragrance. The ancient Egyptians, Persians, and Romans used rose petals to decorate food and flavor syrups. In the eleventh century, the Persian polymath Ibn Sina (Avicenna) is credited with the discovery of the distillation of rose petals to make rose water. In Europe in the Middle Ages, rose water was a key flavoring in sweetmeats, such as marzipan, mainly associated with the wealthy nobility. The petals also make wonderful preserves and conserves, preserved intact within a soft-set, sweet, fragrant jelly.

The culinary use of rose is largely restricted to sweet preparations (such as the innumerable Indian milk-base confectionary and desserts), although the dried petals are found in the North African spice blend *ras el hanout*, and rose water can be sprinkled over biryani and other lavish rice dishes. In the West, the petals are frosted with egg white and sugar and used to decorate cakes, and dark chocolates filled with a rose fondant cream are an old-fashioned British treat.

SAFFRON

Botanical name: Crocus sativus
Part used: Stigma
Main flavor and aroma compounds: Picrocrocin and safranal
Character: Intense, floral, light astringency
Note: Mid
Buy: "Threads" or "strands"

Saffron is gathered from certain varieties of the crocus flower. Each flower has three vivid red stigmas. It takes about 150,000 such stigma to make about 2¼ pounds (1kg) of saffron, making this spice the most expensive of all. However, a couple of threads of this precious spice will go a long way, and have the power to totally transform a dish with saffron's inimitable flavor and fragrance. Always buy the fine whole threads: ground saffron is not only vastly inferior and loses fragrance fast, it is also probably a fake. Safflower is a thistlelike plant with orange flowers that are often dried and passed off as saffron—but the only thing it has in common is a similar color. Look for saffron that is purely red, with no lightly colored wispy filaments. To me, the best saffron comes from Kashmir, but popular growing areas include Iran, Greece, Turkey, Spain, and Morocco.

In the UK, the spice was historically cultivated around the southeast town of Saffron Walden, and it was also grown in Ireland. Cornish saffron rolls use the spice, but there aren't too many British recipes that include it. Saffron is used in Spain's paella, Italy's risotto Milanese, and France's Provençal fish stew bouillabaisse. In Asia, saffron is used in both savory and sweet preparations, notably in dishes with Mughal roots: you'll see it in Persian rice dishes and north Indian biryanis. It also flavors milky Indian confectionery, lassis, and the sweet, festive Muslim rice dish, fruit-and-nut studded *zarda pilau*.

Unusually among spices, saffron's defining flavor compounds are water soluble, so it makes sense to soak it in liquid before use to get the maximum flavor and aroma from each thread—either water or milk as is most appropriate for the dish. To preserve its delicacy, saffron should always be added toward the end of cooking. It can be stored for longer than other spices, around 2 years in a cool, dark cupboard.

STAR ANISE
Botanical name: Illicium verum
Part used: Fruit (pericarp and seeds)
Main flavor and aroma compounds: Anethole
Character: Deep, rich, buttery anise, licorice, intense perfume
Note: Bass
Buy: Whole

The name denotes the appearance, each pod from the evergreen tree resembling an eight-pointed star. Although it contains the same flavor compound, star anise is not related to the Mediterranean anise (*Pimpinella anisum*). Native to southern China and Vietnam, it is also cultivated in India and many other Asian countries, and in Jamaica.

The ground spice is an important component of Chinese five-spice powder, and the whole spice is used in braised dishes. ou will also find star anise in the Vietnamese

noodle soup *pho* and in some Thai, Persian, and Pakistani dishes. In north India, it is used in biryani, garam masala, and masala chai. In the West, the primary use for the spice is as a flavoring for alcoholic drinks.

When using it in a spice blend, restraint is the key. All too often it is given a starring role, beguiling the cook with its dazzling beauty, but this captivating spice can easily smother all flavors it meets.

TAMARIND
Botanical name: Tamarindus indica
Part used: Fruit (pulp)
Main flavor, aroma, and souring compounds: Sugars, tartaric acid
Character: Sweet–sour, tangy, light astringency
Note: Bass
Buy: Paste or dried

The tamarind tree is indigenous to Africa and grows prolifically on the banks of rivers and lakes of southern India; it is also cultivated in other parts of tropical Asia, Latin America, and the West Indies. Its fruit—sometimes called Indian date—is a large beanlike pod, dark brown when ripe, containing a sticky fruity pulp punctuated with large seeds. For ease of use, I generally use the thick, black, concentrated paste of Indian origin available from nearly every Asian store; I have written the recipes with this product in mind, not the more runny brown product normally made in Malaysia or Thailand.

Tamarind is prized for its souring properties, similar to that achieved with lemon, vinegar, or tomato. It is widely used throughout South and Southeast Asia, and in Latin America, in both sweet and savory foods, relishes, sherbets, teas, and other drinks. It's not a traditional component of many Western dishes, except Worcestershire sauce.

In India, tamarind chutney and tamarind water are used to dress all kinds of snack dishes, collectively called *chaat*. In southern India, it's often found in vegetable dishes, such as *sambar* and *rasam*, and as the key flavoring in *puliyogare*, spicy-tangy tamarind rice. Intensely sweet-sour tamarind candies are popular in many countries of Asia, Latin America, and the Caribbean.

TURMERIC
Botanical name: Curcuma longa
Part used: Rhizome (root)
Main flavor and aroma compounds: Turmerone, atlantone, zingiberene
Character: Sweet, earthy, gingery, ethereal astringency
Note: Bass
Buy: Powdered

Fresh turmeric looks much like fresh ginger—until you slice it and reveal the dazzling orange-gold flesh. To transform the knobbly

rhizomes into the more familiar brilliantly colored powder, fresh turmeric is boiled, dried, and ground. Turmeric grows wild in many parts of South and Southeast Asia and is cultivated in India and elsewhere. This wonderful spice has been used medicinally for thousands of years and is now being studied as a treatment for cancer, Alzheimer's disease, and other conditions. The beautiful and auspicious color is readily transferred to food—and to hands and clothes. In fact, it has been used as a dye since at least 600 BC. Turmeric is a staple ingredient in Indian cooking. Its musky perfume imparts an earthy background note that rounds out the flavors in many Indian dishes, although its bitter astringency means it needs to be thoroughly "cooked out," usually in hot oil, and used in small quantities.

VANILLA
Botanical name: Vanilla planifolia
Part used: Fruit and seed
Main flavor and aroma compounds: Vanillin
Character: Deep, heady, enveloping richness, sweet and creamy
Note: Bass
Buy: Pods

A highly distinctive, sweet, mellow, calming aroma, more than 130 trace compounds have been found in vanilla extract, many of which contribute to the flavor of vanilla. They are also the reason that the taste of real vanilla is beyond comparison with artificial.

Although they are referred to as vanilla "beans," what we use is the dried ripe fruit pod of a plant in the orchid family. Around 6–8 inches (15–20cm) long and ½ inch (1cm) in diameter, each bean contains thousands of tiny seeds, which, along with the oil around them, contain most of the fragrance and flavor. The tiny black speckles you see in good-quality vanilla ice cream are the vanilla seeds.

The lengthy drying and curing process explains why good-quality vanilla is expensive. Look for dark brown, waxy, pliable beans with a deep aroma; poor-quality vanilla beans are pale, stiff, and lack aroma. The flavor is mostly in the seeds and the oil that you scoop from the slit bean, but the bean itself contains plenty of flavor. Whole beans can be steeped in warm liquid to impart their flavor, and then reused after washing and drying. The emptied bean can be dropped into your sugar container to make vanilla sugar.

Vanilla is used mainly in sweet dishes, such as ice cream, cookies, and cakes. However, adventurous cooks increasingly use it in savory dishes, where it can subtly lift and smooth other flavors. If you absolutely must; extract is superior to essence and vanilla paste is better again; 1 level teaspoon of paste is equivalent to one juicy bean.

THE SCIENCE OF FLAVOR

Spices are parts of plants, rich in flavor compounds. They offer a complex, diverse, and almost endless palette for us to use as we cook and create flavor combinations. And at the heart of this palette is flavor—a fascinating yet equally complex topic, so I'm going to concentrate on one particular area of flavor: how taste is perceived and how flavor "works."

The understanding of flavor and taste perception is becoming increasingly well explored. In simple terms, taste is perceived in the mouth, flavor in the nose. In our mouths are many different types of specialized receptors called sensors, which are triggered, or "tripped," when food hits them, sending information to our brain to help us form an overall picture of the food we're eating. This is our perception of the information provided by the senses. The parts of food that are soluble in saliva are sensed on the tongue—for example, sugars trigger the taste perception of sweetness. Parts of food that are volatile are detected by the nose—more precisely, the nasal epithelium, which gives us our sense of smell. As we eat, all the information sent from these taste triggers is gathered up and deciphered by our brain. This is how we seamlessly perceive the flavor of food as a whole, which is greater than the sum of all its individual taste parts.

We generally think in terms of five basic taste sensations: salt, sour, sweet, bitter, and umami. The tastes of salt and sour have similar recognition mechanisms. Umami and sweet share a receptor unit, and then there's bitter, perhaps the most complicated of tastes, which has more than 30 receptors on the human tongue. These five tastes all have biological functions. Sweet is our body's way of rewarding us for consuming calorie-rich carbohydrates. Sourness tells us about the acidity of foods, and is a great indicator of things such as the ripeness of fruit. Umami is our method of recognizing proteins, and we need the ability to recognize salt to maintain equilibrium and balance in our bodies. Bitter compounds are often toxic or medicinal, and this might explain why we've developed a more highly tuned receptor system for bitter substances in terms of self-protection and self-nurturing.

Other "tastes" are less well understood. The taste receptor for fat has only recently been found in humans. Some fats make food delicious. Fat can enrich texture and mouthfeel while making flavors and aromas interact for longer with the tongue and nose. It's a flavor carrier. But what most scientists thought was purely a textural, physical sensation seems also to be an actual "taste," with its own dedicated receptor cells. We all sense fat differently and this difference is closely linked to the type of food we each choose to eat. Indeed, many of our sense levels differ; this is why we have individual tastes and like different foods. Some of these differences can be attributed to genetics. There are also some complex interactions with our exposure to sensations, which allow some people to become "used to" certain foods, such as chile.

Kokumi is a taste sensation you've probably never heard of, but have almost certainly experienced. As a mechanism, it's similar to umami in that it recognizes the building blocks of protein. If you cook a stew or a curry, then reheat and eat some the next day, you might perceive it to taste better, richer, deeper than when it was first cooked. My Persian Lamb Tagine with Rhubarb-Orange Salad (see page 65), Beef, Carrots & Ale (see page 49), Asian Sticky Beef Ribs (see page 55), and Tarka Dhal (see page 162) are good examples of dishes that display this trait. This is scientifically explained as an increase in kokumi. As proteins and DNA in the food continue to degrade over time, their simple amino acids and nucleotides are more greatly perceived by the tongue, and so the kokumi taste is enhanced. This is handy information if you're cooking a stew, tagine, or curry for a dinner party; it's better to make it a day ahead.

Astringency and metallic are other tastes less well understood by science. Metallics are thought of as either "zapping" the tongue with a taste hit—a kind of physical reaction to partial oxidation of the receptor cells—or as a sudden increase in the electrical conductivity of our saliva. Astringency is a mix between a taste sensation and a physical reaction: the immediate release of proteins in our saliva when it comes into contact with tannins or similar compounds. Highly tannic red wines, unripe grapes, strong black tea, pomegranates, and floral waters are all examples of this. In fact, I use some of these in my recipes to help cut richness, counteract sweetness, and create balance.

There is another type of taste perception: a physical reaction called chemesthesis, which is associated with the effects that mint and chile have on our bodies. This is the chemical response associated with pain, touch, and heat receptors. The cooling effect of mint and the heat of chile have opposite effects on the tongue, and they both affect our perception of temperature. Menthol, a compound in mint, triggers a receptor on the tongue that responds to cool temperatures. It just happens that we have the same receptors all over our skin, so our bodies are tricked into thinking they're cooling off, when, in fact, this is merely the effect of menthol. Chile has a similar effect, but its tricky trigger compound is known as capsaicin. This triggers a receptor on the tongue that elsewhere on our bodies is linked to the perception of heat, so consuming capsaicin makes us think we're heating up. Our body's cells help us regulate our core temperature by sending signals to the brain when hot or cold is received by the sensors on our tongue and body. You could say that menthol and capsaicin act as receptor "blockers." Menthol raises the temperature at which the cell will send a cold signal, so that even at room temperature, the food we eat feels cold. The opposite happens when we eat chile; the taste receptor would normally trigger and send a warning signal to the brain at around 107.6°F (42°C), but eating food containing capsaicin lowers this threshold to around 95°F (35°C). The result is that we feel hot from eating food containing chile, although the food may be at room temperature.

Chiles are interesting in other ways, too. To digress for a moment, the commonly accepted scale that measures the heat of chiles, the Scoville scale, was devised using a panel of chile tasters drinking various dilutions of capsaicin in water. The system allots Scoville Heat Units (SHU) to different chiles: the higher the number of units, the hotter the chile. My favorite chile, the Thai (or bird's-eye), rates about 50,000–100,000 SHU and the jalapeño 2,500–8,000. The trouble is everyone perceives taste differently, so the scale is unreliable. A second system, the American Spice Trade Association (ASTA) scale, measures the concentration of heat-producing chemicals more scientifically. Roughly, one capsaicin part per million equals 15 SHU, so 1 ASTA is about the same as 15 SHU.

We're the only animals that deliberately consume chiles for pleasure. Our brains respond to the perceived pain by releasing the pleasant and addictive substances known as endorphins, and this in turn perpetuates our desire to eat chiles. Furthermore, chile increases our perception of salt, so you can actually reduce the amount of salt you use in dishes by adding chile.

Incorporating spices in our food has other health benefits, too. Spices improve digestion through increased salivary, gastric, and intestinal secretions, bile production, and healthy bowel function. Pungent food sensations occur not only in the mouth and nose cavity, but also in the respiratory, gastrointestinal, cardiovascular, and nervous systems, suggesting the possibility of more systemic health effects. To get to the point, spices contain many bioactive compounds. On a physiological level, we perceive the flavor of these compounds as exciting, pronounced, and vibrant, but these compounds often work in tandem with many of our other bodily functions, which modern medicine is only just beginning to explore. Many spices have antibacterial, antioxidant, anti-inflammatory, or other beneficial properties, which is why they have a rich history of use both in food preserving throughout many culinary cultures and in Ayurvedic medicine.

AYURVEDA

Ayurveda is an ancient Hindu philosophy, more than 3,000 years old, the basis of which can be summed up as, "Look after your body and your body will look after itself." It is the science of life, the science of longevity.

I happen to believe that the basic principles of Ayurveda can benefit our overall well-being. So how do we get our bodies to look after themselves? Mainly through common sense and a little understanding: regular exercise, managing stress levels, and, more important, thinking about what we eat and how we manage our diets.

Ayurveda is all about maintaining a healthy digestive system. Spices form an integral part of an Ayurvedic diet, and many have proven health benefits; they are traditionally matched with foods not only for their specific taste but also for their digestive properties. Certain meats and vegetables are always paired with certain spices because they have been found over time to help the digestion of the foodstuff. So starchy tubers go with ajwain, lentils with asafetida, gourds with coriander— that kind of thing. "Synergy" is a concept I apply when combining spices in a blend; it derives from two Greek words meaning "working together" and means that every spice has its role to play, not just from a flavor perspective, but also from a digestive, soothing, or stimulating slant.

Ayurveda explains that if you eat seven different *rasas* (tastes) at every meal, then your body can best assimilate and absorb its nutrients. Generally, in the West we recognize five main taste sensations: salt, sweet, bitter, sour, and umami. Ayurveda mentions two more: pungent and astringent. Pungent tastes come from foods, such as garlic, ginger, and asafetida. Astringency comes from floral waters, such as rose, from rhubarb, pomegranates, and certain other fruits, and in the form of tannins found in wine and coffee. Think of pungent garlic and astringent red wine, and the benefits they add to the French diet.

To look at this from a Western perspective, it's like when rose bushes are planted between vines. The roses not only attract insects and pests away from the grapes, but they make the vines compete and work harder for soil nutrients. Or think about getting a vaccination before going on vacation; the vaccination contains a little of the infection, which causes the body to jump into action, helping the immune system to fight it off. Similarly, in Ayurveda, the pungent and astringent elements make our bodies work harder from the inside, keeping us strong and healthy, naturally. It's a question of balance and eating a variety of foods at each sitting. Part of the reason Indian cuisine has so many pickles, chutneys, and relishes is to help bring all the elements into each meal.

Another principle of Ayurveda divides us into three *doshas*, or body types: *vata, pitta,* and *kapha.* Determining which dosha you are helps to determine which foods and spices will keep you in the best of health. Further, your dosha can change as you become "out of balance," overstressed, and underexercised; you can change your diet until balance is restored, bringing you back to your ideal type. This is the essence of food as medicine.

My cousin Guria swears by the traditional remedy of cinnamon mixed with honey to ward off colds and flu, while turmeric in warm milk at night is said to help improve memory. Western medicine is now discovering the beneficial properties of spices. Turmeric has been proven to have anticancer and anti-inflammatory properties. Other scientific studies have shown that fenugreek lowers blood-sugar levels and is particularly useful for managing type-2 diabetes.

I won't go into every spice from an Ayurvedic point of view—that'd be a whole book in itself—but here is just one example in the form of coriander. According to Ayurveda, coriander improves digestion and stimulates hunger. It has antibacterial, antifungal, antispasmodic, carminative (flatulence-relieving), and diuretic properties. It also helps routine function of the stomach, relieves distension, diarrhea, and cold symptoms and may help to lower cholesterol. When steeped in water, the seeds can help regulate overactive peptic acid and relieve morning sickness. The seeds also have a relatively high vitamin B and C content. Sounds a little like a wonder medicine, doesn't it? The point is, eaten as part of a balanced diet, coriander's health benefits shine through. In conclusion, we can all benefit from Ayurveda, simply by eating a balanced diet, with regular meals, regular exercise—and loads of spice.

PORK & BACON

WHEN I MOVED TO IRELAND, PORK (AND PARTICULARLY BACON) JUMPED INTO MY COOKING REPERTOIRE. Green bacon, boiled bacon, smoked ham, ham steak, loin chops, bacon slices … I love them all. The group of spices I use in this chapter are about lifting porcine tastes, enlivening sweet fat with an aromatic buzz and mellowing saltiness.

The Bacon Chops with Glazed Pepper Pineapple and Fenugreek Potatoes is a firm and loving nod to my Irish family, my mother-in-law Rose, and her cooking. Next time you poach a piece of bacon or ham, simply add a mix of green cardamom and turmeric to the water: they balance and counteract the salty cure taste sensations. I've developed this idea in my Bacon Chop recipe, adding the sweetness of pineapple and the crunchy texture of bread crumbs. My Roast Pork Shoulder Vindaloo is a similar case of stretching hands across the water. The combination of coriander, green cardamom, cloves, fennel, vinegar, garlic, ginger, and chiles don't detract from the meat, they compliment, lift, and embellish the ignoble swine!

I twist, tweak, and muddle green (lightly cured) bacon with the highs of green cardamom, fennel, nutmeg, coriander, white pepper, using them in other elements of the dish—the cooking liquid, marinade, or sauce. But there are times when the sweetness of the meat needs no emphasis, for example in my Warm Lentil and Ham Hock Salad, but by accenting the lentils with a little cumin and freshening it all up with peppery watercress and bitter endive, the dish comes together as a whole.

Pork is essentially a sweet-tasting meat: it needs a light touch, but it loves a little "crazy"—try Sichuan pepper, mace, and chile. In my Pig Plate, star anise, clove, and ginger combine with the more traditional juniper to tinge and soften the edges of the choucroute, with green cardamom, black pepper, and nutmeg to define and bring together all the different pork flavors.

Previous page: Fennel adds sweet anise notes, a vibrancy that balances salty sensations and cuts through sweet fat meat.

Roast Pork Shoulder Vindaloo

FOR THE MARINADE

2 teaspoons black peppercorns
1 teaspoon coriander seeds
5 green cardamom pods
1 teaspoon cumin seeds
5 cloves
½ teaspoon fennel seeds
¾ cup (6fl oz/175ml) cider
     vinegar
10 garlic cloves, crushed
3¼-inch (8cm) piece fresh
     ginger (about 4½oz/125g)
2 onions, coarsely chopped
1 heaping tablespoon tomato
     paste
2 tablespoons canola oil
2 teaspoons Kashmiri
     chili flakes
2 teaspoons powdered turmeric
½ teaspoon finely ground cassia
1 teaspoon sea salt
2 teaspoons superfine sugar

FOR THE PORK

4½lb (2kg) piece of shoulder
     pork, boned and scored
2 tablespoons sunflower oil
3 cups (1⅓ pints/750ml) light
     chicken stock or broth
1 red Thai chile, seeded and
     finely diced (optional)
2 tablespoons (1oz/30g) butter,
     cubed
1 handful cilantro leaves,
     chopped
Coconut flakes, toasted

This wonderfully fragrant, almost sweet-and-sour Goan dish has a peppery perfume. Its name hints at its Portuguese heritage—vindaloo is more about vinegar (vin) and garlic (alho) than pure heat—but the chiles reflect Goa's penchant for a little extra kick.

1. Finely grind the marinade spices using a mortar and pestle. Put all the marinade ingredients into a food processor and process to a paste. (Alternatively, grate the garlic, ginger, and onions, then add the remaining ingredients and grind to a paste, using a mortar and pestle.) Taste to judge how much Thai chile, if any, you will need to use later.

2. Put the meat into a large mixing bowl and pour the paste over it. Massage the meat with the paste, then cover, put it into the refrigerator, and let marinate for at least 4 hours or preferably overnight.

3. Preheat the oven to 350°F (180°C). Put a large roasting pan over high heat. Lift the meat from its marinade, reserving the marinade in the bowl. Sear all sides of the meat to achieve a golden, nutty brown. Remove from the heat.

4. Next, pour the oil over the meat, followed by the marinade, coating the meat all over. Add the stock or broth and the Thai chile, if using, to the roasting pan, then give it a quick stir. Dab the butter over the meat and cover loosely with aluminum foil or moistened wax paper. Put on the middle shelf of the oven and roast for 2 hours.

5. Remove the foil, give the cooking liquid a quick stir, then put the roast back into the oven, uncovered, for another 10 minutes or until the meat and sauce are just browned. Remove from the oven and put the meat on a board to rest. Stir the sauce, then put it over high heat until reduced to the consistency of heavy cream, stirring frequently. Remove from the heat and set aside.

6. Carve generous slices of the pork and put on a warmed serving plate. Coat the slices with the sauce, sprinkle with fresh cilantro and coconut flakes, and serve with fragrant basmati rice or other long-grain rice.

WARM LENTIL & HAM HOCK SALAD

This dish takes a little time to make, but it's actually a simple process. Earthy lentils combine with the earthy-citrus notes of cumin. Sweet, tender ham adds texture and contrast, and semi-dried tomatoes, parsley, and fresh mint add a clean lift at the end. The use of hot ham stock in the mayonnaise emulsion balances the dish, coating peppery salad greens for freshness and bite.

SERVES 6

FOR THE HAM HOCKS
**2 ham hocks or knuckles, about
   1¾–2¼lb (850g–1kg) each
2 carrots, chopped into chunks
1 leek, chopped into chunks
1 onion, chopped into chunks
3 celery sticks, chopped into
   chunks
3 ripe tomatoes
2 garlic cloves, crushed
2 teaspoons cumin seeds**

FOR THE LENTILS
**1¾ cups (12oz/350g) French
   green Puy lentils or beluga
   lentils
2 cups (18fl oz/500ml)
   ham-hock cooking liquid
2 cups (18fl oz/500ml) vegetable
   stock or broth
2 teaspoons cumin seeds,
   finely ground**

FOR THE VEGETABLES
**3 tablespoons light olive oil
2 shallots, finely chopped
1 small carrot, finely chopped
2 celery sticks, finely chopped
1 garlic clove, crushed**

1. To cook the ham hocks, put all the ingredients in a large saucepan and cover with cold water. Bring up to a simmer over low heat, partly cover, and let simmer gently for 4–5 hours, until the meat is meltingly tender and soft. Top up the water from time to time to make sure it doesn't go below the level of the meat.

2. Leave the hocks in the cooking liquid until cool enough to handle, then remove to a plate. Strain the liquid into a small bowl.

3. Put the lentils, cooking liquid, stock or broth, and cumin seeds in a large, heavy saucepan. Bring up to a gentle simmer and cook over low heat, partly covered, for about 20 minutes, until only a couple of teaspoons of liquid run around the pan and the lentils are only just soft. Remove from the heat, cover completely, then set aside and keep warm.

4. Heat the olive oil in a sauté pan or skillet, then add the vegetables and garlic and cook over medium–low heat for a couple of minutes. Turn out onto a plate, set aside, and keep warm.

[*Continued*]

FOR THE MAYONNAISE

⅔ cup (5fl oz/150ml) ham-hock cooking liquid
2 large egg yolks
1 teaspoon Dijon mustard
1 tablespoon white wine vinegar
1 cup (9fl oz/250ml) light olive oil
Grinding of white pepper
Sea salt

FOR THE SALAD

12 semi-dried tomatoes (see Tip) or fresh plum, roma, or cherry tomatoes, quartered
1 handful curly parsley leaves, chopped
1 small handful mint leaves, finely shredded

TO GARNISH

1 large bunch watercress, leaves and thin stems
2 heads endive, sliced lengthwise into thin shards

5. To make the mayonnaise, heat the cooking liquid in a small saucepan to a gentle simmer. Put the egg yolks, mustard, and vinegar into a food processor and pulse to combine. With the processor on slow, slowly trickle the oil down the spout. With the processor still running, carefully trickle in the hot ham stock, then add the white pepper and salt to taste. (Alternatively, make the mayo in a bowl, using a balloon wire whisk and plenty of elbow grease.)

6. If not using immediately, let cool, pour into a sterilized jar (see page 255) and put a circle of wax paper on the top of the dressing. Cover with a lid and store in the refrigerator. It keeps for at least two weeks.

7. When ready to serve, remove the jellied skin from the ham hocks and chop into small dice, then pull off the meat, trying to keep it in nice strips.

8. Warm the dressing, if necessary. Put the lentils, vegetables, and salad ingredients into a large mixing bowl and add a small handful of the chopped hock skin, together with about 2 tablespoons of the warm dressing—just enough to coat. Gently mix all the ingredients together.

9. In another bowl, combine the watercress and endive with 1 tablespoon of the dressing.

10. Serve the warm lentils and ham in generous amounts with some dressed salad greens.

Tip

To make your own semi-dried tomatoes (sometimes called sun-blush tomatoes), place halved plum, roma, or cherry tomatoes on a baking sheet, skin side down, and bake in a preheated oven at 250°F for about 4 hours.

Slow-Roast Pork Neck Chops

The rich roast pork, soft spicy beans, and zingy llajua *("hot sauce") come together to create a wonderful combination of flavors, textures, and heat.*

SERVES 4–6

8 pork neck chops, about
    4½ oz (125g) each
Sea salt
1 tablespoon light olive oil
2 onions, halved and thinly
    sliced
1 teaspoon superfine sugar
1 teaspoon white peppercorns
2 teaspoons fennel seeds
Seeds of 2 black cardamom pods
3½ cups (1½ pints/850ml)
    chicken stock or broth
1 cup (7fl oz/200ml) sweet hard
    cider, preferably local
2 strips of lemon zest, pared
    with a vegetable peeler
2 (15-oz/425-g) cans
    navy beans or lima beans,
    drained and rinsed

FOR THE LLAJUA

5 jalapeño peppers, seeded and
    coarsely chopped
½ onion, coarsely chopped
1 small handful cilantro leaves,
    with thin stems
4 ripe tomatoes, coarsely
    chopped
1 teaspoon sea salt

1. Preheat the oven to 275°F (140°C). Sprinkle a little salt on both sides of each chop. Add a splash of olive oil to a large flameproof casserole, Dutch oven, or deep roasting pan and put over high heat.

2. When hot, add the chops and sear for 1 minute on each side or until the meat is a nice nutty brown (you may need to do this in a couple of batches). Remove from the casserole and set aside.

3. Turn down the heat, add a little more oil, the onions, and sugar, and sauté gently for 12–15 minutes, until they take on a little color and become really soft.

4. Finely grind the peppercorns, fennel, and cardamom seeds, using a mortar and pestle. Add the stock or broth to the casserole, followed by the cider, lemon zest, and spices, stir well, then put the chops on top of the onions, pouring in any juices. Cover tightly with aluminum foil and cook on the middle shelf of the oven for 3½ hours.

5. Meanwhile, make the llajua. Put the chiles, onion, and cilantro into a food processor or blender and process to a smooth paste, then add the tomatoes and salt, and pulse to a chunky consistency. Set aside. (Alternatively, grind everything together, using a mortar and pestle.)

6. When the meat is cooked, still moist, and tender, remove the foil, take out the chops, and keep them warm. Remove and discard the lemon zest.

7. Add the beans to the casserole, put over medium heat, and stir gently to combine them with the cooking liquid. Bring up to a gentle simmer and cook for 3–5 minutes, until the beans are warmed through.

8. Take off the heat, pour the beans into a warmed serving dish, put the chops on top, drizzle with a little of the llajua, and serve the remainder in a side bowl.

BLOOD SAUSAGE SALAD

SERVES 2

FOR THE DRESSING

1 teaspoon caraway seeds
½ teaspoon fennel seeds
½ teaspoon black peppercorns
1 teaspoon English mustard
   powder
2 tablespoons red wine vinegar
½ cup (3½ fl oz 100ml) light
   olive oil
1 teaspoon sea salt
3 tablespoons boiling water

FOR THE CROUTONS

1 teaspoon caraway seeds
½ teaspoon cumin seeds
4 thin slices sourdough bread
A splash fruity olive oil
1 garlic clove, halved
1–2 pinches sea salt

FOR THE SALAD

1–2 splashes light olive oil
10½–14oz (300–400g) blood
   sausage, sliced on the
   diagonal
1 head each white endive, red
   endive, and radicchio, leaves
   separated
2 bunches of watercress
   (about 7oz/200g) or other
   peppery salad greens
A splash black truffle oil
8 quail eggs
1 pinch sea salt
8 pickled walnuts, sliced into
   disks, ends discarded

The types of black sausages vary, from the almost solid, meaty ones with a strong piggy flavor to the cereal-flecked ones to delicate, almost mousselike versions. All are perfect for this recipe. This salad has real earthy notes, ethereal truffle oil, crisp winter leaves, peppery watercress, and a delicate touch of fragrant anise.

1. Finely grind the spices for the dressing, using a mortar and pestle. Put all the dressing ingredients into a clean screw-top jar, pouring in the boiling water last, then shake well and set aside.

2. Finely grind the spices for the croutons and set aside. Drizzle the sourdough slices with a good glug of olive oil, put them under a hot broiler, and toast until the edges char. Let them cool slightly, then rub with the cut side of the garlic clove and sprinkle with the spices and sea salt. Cut each slice in half lengthwise to make dramatic, long triangular pieces. Set aside on a wire rack.

3. For the salad, heat a small splash of oil in a nonstick skillet over medium heat, then add the black sausage. Cook on one side for a few minutes until crisp, then turn over with a spatula and cook the other side. Remove from the pan and set aside to keep warm. Wipe the pan clean with paper towels.

4. Put the endive, radicchio, and watercress into a large bowl. Shake the dressing jar, add 2 tablespoons to the bowl, and gently mix the leaves, using your hands, adding a little more dressing, if you desire. Set aside.

5. Pour another slug of olive oil and a generous splash of black truffle oil into the wiped skillet. Break the eggs into it and put over medium–low heat. Gently cook for 2 minutes, until the whites are just set, sprinkle with sea salt, then spoon some of the oil over the eggs. Take off the heat.

6. Working fairly quickly, warm the croutons under the broiler, then carefully spread the dressed leaves over a large serving plate. Remove the croutons from the heat and put an egg onto each. Put these, and the sausage slices, among the leaves, sprinkle the pickled walnuts on top, and, finally, drizzle with a little more of the dressing. Serve immediately.

Bacon Chops with Glazed Pepper Pineapple & Fenugreek Potatoes

From my first trips to fast-food restaurants around English northern towns in the 1970s, to school lunches and then the occasional "greasy spoon" café, I developed, loved, and nurtured a taste for ham and pineapple. This is my version: spiced pineapple paired with a breaded bacon chop for texture and satisfying crunch. The potatoes are something Dad taught me more recently, and the bitter fenugreek also works well with the pineapple's sweetness. Prepare the glazed pineapple the day before, because it really benefits from 24 hours marinating.

SERVES 6–8

FOR THE GLAZED PEPPER PINEAPPLE

- **1¼ cups (9oz/250g) demerara sugar or other raw sugar**
- **1 (15-oz/425-g) can pineapple slices in syrup, drained and syrup reserved**
- **1 red finger chile, seeded and chopped into 3 pieces**
- **⅓ cup (1½oz/40g) coarsely chopped fresh ginger**
- **1 thyme sprig, leaves only**
- **1 strip of orange zest, pared with a vegetable peeler**
- **1 teaspoon black peppercorns**
- **½ teaspoon Sichuan pepper**
- **½ long pepper spike, smashed**
- **½ nutmeg, smashed**
- **3 cloves**

1. Put a large, heavy sauté pan over medium heat. Add the sugar and 2 tablespoons of the pineapple syrup, give it a quick stir, and let dissolve gently—about 6 minutes. Meanwhile, pat the pineapple slices dry with paper towels and set aside.

2. Once the sugar has dissolved, add the chile, ginger, thyme, zest, and spices and cook for 1–2 minutes, then add the pineapple slices.

3. Cook in the syrup for 2 minutes, turn them over, then cook for another 2 minutes. Take the pan off the heat, leaving the pineapple in the syrup, and set aside overnight, covered with a clean dish towel.

4. Next day, lift the pineapple onto a wire rack. Strain the syrup through a fine strainer into a small bowl.

[*Continued*]

FOR THE CHOPS

1 teaspoon white peppercorns
1 teaspoon cumin seeds
¾ cup (3½oz/100g) all-purpose
    flour
½ teaspoon powdered turmeric
1 teaspoon sea salt
1¼lb (600g) boneless loin
    of bacon, loin roast, or
    tenderloin roast
5 green cardamom pods, lightly
    crushed
2 large eggs, lightly beaten
1 cup (1¾oz/50g) fresh
    bread crumbs
Canola oil, for frying

FOR THE POTATOES

4–5 large red-skinned or white
    round potatoes, peeled and
    cut into bite-size chunks
2 tablespoons sunflower oil
2 teaspoons fenugreek seeds
1 heaping tablespoon coriander
    seeds, finely ground
2 teaspoon sea salt

5. Finely grind the peppercorns and cumin, using a mortar and pestle. Mix the flour, spices, turmeric, and salt and set aside on a dinner plate.

6. Put the bacon loin into a large saucepan, cover the meat with cold water, and bring to a boil. As the bubbles burst to the surface and a scum forms, take the pan off the heat, discard the water, then repeat. Do this three times.

7. Cover the meat with cold water as before, but this time add the cardamom pods. Bring to a boil, then turn down the heat to a gentle simmer, partly cover, and cook for 40 minutes.

8. Remove the bacon from the water, put on a cutting board, and cut away the rind and excess fat. Slice the loin into chops, about ⅝ inch (1.5cm) thick, coat in the spiced flour, then in the eggs, then in the bread crumbs. Set aside.

9. Boil the potatoes in lightly salted water for about 5 minutes, so that they are no longer raw but still holding their shape with a delicate "give" to their flesh. Drain.

10. Add the sunflower oil to a skillet and put over medium heat. Sprinkle in the fenugreek seeds and cook until they are a dark color, appearing burned, then quickly add the coriander seeds and salt, and stir to combine. Add the potatoes and toss to coat well with the spice mix, then cook for about 8 minutes, until tender but before they begin to break up. Take the pan off the heat and keep warm.

11. Add the canola oil to a heavy sauté pan and put over medium heat. Gently cook the chops, in batches, if necessary, until lightly golden, then remove them and drain on paper towels until you've fried all the chops.

12. Meanwhile, warm the pineapple syrup in a small saucepan, then pour it into a warmed small bowl. Serve the chops on warmed plates, with the glazed pineapple slices on top, and serve with the small bowl of pineapple syrup. Serve the potatoes in a separate bowl.

My Mom's Sausage & Potato Pie

Sausage "pie," or casserole, is great whenever we're looking for a little comfort from a meal.

SERVES 4–6

6–8 best-quality pork sausages

7 tablespoons (3½oz/100g) unsalted butter, diced, at room temperature

2 tablespoons canola oil

3 onions, halved and thinly sliced

1 teaspoon superfine sugar

1 teaspoon white peppercorns

Seeds of 2 green cardamom pods

1 star anise

Scant ¼ teaspoon finely ground mace

½ teaspoon powdered ginger

1 tablespoon sea salt

1 cup (9fl oz/250ml) sweet hard cider, preferably local

1 thyme sprig, leaves only

7 russet or Yukon Gold potatoes (about 2¾lb/1.25kg), peeled

⅓ cup (2½fl oz/75ml) whole milk

1 teaspoon English mustard

3 scallions, finely sliced on the diagonal

2 (14½-oz/400-g) cans diced tomatoes

1 teaspoon black peppercorns, coarsely ground

½ cup (1¾oz/50g) finely grated cheddar cheese

1 small handful curly parsley leaves, finely chopped

1. Preheat the oven to 400°F (200°C). Put the sausages on a baking sheet and bake in the oven for 35–40 minutes, turning them over after 20 minutes, until cooked and lightly browned. Let cool slightly, then cut in half lengthwise and set aside.

2. Meanwhile, heat 4 tablespoons (50g/1¾oz) of the butter and 1 tablespoon oil in a large, heavy skillet over medium heat. Add the onions and sugar. Stir, cover with a sheet of wax paper, and cook gently for 20 minutes or until the onions are meltingly soft. Finely grind the whole spices, using a mortar and pestle. Remove the paper from the pan and add all the spices and 1 teaspoon salt. Stir, then add the cider and thyme leaves. Turn up the heat slightly. Cook for 25–30 minutes, until all the cider has reduced and the onions are glossy. Set aside.

3. Put all but one of the potatoes into a saucepan and cover with water. Add 1 teaspoon salt. Bring to a boil over high heat, then reduce the heat and cook until tender. Drain. Heat the milk in a saucepan, add the remaining butter, and bring up to a boil. Add the mustard, 1 teaspoon salt, and the scallions. Stir, then pour a little over the boiled potatoes and mash until creamy, adding more of the milky mixture as required. Set aside. Put the tomatoes in a saucepan over medium heat, bring up to a good boil, and reduce by half, then take off the heat and set aside.

4. Using a sharp knife or mandoline slicer, slice the raw potato thinly—about ⅛ inch (2mm). Put in a colander, rinse well under cold running water, then turn out onto a clean dish towel and pat dry completely. In a small bowl, mix the potato slices with the ground pepper, 1 tablespoon oil, cheese, and parsley. Set aside.

5. Spread the onions over the bottom of a large ovenproof dish or roasting pan, then add the tomatoes, sausages, and mashed potatoes, spreading it evenly. Push in the potato slices so that they stick up at interesting angles. Bake for 1 hour, until the sliced potato crisps and colors slightly. Serve with peas and a glass of mulled cider or wine.

POTTED PEPPER PORK

Potted pork is perfect for picnics or appetizers served with crostini, Melba toast, or crusty sourdough bread, plus cornichons and assorted pickles, crunchy radishes, and celery. If you're using really good pork, the apple brandy and scorched orange zest may seem a little extravagant, but it adds a lovely depth of flavor that works well with the clove notes.

MAKES 1½LB (700G)

FOR THE MIREPOIX

2 carrots, cut into ⅜ inch (8mm) dice

1 onion, cut into ⅜ inch (8mm) dice

3 celery sticks, halved

6 garlic cloves, peeled and gently smashed

1 large cooking apple, such as Granny Smith, peeled, cored, and cut into 8 pieces

FOR THE POTTED PORK

3 Indian bay leaves (tejpatta), lightly crushed

2¼lb (1kg) pork belly, rind removed

⅔ cup (5fl oz/150ml) dry hard cider, preferably local

½ teaspoon white peppercorns

4 cloves

1 piece blade mace

1 allspice berry

1 teaspoon fine sea salt

½ teaspoon finely ground cinnamon

3–4 gratings nutmeg

2 tablespoons apple brandy

Zest of ¼ orange, pared with a vegetable peeler

5½–7 tablespoons (2¾–3½oz/ 75–100g) unsalted butter, melted

1. Preheat the oven to 325°F (160°C). Spread all the mirepoix ingredients over the bottom of a deep baking pan. Sprinkle with the Indian bay leaves, then put the pork belly on top. Add the cider, cover, and seal tightly with aluminum foil. Slow-roast for 3–4 hours, until the meat is meltingly tender. Let rest in the pan to cool to room temperature. Finely grind the whole spices, using a mortar and pestle; set aside.

2. Transfer the pork to a cutting board. Strain the cooking juices and reserve. Cut off and discard the pork rind, then cut the white fat away from the meat. Carefully remove the thin sinew from the meat and discard. Pull about one-quarter of the pork meat into "single-thread" strips. Coarsely chop 2 tablespoons of the white fat into small dice.

3. Discard the bay leaves, celery, and garlic. Put the pork threads into a large bowl and add the diced fat, the braised carrots, onion, and apple. Set aside. Put the remaining meat and white fat into a food processor. Pulse until it forms a velvety, airy emulsion. (Alternatively, chop the meat and fat as finely as you can, then put it into a bowl and beat well with a wooden spoon.) Sprinkle the salt, cinnamon, nutmeg, and ground spices over the meat, and briefly pulse or stir again. Using a rubber spatula, scrape the emulsion into the bowl of pork threads. Set aside.

4. Put the apple brandy and orange zest into a heavy saucepan. Warm the alcohol, then set it alight and let it burn for 10 seconds. Put the lid on to extinguish the flame, discard the zest and set aside to cool. Add the apple brandy and ¼ cup of the reserved cooking juices to the pork. Mix together with your fingers to form a spreadable consistency, adding a little more of the juices, if needed. Season to taste. Transfer to sterilized jars (see page 255) and pour melted butter on top to about ⅛ inch (3mm). Store in the refrigerator for two to three days before serving. Bring to room temperature and serve with pickles and toast. Store in the refrigerator unopened for six months; once opened, use within seven days.

PIG PLATE

This dish is a celebration of all things pig, and is something I first tried on a hazy day spent in Paris. Salt-cured cabbage, aka choucroute, or "sauerkraut," the stalwart of the brasseries, forms the backbone of this beautiful dish and is the foil to a selection of salted, cured, or smoked pork cuts and charcuterie. Look for pure pork poaching sausages at your local master butcher, farmers' markets, East European delis, or even larger supermarkets. Buy sauerkraut in jars—it's a tricky thing to make from scratch. This makes a generous quantity, so is ideal for family celebrations, because you can really push the boat out, and have a feast of different cuts garnished with a whole host of vegetables.

SERVES 6–10

2¾lb (1.2kg) boneless smoked cured ham

3¼lb (1.5kg) salted, unsmoked pork belly bacon

1¾lb (800g) pure pork sausages: French, German, or Polish poaching sausages

FOR THE COOKING LIQUID

2 leeks

2 celery sticks

1 small handful parsley stalks

2 carrots

1 large onion

1 red chile, split in half and seeded

20 black peppercorns

8 green cardamom pods, smashed

1 whole nutmeg

1. Put the ham and belly cuts into a large saucepan, cover the meat with cold water, and bring to a boil. As the bubbles burst to the surface and a scum forms, take the pan off the heat, pour away the water, then repeat. Do this three times.

2. Cover the meat with cold water as before, but this time add all the cooking liquid ingredients. Bring to a boil, then turn the heat down to a gentle simmer, partly cover, and cook for 40 minutes.

3. Add the sausages and cook for another 35 minutes, then lift out all the meat, set aside, and keep warm. Strain the cooking liquid into a large small bowl or bowl. Preheat the oven to 250°F (120°C).

4. Finely grind the spices for the choucroute, using a mortar and pestle.

5. Put the goose fat into a large, cast iron Dutch oven or heavy roasting pan. Add the choucroute, sprinkle in the spices, then add the orange zest, 3 cups (1⅓ pints/750ml) of the strained cooking liquid, the wine, ginger, celery, carrots, and onion quarters. Cover with wax paper, then seal the Dutch oven or pan with a close-fitting lid and aluminum foil.

6. Put in the oven and cook for 45 minutes or until most of the liquid has been absorbed into the cabbage. If the vegetables are not quite cooked, add a little more cooking liquid and return to the oven until they're only just able to hold their shape.

FOR THE CHOUCROUTE

1 small piece blade mace

1 star anise

½ teaspoon Sichuan pepper

2 juniper berries

½ long pepper spike

3 cloves

¼ cinnamon stick

1½ tablespoons goose fat, duck fat, or bacon dripping

9 cups (4½lb/2kg) cooked choucroute (sauerkraut), drained through a colander, pressing down with a plate to be sure all liquid is removed

Zest of ½ an orange, pared with a vegetable peeler

1¾ cups (14fl oz/400ml) good white wine

1¼-inch (3-cm) piece fresh ginger, peeled (about 1¾oz/50g)

1 celery heart, quartered

10 carrots

3 onions, quartered

7. Remove the vegetables, using a slotted spoon, and transfer to a large, warmed oval serving plate, piling them in a mound on one side.

8. Remove the cabbage with a slotted spoon (so that the juices remain in the casserole) and pile it onto the other side of the serving plate. Slice the ham into generous chunks and place on top of the cabbage. Slice the pork belly into ½-inch (1-cm)-thick pieces and add to the plate, placing them on top of the ham along with the sausages, left whole.

9. Pour a little of the cooking liquid over the vegetables and the meats to moisten them.

10. Take the choucroute and vegetables to the table and serve with a generous quantity of boiled new potatoes, Dijon mustard, and a well-chilled Riesling, Pinot Blanc, or Pilsner lager. Spectacular!

BEEF & VENISON

DARK AND RICH, BEEF AND VENISON need spice notes that will cut through richness. Chiles do this effectively and I love using such varieties as dried Kashmiri or chipotle chiles; they introduce a smoky, fruity element that's more than just pure heat. In my Chile Beef Hash, Kashmiri chiles add subtle heat and "kick" to liven up a favorite family dinner.

Try to find beef where the animal has been grass-fed on lush pastures and suitably aged (preferably for no less than 21 days). Aging brings out an iodine-rich, almost fresh leathery perfumed flavor in the meat (beasts less loved, less carefully raised and slaughtered, tend to produce meat with a "metallic" edge). Venison is also aged, or hung, before eating, and has a deeper flavor than beef, typically referred to as "gamy." And it's these characteristics I pick up on when it comes to spices.

Dark, aged, strong-flavored meats with hearty, "meaty" textures can carry off dark, sultry spices. Black cardamom, black pepper, nutmeg, and star anise are used in the blend for Beef, Carrots, and Ale; the deep, smoky notes add depth to the dish, but also bring a clarity to the richness of the stew.

Black cardamom has a kind of twisted perfume, as does long pepper, and I think these two work really well together. Ginger has a lovely sweet perfume, while still a little "mottled," sitting in the background to nutmeg's heady dominance. All these spices combine with the rich, warm aromatics of beautiful star anise in my Asian Sticky Ribs, creating a stunning effect.

Mace is great for defining flavors, with its floral perfume and touch of astringency—just a small amount can make a big difference. I use mace in the Smoked Chili Sauce of my "Dog" to help balance and add definition to the smoky eggplant.

Previous page: The subtly perfumed, slightly astringent qualities of mace help define and lengthen the finish of rich, dark meats.

CHILE BEEF HASH

Here's a spicy take on a dish we used to have as kids: corned beef hash and baked beans. This is wonderful comfort food and really tasty. I like to use up leftovers for my hash and find that a mix of meats is excellent. Poultry, pork, and beef work well together.

SERVES 4

1lb (450g) new potatoes,
5½ tablespoons (2¾oz/75g)
    unsalted butter
1 onion, diced
2 teaspoons cumin seeds
2 teaspoons Kashmiri
    chili flakes
½ teaspoon sea salt
1lb 2oz (500g) cooked beef
    brisket, diced and torn, or a
    mix of leftover cuts
3½oz (100g) fresh mushrooms
    (porcini, chanterelles, or
    blewits work well), coarsely
    chopped
½ cup (3½fl oz/100ml)
    good-quality chicken
    stock or broth
A little sunflower oil
4 eggs
1 handful curly parsley leaves,
    finely chopped

1. Put the potatoes into a saucepan and cover generously with water. Bring to a boil over high heat and cook until only just tender. Drain and cut into 1-inch (2.5-cm) pieces. Set aside.

2. Put a heavy, nonstick skillet over medium–low heat. Add 4 tablespoons (50g/1¾oz) of the butter and let melt, then add the onion and cook gently until soft and translucent.

3. Turn up the heat slightly and sprinkle in the cumin seeds, Kashmiri flakes and salt. Stir to combine, then add the diced potatoes and the meat. Don't stir them, just let them cook until they begin to brown slightly.

4. Turn the mixture over with a spatula and add the mushrooms. Add the remaining butter and cook for 5–6 minutes, until the potatoes and meat are lightly browned all over.

5. Add the stock or broth, turn up the heat to a simmer, and give the mixture a little stir. Let the stock simmer and reduce.

6. Meanwhile, heat the oil in another skillet, crack in the eggs, and cook them until they're cooked just as you prefer. Set aside.

7. Check that the potatoes are cooked, then spoon a generous amount of the hash onto each of four warmed plates. Put a fried egg on top of each mound of hash, sprinkle with the parsley, and serve immediately.

Beef-on-Beef "Dog" with Smoked Chili Sauce & Gubbeen Cheese

This is a delicious and simple way to use up leftovers of beef brisket—the addition of my aromatic smoked chili sauce gives this hot dog the edge. Gubbeen cheese is a semisoft, washed-rind cheese made by Tom and Giana Ferguson at the Gubbeen Farmhouse in West Cork, Ireland. If you can't get your hands on it, then simply use your favorite melting cheese instead: Comté or a mild cheddar are perfect.

SERVES 4

10½ oz (300g) poached brisket
    (see Tip)—or any cooked
    beef or pork leftovers (about
    2 heaping cups of chunks)

FOR THE DOG DRESSING
½ teaspoon black peppercorns
4 cloves
½ star anise
1 teaspoon Kashmiri chili flakes
2 tablespoons ketchup
1 teaspoon Worcestershire sauce
2 teaspoons maple syrup
1 garlic clove
1 cilantro sprig, hard stems
    removed

1. To make the dressing, finely grind the peppercorns, cloves, and star anise, using a mortar and pestle, then add the Kashmiri flakes. Put all the dressing ingredients into a food processor and pulse until just smooth.

2. Put the brisket on a large plate and use your fingers to break up about 1¾ cups (9oz/250g) of the meat into large chunks, reserving the remaining ⅓ cup (1½oz/50g).

3. Spoon the dressing over the chunks of brisket, coating the meat well. If you'll be using in it the next hour or so, let it marinate at room temperature. If not, cover loosely with wax paper and put it in the refrigerator for up to 12 hours.

Tip

To cook brisket, put the brisket into a large saucepan and cover with water. Add a few peppercorns and a carrot, then bring to a boil. Reduce the heat and simmer for 2 hours or until the meat is meltingly soft. Serve hot, or drain and let cool.

[Continued]

SMOKED CHILI SAUCE

2 teaspoons coriander seeds
1 teaspoon cumin seeds
1 small piece blade mace
¼ teaspoon Kashmiri chili flakes
2 firm eggplants
1 tablespoon light olive oil, plus
**   extra if needed**
1 onion, diced
2 garlic cloves, finely diced
2 teaspoons molasses
⅓ cup (50g/1¾oz) brisket strips
**   (see above, pulled apart)**
½ cup (2¾oz /75g) drained,
**   canned chickpeas, rinsed,**
**   lightly crushed with a fork**
2 teaspoons tomato paste
Sea salt

1. Finely grind the coriander and cumin seeds and the mace, using a mortar and pestle, then add the Kasmiri flakes.

2. Insert a metal skewer lengthwise through each eggplant so you can turn them easily, prick them with a fork, then put them on the open flame of a gas stove or under a preheated broiler.

3. When the eggplants are nicely charred all around—this is what gives the eggplant its delicious smoky flavor—cut each one in half, remove the flesh, and coarsely chop it up. Discard the skins.

4. Heat the oil in a skillet over medium heat and sauté the onion for 1 minute, then add the eggplant flesh, the garlic, and the ground spices and cook for about 5 minutes, until it's all lovely and soft.

5. Add the molasses to the pan, followed by the brisket, the chickpeas, and the tomato paste; cook for 2 minutes, adding a little more oil, if required, then set aside and let cool before adjusting the seasoning.

TO FINISH

4 soft hot dog rolls
¼ head iceberg lettuce,
**   finely shredded**
½ red onion, thinly sliced
1¼ cups (5½oz/150g) shredded
**   Gubbeen cheese, mild**
**   cheddar cheese, or your**
**   favorite**
1 small handful cilantro leaves,
**   coarsely chopped**

1. To assemble your dog, bring the marinated brisket back to room temperature, if necessary. Preheat the broiler to its hottest setting.

2. Slice open a roll and gently pull it apart, leaving a "hinge," then put onto a baking sheet or broiler pan.

3. Put a little lettuce on the butterflied roll, then spread a couple of spoons of the Smoked Chili Sauce evenly along the roll. Add some of the marinated brisket, and top with the onion and cheese. Repeat for all the rolls.

4. Put the pan under the hot broiler and glaze the hot dogs until they're just colored: about 30 seconds to 1 minute.

5. Finish with some chopped fresh cilantro and serve immediately. One "dog" may not be enough!

BEEF, CARROTS & ALE

This is an unbelievably rich, unctuous, "eat-with-a-spoon" beef dish. I love using beef shin for this recipe; it's one of my favorite cuts for slow cooking. The naturally gelatinous meat adds beautiful body and general oomph! If you use stewing beef, ask your butcher for a couple of marrow bones to throw into the cooking pot for extra flavor. You will need to start two days in advance to let for the long marinating time—or better still, three days, so you can reheat the stew for maximum flavor development. Served with Coconut Mashed Roots (see page 51), it's a total comfort treat!

SERVES 4–6

1kg (2lb 4oz) beef shank, cut coarsely in half, keeping the central bone in one half, or chuck beef, plus 1–2 marrow bones, sawn in half by the butcher

FOR THE MARINADE

1 teaspoon black peppercorns
½ star anise
3 cloves
½ teaspoon fennel seeds
2 teaspoons Garam Masala blend (see page 267)
1 teaspoon red pepper flakes
4¼ cups (1¾ pints/1 liter) stout, use a dark, rich brand
3 small thyme sprigs
1 garlic bulb, cloves peeled

FOR THE STEW

2 tablespoons all-purpose flour
1 teaspoon sea salt
2 tablespoons canola oil
7oz (200g) pearl onions or shallots, peeled

1. Finely grind the peppercorns, star anise, cloves, and fennel seeds, using a mortar and pestle, then add the Garam Masala and red pepper flakes. Set aside 2 teaspoons of the spice mix to use later.

2. Put all the marinade ingredients into a nonmetallic bowl and add the beef. Cover with wax paper, weigh it down with a small plate to make sure everything is submerged, then cover the bowl with plastic wrap and put it into the refrigerator. Let marinate for 40–48 hours. After 24 hours, gently move the meat around, then replace the cover.

3. To make the stew, mix the flour, the reserved 2 teaspoons spice mix, and the salt in a small bowl. Remove the meat from the marinade, dry well with paper towels, then lightly coat with the flour mixture and put it on a plate. Set aside.

4. Put a heavy flameproof casserole or Dutch oven over medium heat. Add the oil. Shake any excess flour from the meat. When the oil is hot, cook the beef in a couple of batches so that each piece is nicely caramelized on each side. Preheat the oven to 325°F (160°C).

5. Transfer the meat to a clean plate. Turn down the heat slightly, then add the onions and celery, stir, and cook for 30 seconds. Add the carrots, turnips, meat, and marrow bones, if using, and all the marinade, bring to a gentle simmer (no more than a bubble or two), then cover with aluminum foil, put on the lid, and put into the oven to cook for 3–3½ hours, until tender.

[*Continued*]

2 celery sticks, cut into chunky
batons
2 large carrots, peeled and cut
into chunks
8 small turnips (about 1½lb/
700g), peeled and halved, or
3 large turnips, peeled and
diced into 1¼-inch (3-cm)
cubes
1 tablespoon red wine vinegar
1 handful curly parsley leaves,
chopped

6. Remove the casserole from the oven. Using a slotted spoon, carefully transfer the meat, celery, turnips, carrots, and onions to a large, shallow serving dish and skim any surplus fat from the cooking liquid.

7. Put the casserole over high heat and reduce the liquid to about half, until the gravy is rich and unctuous. Add the wine vinegar, stir, then put all the meat and vegetables back into the sauce. (If making this the day before you serve, let cool, cover, and keep in the refrigerator overnight. Reheat the stew when the mashed roots are nearly ready.) Sprinkle with the parsley, give it a quick stir, and let rest while you make the Coconut Mashed Roots.

Coconut Mashed Roots

2 small–medium (about 1lb 2oz/
500g) rutabagas, cut into
chunks
8 carrots (about 500g/1lb 2oz),
chopped into chunks
4 russet or Yukon Gold potatoes
(about 500g/1lb 2oz), peeled
1⅔ cups (14fl oz/400ml)
coconut milk
4 tablespoons (1¾oz/50g)
salted butter
2 heaping teaspoons black
peppercorns, coarsely ground
Sea salt

1. Put the rutabagas and carrots into a saucepan, add warm, salted water to cover, and boil for 35 minutes or until soft. Drain, set aside, and let steam-dry.

2. Put the potatoes into a second saucepan. Just cover with warm, salted water and boil for 25 minutes or until soft. Drain, set aside, and let steam-dry.

3. Put the coconut milk, butter, and peppercorns into a third saucepan, bring to a gentle simmer, and reduce to about ⅔ cup (5fl oz/150ml)—this will take about 35 minutes.

4. Combine all the ingredients, mash to a chunky texture, and serve hot.

ROAST SIRLOIN IN A TAMIL CRUST

This is a roast cut of meat like no other! I've taken a southern Indian influence to add a little extra dimension to what is an economical, wonderful cut of meat for a Sunday (or any day) roast. The buttery crumb and cooking juices add an extra depth of flavor. You will need to start a day ahead to allow for marinating. Don't forget to keep any leftovers for my Chile Beef Hash on page 45.

SERVES 4

3¼lb (1.5kg) sirloin beef, aged
    for at least 21 days, with a
    nice dark hue
3 onions, halved through the
    root, then each half sliced
    into 4 wedges
Canola oil, for frying

FOR THE MARINADE
1 tablespoon coriander seeds
2 teaspoons cumin seeds
1 star anise
5 cloves
1 teaspoon dried rose petals
2 teaspoons finely ground cassia
1 teaspoon Kashmiri chili flakes
¾ cup (2¾oz/75g) coarsely
    chopped fresh ginger
6 garlic cloves, coarsely chopped
1 handful mixed soft herbs,
    such as parsley, cilantro, dill,
    coarsely chopped
⅓ cup (2½fl oz/75ml) canola oil
½ cup (4fl oz/125ml)
    lemon juice
2 tablespoons lime juice
1 tablespoon sea salt

1. First grind the coriander seeds, cumin seeds, star anise, cloves, and rose petals to a fine powder, using a mortar and pestle. Add the cassia and Kashmiri flakes. Put the ginger, garlic, herbs, oil, spice blend, lemon and lime juices, and salt into a food processor and blend to a smooth paste.

2. Trim the meat, then, using the point of a knife, make plenty of jabbed incisions over both sides. Put the meat into a large nonmetallic bowl and coat it in the marinade paste. Rub the marinade in all over. Cover the bowl with plastic wrap and let marinate in the refrigerator for 24 hours. Turn the meat over at least three or four times during this time.

3. When you're ready to cook, let the meat come to room temperature (it will take about 40 minutes). Preheat the oven to 400°F (200°C).

4. Put a large roasting pan over medium–high heat, add the onion wedges and a little oil, and sauté gently for 5 minutes, tossing them around occasionally, until they're just beginning to soften.

5. Remove the meat from the bowl and shake or scrape off any excess marinade. Reserve the marinade. Put the meat on top of the onions, then put the pan in the oven.

6. Roast for about 50–55 minutes for rare (120–130°F/50–55°C core temperature if using a meat thermometer), or up to 1¼ hours for medium (140–150°F/60–65°C core temperature). Use a slotted spoon to remove the meat and onion wedges from the pan and put them on a warmed plate. Cover with aluminum foil and set aside to rest for 20–25 minutes.

FOR THE SAUCE

3 tablespoons packed jaggery or dark brown sugar

4 tablespoons red wine vinegar

3 tablespoons finely chopped flat-leaf parsley

Sea salt

FOR THE CRUMB MIX

3 tablespoons (1½oz/40g) unsalted butter

2 cups (3½oz/100g) fresh bread crumbs

½ cup (1½oz/40g) finely grated fresh Parmesan cheese

½ teaspoon cayenne pepper

1 small handful flat-leaf parsley, very finely chopped

7. Meanwhile, make the sauce in the roasting pan over medium–low heat. Add the reserved marinade, the jaggery or brown sugar, and the vinegar to the meat juices. Bring to a gentle simmer and whisk everything together, incorporating all the cooked, sticky sediment. Cook for a couple of minutes, stirring continuously. Check the seasoning, then add the parsley and any cooking juices from the resting meat and stir through; set aside.

8. To make the crumb, put a heavy skillet over medium heat and add the butter. When it's just beginning to foam, add the bread crumbs and sauté gently for a few minutes, until golden, then add the Parmesan, cayenne, and parsley; set aside.

9. To serve, warm a large serving plate. Put the meat on a carving board and carve it into chunky slices. Put the slices onto the warm plate, spread the onion wedges on top and sprinkle with the crumb mix. Pour the sauce into a small, warmed bowl and let everyone help themselves.

ASIAN STICKY BEEF RIBS

I love getting a piece of a charred crunch along with the succulent, fall-off-the-bone action, a kick of chile, and a big hit of deep, glorious flavor, matched by an equally rich yogurt and cilantro dipping sauce. Ideally, you need to marinate everything the night before—but it's worth it!

SERVES 4–6

4½lb (2kg) beef short ribs
(cut as racks)

FOR THE MARINADE

3 star anise
1 cinnamon stick
Seeds of 2 black cardamom pods
1 tablespoon black peppercorns
½ nutmeg, grated
½ teaspoon long pepper spike,
    finely grated (optional)
⅔ cup (2¼oz/60g) peeled and
    finely grated fresh ginger
3 garlic cloves, lightly smashed
⅓ cup firmly packed (2¾oz/75g)
    light brown sugar
Zest and juice of 1 orange
2 red finger chiles, cut into thin
    disks, seeds and all
1 teaspoon sea salt
1 lemongrass stalk, bruised,
    then halved lengthwise
1 teaspoon unsweetened
    cocoa powder
1 tablespoon freshly made
    espresso coffee
½ cup (4fl oz 125ml) tamari or
    light soy sauce
⅓ cup (3½oz/100g) molasses
2 teaspoons Thai fish sauce
½ cup (4fl oz/125ml) rice wine
    vinegar
4 tablespoons white wine vinegar
½ cup (4fl oz/125ml) water
½ cup (4fl oz/125ml) dry sherry
1 tablespoon sunflower oil

1. Finely grind the star anise, cinnamon, cardamom seeds, and black peppercorns, using a mortar and pestle. Add the grated nutmeg and long pepper, if using.

2. Put the spices and all the remaining marinade ingredients into a large nonmetallic bowl and stir throughly to combine. Add the ribs, cover, and let marinade in the refrigerator for at least 4 hours or overnight. Turn the ribs over once or twice during this time so that everything is well coated.

3. The next day, preheat the oven to 325°F (160°C). Put the ribs into a roasting pan, pour the marinade over them, then cover tightly with aluminum foil and put onto the middle shelf of the oven to cook for 3 hours.

4. After 3 hours, the racks should be floppy. If they're not, return them to the oven for another 20 minutes or so.

5. Remove the racks from the roasting pan and set them aside on a plate.

6. Pour all the juices through a strainer into a saucepan, put over medium heat, bring up to a simmer, then gently reduce to a syrupy consistency—a little like honey. Set aside and keep warm.

7. Preheat your broiler to high. Put the racks under the broiler and cook until they start to sizzle. Remove them from the heat, brush generously with the reduced marinade, then put them back under the broiler until they start to spit, char, and caramelize slightly.

[*Continued*]

FOR THE DIPPING SAUCE

**1 cup (7fl oz/200ml) plain
    yogurt**
**½ cup (3½fl oz/100ml) crème
    fraîche, sour cream, or Greek
    yogurt**
Juice of 1 lime
**2 teaspoon tamari or light soy
    sauce**

TO GARNISH

1 small handful cilantro leaves
**1 red finger chile, seeded and
    diced**
**2 scallions, thinly sliced on
    the diagonal**

8. In a small bowl, mix together all the dipping sauce ingredients, pour into a serving dish, and set aside.

9. Cut the racks into individual ribs. Pour the remaining marinade onto a warmed serving plate, and put the ribs on top. Sprinkle the fresh cilantro, chile, and scallions over the ribs and sauce, and serve immediately.

Tip

To get ahead of the game in a party situation, complete all the steps up to and including number 6, then wrap and chill in the refrigerator for up to two days. Come party time, let the meat to come to room temperature, then zoom straight into step 7.

VENISON TARTARE

Steak tartare has to be one of my all-time top meaty dishes. There's just something about being presented with a plate of "raw," seasoned, hot, textured red meat, crisp, salted fries, and fresh green leaves. Although easy to put together at home, it's a little tricky to get absolutely right. The key thing is to take a little time and care.

Use farm-raised venison and purchase it from a reputable butcher; inform the butcher that it will be used raw for tartare. You can use a hand meat grinder and grind the meat only once on a coarse blade, but at home I just chop with a sharp, heavy knife. Either way, it shouldn't be too chunky or lumpy; the meat should "melt" while still retaining a little texture and bite. In any case, try not to get flustered, but get the seasoning just as you like it.

SERVES 4

1 ½ lb farm-raised venison, such
    as backstrap, trimmed of all
    excess fat and sinew
1 red finger chile, seeded and
    finely diced
2 teaspoon finely chopped chives

FOR THE DRESSING

4 large egg yolks (use the egg
    whites to make meringues,
    see page 206)
3 tablespoons sour cream
A drizzle peppery virgin olive oil
4 small shallots, finely diced
2 teaspoons thick, black Indian
    tamarind paste
2 teaspoons finely grated and
    chopped fresh horseradish
2 teaspoons drained and coarsely
    chopped fine capers
1 teaspoon coarsely ground
    black peppercorns
½ teaspoon dried red pepper
    flakes
Seeds of 1 black cardamom pod,
    finely ground
Sea salt

1. First make the dressing. Put the egg yolks, cream, olive oil, shallots, tamarind paste, horseradish, and capers into a shallow bowl. Mix them together with a fork.

2. Season with the pepper, red pepper flakes, cardamom, and a light touch of salt, and mix well again.

3. Put the well-trimmed venison on a cutting board and, using a sharp, heavy knife, chop it very finely. Add the chopped venison to the dressing, then sprinkle in the fresh chile and chives.

4. Next, take two forks and gently but firmly bring the dressing into the meat so that it combines really well, while being careful not to overwork it. Check the seasoning and adjust it, if necessary.

5. Serve immediately, with french fries and a green salad. You could use ring molds to give it some shape, if you desire.

LAMB & MUTTON

WHETHER IT'S YOUNG LAMB OR RICHLY flAVORED MUTTON, THE MEAT OF SHEEP IS IN ITSELF AROMATIC, A WORTHY MATCH FOR SPICES. Use spices to emphasize the floral sweetness in younger meats, or to cut through and "warm" the more pungent flavors of hogget and mutton. What is the difference between lamb, hogget, and mutton? In some countries, when a sheep is 7 months or younger, you will find reference to spring, "suckling," or milk-fed lamb: these have a really tender, sweet-tasting flesh. Up to 12 months, the meat is correctly called lamb. An animal slaughtered at 12 to 24 months would be termed hogget; older than that, it becomes mutton. Interestingly, mutton can also refer to goat meat. In the United States, lamb is the only term used regardless of the age of the animal; in general, the darker the color, the older the animal was when slaughtered.

Lamb is the sweetest meat, with a rich fat. In Western cuisine, the fat is usually offset with strong, astringent herby flavors, such as rosemary or mint. I think spices are a wonderful alternative. Cardamom, nutmeg, allspice, and cassia all offer heady perfume, and these are some of the spices in the tagine spice blend that I use for the "Park Railings" (the name refers to the appearance of the ribs of a breast of lamb), while the ginger, turmeric, and sweet paprika of the blend add earthy notes to help ground the richness of the dish.

The meat you'll use for the Spiced Lamb Cutlets and Winter Salad will more than likely be hogget, even though it may be labeled lamb at the butcher's and on supermarket shelves. And that's totally fine. Hogget has firm flesh and rich flavor. The spices and flavors in this recipe echo the breadth of flavors in the meat, from the bass notes of cumin to the highs of allspice, the tangy sensations of pomegranate molasses and the floral perfume of rose.

Then there's mutton, with its more pronounced pungent note and aged protein structure, giving it a tougher texture. I reflect those pungent notes in my choice of spices. Star anise, fennel, and cumin—and anardana to add tangy punch—work particularly well in my Poached Mutton Shoulder, with lemon zest and red wine to bring much-needed astringency and even more wonderful perfume to the deep, rich notes of the glorious mutton.

Previous page: Dried pomegranate seeds (anardana in Hindi) add a subtle sweet–sour element and glorious crunchy texture.

Lamb "Park Railings" with Wally-Wally Pickle

FOR THE "PARK RAILINGS"

1 whole lean breast of lamb,
    2–2¼lb (900g–1.1kg)
    trimmed of cartilage and
    excess fat, outer skin removed
1 tablespoon Tagine spice blend
    (see page 266)
½ teaspoon sea salt
1 garlic bulb, halved
3 large eggs
Light olive oil, for pan-frying

FOR THE WALLY-WALLY PICKLE

1 cup (9oz/250g) mayonnaise
1 cup (5½oz/150g) gherkins or
    cornichons, finely chopped
2 tablespoons chopped shallots
1 tablespoon Dijon mustard
2 red finger chiles, seeded and
    finely chopped
1 tablespoon chopped tarragon
    leaves
2 tablespoons chopped mint leaves
2 teaspoons fennel seeds,
    finely ground
1 teaspoon black peppercorns,
    finely ground
½ teaspoon finely ground cassia
2 teaspoons black mustard seeds,
    cracked

FOR THE BREAD CRUMBS

4 cups (14oz/400g) dried
    bread crumbs
1 tablespoon Tagine spice blend
    (see page 266)
Zest of 2 lemons
1 teaspoon sea salt

My version of a classic modern British bistro dish is a nod to my friend chef Mark Broadbent. "Park railings" refers to the ribs in the breast of lamb. I serve them with a zingy dipping mayo that I call Wally-Wally Pickle—wally being an old East End slang name for gherkins, a type of small pickle.

1. Preheat the oven to 350°F (180°C). Rub the lamb breast with the Tagine spice blend, then put it into a roasting pan, add ½ cup (3½fl oz/100ml) water, the salt and garlic, and cover tightly with aluminum foil. Cook on the middle shelf of the oven for 2 hours or until soft and melting.

2. Remove from the oven, let cool for 2–3 minutes, then carefully remove the meat from the roasting pan. Put the meat on a baking sheet, then put another baking sheet on top and gently press down on the meat. Put a couple of food cans on the pan to weigh it down and let cool completely, then put it in the refrigerator to chill for 4–6 hours.

3. Meanwhile, combine all the pickle ingredients in a bowl, then set aside in the refrigerator. (Stored in a sealed jar in the refrigerator, it will keep for two weeks.)

4. Mix all the bread crumb ingredients in a nonmetallic bowl, then spread out on a plate ready for bread crumbing the lamb. Remove the lamb breast from the refrigerator, put onto a cutting board, and cut into "park railings" about ⅝ inch (1.5cm) wide by 3–4 inches (7.5–10cm) long.

5. Lightly whisk the eggs and pour onto a large dinner plate. Dip each "park railing" in the egg wash, then roll it in the spiced bread crumbs so that it's nicely covered all over. Do this twice for each "railing."

6. Put a large sauté pan over medium–high heat, add a splash of oil, and cook the lamb for about 5 minutes, until golden brown and crisp, cooking the "railings" in batches and draining them on paper towels as you work. Serve immediately, on a warmed serving plate, with the Wally-Wally Pickle in a bowl. Perfect for movie nights!

Lamb Biryani Ka Kesar

2¼lb (1kg) lamb stew meat, diced

1 tablespoon ghee, sunflower oil, or unsalted butter

FOR THE MARINADE

5 large garlic cloves, crushed

⅔ cup (2¼oz/60g) grated fresh ginger

½ cup (4fl oz/125ml) plain yogurt

1 green Thai chile, seeded and finely chopped

2 onions, diced

2 tablespoons sugar

1 tablespoon sea salt

2 teaspoons powdered turmeric

2 teaspoons black peppercorns, finely ground

1 teaspoon red pepper flakes

2 teaspoons Garam Masala blend (see page 267)

½ teaspoon freshly grated nutmeg

Zest and juice of ½ lemon

1 handful mint leaves, chopped

FOR THE RICE

1¾ cups (11½oz/330g) aged basmati rice or other long-grain rice

1 tablespoon cumin seeds

3 cloves

Seeds from 3 green cardamom pods

Seeds from 1 black cardamom pod

½ teaspoon finely ground mace

10 saffron threads

2 teaspoon sea salt

This is my version of an Indian classic; ka kesar means "with saffron." From the glorious Nizam Hyderabadi palaces to the Moghul territories of Lucknow, Delhi, and Agra, across to Kashmir, Lahore, and Karachi, and back to Persia, biryani has many regional variations. Lamb, hogget, mutton—even goat—are all traditional. The key is undoubtedly the beauty of the basmati rice and a slow, dum *cooking method.* Dum *refers to cooking in a sealed pot; traditionally the pot is sealed with dough but here we use a tight-fitting lid.*

1. Combine all the marinade ingredients in a nonmetallic bowl and mix well. Add the meat, cover, and set aside for at least 4 hours (or preferably overnight) in the refrigerator.

2. Put the ghee in a large, heavy saucepan, Dutch oven, or flameproof casserole or with a tight-fitting lid. Put over medium heat, add the meat and all its marinade, and cook for 25 minutes. Set aside.

3. Wash the rice throughly and drain it. Finely grind the whole spices, except the saffron, using a mortar and pestle. Put 5 cups (2 pints/1.2 liters) water into a large saucepan, add all the spices, the rice, saffron, and salt, and bring to a boil. Cook, uncovered, for 10 minutes.

4. To assemble the dish, strain the remaining water from the rice into the meat mixture, stir throughly, and then level the meat out evenly.

5. Spread the rice in an even layer over the meat. Cover the pan and cook over high heat for 5 minutes.

6. Turn down the heat to its lowest setting and cook gently for 30 minutes, keeping the lid on and not stirring at all. (Alternatively, put the casserole into the oven, preheated to 350°F/180°C.)

7. Remove the dish from the heat and let it rest for 5 minutes before taking it to the table, lifting off the lid with a flourish, and leting everyone get the full, fragrant Eastern aroma. Biryani made simple!

Persian Lamb Tagine with Rhubarb & Orange Salad

The wonderfully sticky texture of this dish has its roots in Arabic Bedouin tradition, but I've taken influences from Persia for its perfumed flavor and nutty crunch. The tangy rhubarb and orange salad helps cut through the sweet richness of the tagine. I'm really pleased with it and I'm sure you will be, too.

SERVES 4–6

1½ tablespoons (¾oz/20g) unsalted butter

1 tablespoon light olive oil

2 onions, cut into chunky dice

2 teaspoons sea salt

2lb 4oz (1kg) lamb stew meat, cut into 2¾-inch (7-cm) chunks

2 teaspoons black peppercorns, finely ground

1 teaspoon powdered turmeric

2 teaspoons finely ground cinnamon

2½ tablespoons finely grated fresh ginger

1¾ cups (9oz/250g) pitted dates

1 tablespoon honey

1. Add the butter and oil to a large, heavy flameproof casserole or Dutch oven and put over medium heat. Add the onions and salt. Stir and sauté gently for 10–12 minutes, until the onions are soft and nutty brown.

2. Add the meat, spices, and ginger. Stir to combine everything, then pour in 3 cups (1¼ pints/700ml) water and stir again.

3. Turn up the heat, bring to a boil, and let simmer, uncovered, for 30 seconds. Turn down the heat to a gentle simmer, cover, and let simmer gently for about 1½ hours, until meltingly soft.

4. Take off the lid, add the dates and honey, stir, and continue to cook at a gentle simmer, uncovered, stirring occasionally, for another 30–40 minutes, or until the meat is tender and the sauce is sticky and unctuous.

[*Continued*]

FOR THE RHUBARB & ORANGE SALAD

2 small oranges
1 green crisp, sweet apple
Olive oil, for drizzling
9 rhubarb stalks (about 1lb/450g), cut on the diagonal into 3-inch (7.5-cm) batons
Juice of 1 lemon
1 tablespoon honey
¼ preserved lemon, finely diced (optional)
Seeds of 2 green cardamom pods, finely ground
1 small handful mint leaves, bigger leaves torn

FOR THE GARNISH

1 teaspoon butter
Splash olive oil
1 small handful blanched almonds
1 small handful pistachio nuts, shelled
2 teaspoon orange blossom water
1 small handful flat-leaf parsley leaves
1 small handful mint, big leaves torn, small leaves left whole

5. Meanwhile, make the salad. Preheat the oven to 400°F (200°C).

6. Using a bowl to catch the juice, cut a thin slice off the top and bottom of each orange, then sit it on its freshly cut flat surface and slice off its skin and pith. Turn each orange onto its side and slice it into thin disks, retaining the juice. Remove any seeds and discard.

7. Core and peel the apple and cut it in half. Put it, flat side down, on a cutting board and cut it into thin slices, about ⅛ inch (3mm) thick. Put the apple slices onto a baking sheet, coat lightly with olive oil, and roast for 10 minutes.

8. Take the baking sheet out of the oven, add the rhubarb, drizzle with a little more oil, the lemon juice, and honey, and return to the oven for another 12 minutes or until the rhubarb is just soft but still holds its shape. Take the fruit from the oven and let it cool on the baking sheet.

9. Arrange the orange slices on a serving plate, put the apple slices and rhubarb on and around them, then mix the reserved orange juice with the roasting juices, drizzle over the salad, and sprinkle with the preserved lemon pieces, if using. Sprinkle with the ground cardamom and the mint. Cover the plate with plastic wrap and put it in the refrigerator until it is time to serve.

10. Meanwhile, make the tagine garnish. Melt the butter and oil in a small skillet over medium heat. Add the nuts and sauté gently, tossing and stirring them, until lightly brown. Remove the nuts from the pan, set aside, and keep warm.

11. Take the casserole off the heat, sprinkle the orange water over it, and stir, then sprinkle with the garnish herbs followed by the nuts. Take straight to the table and serve with the Rhubarb and Orange Salad.

Olive's Irish Stew Skewers

Irish stew is somewhat of an institution where I live on the Emerald Isle, and everybody has their own preferred recipe—normally "Mammy's." This is my take, based on my wife Olive's favorite all-time dinner. It's worth trying to find the best local lamb, potatoes, and carrots you can, because the simplicity of the cooking brings focus to the ingredients. You'll need four long metal skewers to assemble the dish.

SERVES 4

4 large carrots
4 large new potatoes, peeled
6 lamb loin chops, fat trimmed
    and reserved, cut into
    chunky dice
3 teaspoon sea salt
A splash canola oil
1½ cups (12fl oz/350ml)
    chicken stock or broth
2 thyme sprigs, leaves only

FOR THE COATING SAUCE

2 teaspoons white peppercorns,
    finely ground
5 gratings nutmeg
5 gratings long pepper
¼ teaspoon finely ground mace
2 tablespoons honey
2 teaspoons cider vinegar
1 big handful curly parsley
    leaves, chopped

1. Put the carrots and potatoes into separate saucepans, cover generously with water, and boil until only just soft. Drain and cut into chunky dice. Season the lamb with 2 teaspoons of the salt. Set aside.

2. Put the lamb fat trimmings in a large flameproof casserole or Dutch oven and melt them over medium heat. Add the lamb, turn up the heat, and cook, adding a little oil, if needed. It might be best to do this in batches so that you don't overcrowd the casserole and stew the meat.

3. When the meat has a nutty brown color, add the stock or broth, bring to a simmer, then add the thyme and turn down the heat. Cover and simmer gently for 2 hours or until the meat is tender.

4. Once the meat is cooked, remove it from the casserole with a slotted spoon, put on a plate, and set aside.

5. To make the coating sauce, mix all the spices together and add them, the honey, and the vinegar to the casserole. Turn up the heat and reduce to a thick, heavy cream consistency, then add the parsley. Stir through and set aside.

6. Preheat your broiler to its highest setting (or light the barbecue, if the weather's right). Take a skewer, and slide alternate pieces of meat, carrot, and potato along its length until there's no more room. Repeat for the other three skewers, then pour the plate juices into the sauce and stir to combine. Coat the skewers generously all over with the sauce and put them on a broiler pan or barbecue rack.

7. Let simmer and char slightly, then turn and repeat. Remove and serve immediately with sliced bread and butter and a cup of tea or wine, depending on your mood!

MEATBALLS WITH RAS EL RELISH

I love meatballs. They're quick and simple to make and are an economic use of inexpensive cuts of meat. They can be sandwiched in sourdough or flatbread with mayonnaise and relish, served in a ragu with spaghetti or couscous, used with salad, or dressed in a curried sauce.

MAKES ABOUT 20

FOR THE MEATBALLS
1 teaspoon allspice
2 teaspoons cumin seeds
1 teaspoon fennel seeds
2 teaspoons black peppercorns
1 teaspoon Mixed Spice blend (see page 266)
1 pinch dried rose petals
¼–⅓ cup plain yogurt
1 red finger chile, seeded and finely diced
2¼lb (1kg) ground lamb
2 teaspoons rose water
2 tablespoons chopped mint leaves
1 heaping tablespoon coarsely chopped curly parsley leaves
1½ teaspoons coarsely chopped cilantro leaves
2 teaspoons sea salt
1 tablespoon sunflower oil

1. Finely grind the allspice, cumin, fennel, and peppercorns, using a mortar and pestle. Mix the spices together in a large mixing bowl, then add the remaining meatball ingredients, except the oil, and mix together throughly. If the mixture feels a little dry and doesn't hold together when you squeeze it, just add a little more yogurt. Cover and let rest in the refrigerator overnight or for at least a couple of hours.

2. Preheat the oven to 350°F (180°C). Divide the spiced meat mixture into approximately 20 mounds. Roll each one into a meatball shape.

3. Put the oil in a heavy, ovenproof sauté pan, Dutch oven, or flameproof casserole over high heat, then gently add the meatballs and lightly brown on all sides. Be careful: These little fellas break up easily and you may need to do this in a couple of batches to be sure they cook more evenly. After 4–5 minutes, when they're a light nutty brown, put the pan in the oven for 15–20 minutes, until they're cooked through.

4. Remove the pan from the oven and carefully spoon out the meatballs. Serve immediately with the Ras el Relish.

FOR THE RAS EL RELISH
⅔ cup (5½oz/150g) firmly packed dark brown sugar
¾ cup (6fl oz/175ml) cider vinegar
1 (14½oz/400g) can dice tomatoes
½ cup (3oz/85g) chopped dried dates
3 tablespoons grated fresh ginger
1 teaspoon ras el hanout (see page 266)
2 teaspoon pomegranate molasses

1. Put the sugar and vinegar in a large saucepan over medium heat and cook until the sugar dissolves into the liquid, swirling the pan around occasionally.

2. Add the tomatoes, dates, ginger, and ras el hanout, and stir carefully. You'll be able to gauge when the relish is ready because it will begin to look like warm preserves.

3. Remove from the heat, add the pomegranate molasses, and serve immediately.

SPICED LAMB CUTLETS
& WINTER SALAD

This Persian-inspired dish is quick to make, pretty healthy, and contains all kinds of taste and flavor sensations: hot and sour dressing; crunchy walnuts; fresh, clean mint; succulent, satisfying lamb … all brought together in one delicious spicy, colorful plate.

SERVES 2

**6 lamb cutlets, trimmed
of excess fat**
A little olive oil
A little sea salt

FOR THE DRESSING
¾ cup (3oz/85g) walnuts
**⅔–1 cup (5–7 fl oz/150–200ml)
good-quality chicken stock
or broth**
**3 tablespoons pomegranate
molasses**
1 tablespoon sugar
Zest and juice of ½ lemon
½ teaspoon allspice berries
1 teaspoon cumin seeds
2 teaspoon coriander seeds
**⅓ cup (2½ fl oz/75ml) light olive
oil, plus extra to drizzle**
1 red onion, diced
½ teaspoon sea salt
**¼ teaspoon freshly grated
nutmeg**
2 teaspoons red pepper flakes
2 teaspoons rose water
**1 handful mint leaves, finely
sliced at the last minute**

FOR THE WINTER SALAD
**endive, watercress, radicchio, or
frisée leaves**

1. Preheat a ridged grill pan until it's nice and hot. Rub a little olive oil (not too much) onto the cutlets, then put on the pan for 60 seconds. Turn 60 degrees and cook for another 60 seconds.

2. Turn over and repeat so that you get an attractive bar mark, then remove from the pan, sprinkle both sides with salt, and keep warm on a plate, loosely covered with wax paper.

3. To make the dressing, put the walnuts in a heavy skillet and lightly toast for 2–3 minutes. Transfer to a clean dish towel, gather up the corners, and rub vigorously to remove the skins. Lightly crush the walnuts.

4. To make the pomegranate syrup, put a small saucepan over medium–high heat. Add the chicken stock or broth, pomegranate molasses, sugar, and lemon juice. Cook for 3 minutes or until it reduces and becomes slightly syrupy.

5. Finely grind the allspice, cumin, and coriander seeds, using a mortar and pestle. Put a skillet over medium heat, add the olive oil, onion, salt, and all the spices, and sauté gently for 30 seconds. Add the walnuts and cook for a maximum of 2–3 minutes, so that the onions still have a little bite but no raw flavor. Add the pomegranate syrup to the skillet, stir, and cook for 1 minute over gentle heat.

6. Remove the pan from the heat, add the lemon zest and any meat juices from the cutlet plate, then add a generous slug of olive oil, the rose water, and the fresh mint leaves.

7. Put the cutlets onto a warmed plate. Dress the winter salad with some of the dressing, seasoning to taste, and serve with the cutlets. Spoon the remaining dressing over the lamb cutlets.

EAT-ME-WITH-A-SPOON MASALA

This dish is an absolute peach of a comfort recipe, even if I do say so myself! Cooked this way, the meat on a lamb shank becomes so soft, so tender and delicious, it not only falls off the bone but it can be eaten with a spoon. The asafetida is the secret ingredient that makes all the difference. My friend Jim, from cooking school, was always trying to add secret ingredients to everything he made. This one's for you, sir: "Sláinte!"

SERVES 4

4 large meaty lamb shanks
    (about 14oz–1lb/400–450g)
3 tablespoons (1½oz/40g)
    unsalted butter, diced
4 onions (about/1lb 2oz 500g),
    thinly sliced
⅓ cup (1¾oz/50g) finely
    chopped garlic cloves
⅔ cup (2¼oz/60g) finely
    chopped fresh ginger
2 teaspoons fennel seeds
Scant ¼ teaspoon asafetida resin
1 tablespoon Garam Masala
    blend (see page 267)
2 cups (18fl oz/500ml) Greek
    yogurt
1 (14½-oz/400-g) can diced
    tomatoes
½ cup (3½fl oz/100ml) chicken
    stock or broth
2 tablespoons dry vermouth
2 tablespoons honey
1 tablespoon red wine vinegar

1. Preheat the oven to 275°F (140°C). Wrap a 2-inch (5-cm) wide strip of aluminum foil around the end of the shank bones, and tie the foil cap securely with kitchen string.

2. Melt the butter in a deep flameproof casserole or Dutch oven over medium heat and gently sauté the onions for 5 minutes or until they're soft. Add the garlic, ginger, fennel seeds, asafetida, and 2 teaspoons of the Garam Masala, and stir well to combine. Add the yogurt, tomatoes, and stock or broth, and stir well.

3. Put the shanks upright in the sauce, cover with foil and the lid, and put into the oven for 4 hours, or less if the shanks are a little skinny. When finished, the meat should be meltingly tender.

4. Carefully take the shanks out, trying to make sure they hold their shape, and set aside on a warmed plate.

5. Put the casserole over medium heat, add the vermouth, honey, vinegar, and the remaining 1 teaspoon of the Garam Masala, and cook for 5 minutes, stirring well to combine, until the sauce is glossy and smooth.

6. Put a lamb shank on each of four warmed dinner plates and remove the foil caps. Coat each shank generously with the sauce and serve with creamy mashed potatoes, green vegetables, such as kale or sautéed spinach, and a squeeze of lemon juice.

POACHED MUTTON SHOULDER

In this hearty, warming dish, I've combined French technique with spicy temperament for a totally indulgent meal. Just be aware that it takes a little time to cook, so get prepared ahead of time.

SERVES 4–6

5½ lb (2.5kg) mutton shoulder
on the bone, outer membrane
removed, tied with kitchen
string to hold its shape
1¾ oz (50g) piece fatback bacon
or pancetta, cut into 24 dice
and blanched for 3 minutes
½ star anise
2 teaspoons fennel seeds
1 teaspoon cumin seeds
1½ sticks (6oz/175g) unsalted
butter, at room temperature
2 garlic cloves, finely chopped
Zest of 1 lemon
Scant ¼ teaspoon finely ground
mace
4 teaspoons dried pomegranate
seeds
9oz (250g) smoked bacon, cut
into chunky strips
8 shallots
5–6 small white turnips, cut into
about the same size as the
shallots
3 carrots, chopped into chunks
on the diagonal
generous 1½ cups (13fl oz/
375ml) red wine, such as
Beaujolais or Pinot Noir
At least 1⅔ cups (14fl oz/400ml)
ham or chicken stock
or broth
1 tablespoon red wine vinegar
1 big handful curly parsley
leaves, finely chopped
1 tablespoon capers, drained
Sea salt

1. Preheat the oven to 275°F (140°C). Make 24 incisions all over the meat with the point of a sharp knife, then poke the bacon cubes snugly in.

2. Finely grind the star anise, fennel, and cumin seeds, using a mortar and pestle. In a small bowl, mix the butter, garlic, lemon zest, all the spices, and the pomegranate seeds. Spread this mixture all over the meat, coating it generously. Set aside.

3. Take a large flameproof casserole, Dutch oven, or deep roasting pan that will hold the meat comfortably and put it over medium heat. Gently fry the smoked bacon until softened, then add the shallots, turnips, and carrots and continue to sauté gently for 5 minutes to brown them a little. Remove from the heat.

4. Put the meat into the casserole on top of the vegetables, add the wine, then add enough stock or broth to come about 1 inch (2.5cm) or so up the meat. Cover tightly with aluminum foil and the lid. Cook in the oven for 6 hours or until meltingly soft.

5. Uncover the casserole and increase the heat to 400°F (200°C). Cook for another 15 minutes to crisp, then remove the meat to a warmed serving plate. Scoop up the bacon and vegetables with a slotted spoon, arrange around the meat, then set aside and keep warm.

6. Strain the juices through a strainer into a saucepan and skim to remove most of the fat. Put over medium heat, bring to a rapid boil, and reduce by half—about 15 minutes. Add the vinegar, parsley, and capers, then taste and adjust the seasoning, if necessary. Spoon a little of the sauce over the mutton, then pour the remainder into a small bowl.

7. Take the meat to the table, carve, and serve with boiled new potatoes and the sauce.

BAKED HOGGET & SQUASH

As the nights start to close in and the north wind brings its inevitable chill, this simple, all-in-one roasted dish makes perfect warming comfort food—ideal for eating by an open fire on a cold evening as the leaves change color. The mix of seasonal squash, hearty chunks of meat, and thick tomato sauce fired up with a blend of fragrant spices, lemon zest, and thyme will warm the cockles of anyone's heart. Hogget is another term for lamb that's between 12 and 24 months old; the flesh is firmer, the flavor richer, so ask your butcher if he or she can get hold of some slightly older lamb.

SERVES 4

2 teaspoons coriander seeds
8 cloves
1 small piece blade mace
1 teaspoon Sichuan pepper
1 heaping teaspoon red
    pepper flakes
1 teaspoon finely ground
    cinnamon
4 tablespoons olive oil
1 garlic clove, crushed
Zest of ½ lemon
1½ teaspoons sea salt
8 bone-in lamb chops, about
    1 inch (2.5cm) thick
6 cups (2lb/900g) cherry
    tomatoes
1½ butternut squash (about
    2¾lb/1.2kg), peeled, seeded,
    and chopped into ⅝-inch
    (1.5-cm) chunks (about
    4½–5 cups/1½lb/650g
    prepared)
4 thyme sprigs
1 handful mint, chopped into
    ribbons

1. Preheat the oven to 375°F (190°C). Finely grind the whole spices, using a mortar and pestle, then mix in the red pepper flakes and the cinnamon.

2. Pour the oil into a large nonmetallic bowl and add the spices, garlic, lemon zest, salt, lamb chops, tomatoes, squash, and thyme.

3. Using your hands, mix everything around in the bowl, then take out the chops, put them onto a plate, cover, and set aside.

4. Carefully pour the spiced squash and tomato mixture into a large roasting pan, scraping in every last scrap. Gently spread the mixture into an even(ish) layer and bake in the oven for 15 minutes.

5. Give everything in the dish a thorough, but gentle, stir, then take the chops from the plate, put them on top of the squash mixture, cover with a sheet of aluminum foil and put back into the oven for another 15 minutes.

6. Remove the foil and continue to cook for another 10 minutes. When the chops have taken on a nutty brown color, take the pan out of the oven.

7. Carefully remove the twigs of thyme, sprinkle the fresh mint on top, then stir to combine all the flavors. Serve immediately with your favorite crusty bread, couscous, or cornmeal.

BIRDS

Ranging across a broad spectrum of flavors, from subtle, sweet Cornish game hens through to the earthy, gamey flavors of guinea fowl, pheasant, and pigeon, when it comes to spicing, this chapter is all about playful, happy, uplifting spice notes. Soft citrus, teasing exotic aromatics, the faintest hint of menthol from green cardamom to cut through and lift the perfume of the spice blend.

For the Butterflied Jerk Game Hen I've gone for a strong jerk seasoning of black pepper and clove, brightened with allspice, coriander, and nutmeg, then combined with a hot and tangy sauce of Scotch bonnet chile, ginger for length of finish and grapefruit for playful citrus zest and balance. Opposing flavors working in harmony with one another, their taste profiles bridged by spice.

Poached Chicken with Lemongrass and Herbs sets off along a well-trodden path of Southeast Asian flavors, combining lemongrass, cilantro, ginger, and star anise, but the unexpected addition of Gewürztraminer wine (appropriately, *Gewürz* is the German word for spice) results in a wonderful cooking liquid to serve as a sauce or use as the base of a comforting broth. The freshness of herbs and fruitiness of orange zest accent the sweet flesh of chicken.

Pheasant is often referred to as an "Indian chicken." In my Pot-Roasted Pheasant, I've chosen spices for their light, happy, citrus, perfumed characters: green cardamom, juniper, Sichuan pepper. Green cardamom for high, "pingy" notes, cubeb for mid–high notes of subtle bitterness, and camphor, grounded with star anise and rounded out by cassia: all compliment the unique taste of pheasant.

In the main, I try to convey a light, happy mood in all the dishes in this chapter, from the everyday to the exotic. Visualizing colors I associate with foods helps me build a better dish; for birds of all types it's deep golden yellows, light greens, nutty browns, warm oranges, reds, and purples. In the Spiced Wood Pigeon Salad, I've included purple-red beets, nuts, and green artichokes, all brought together by the black cardamom in the dressing, giving it an edge and helping define the dish as a whole.

BUTTERFLIED JERK GAME HEN

I love jerk chicken. It brings back happy memories of the Notting Hill Carnival in London, moving from one smoky grill stall to another to choose corn, slaws, and the hallowed jerk. In Ireland I use poussins with the citrus and spicing, but Cornish game hens work well, too. Orange is the traditional citrus for a jerk marinade, but I have chosen grapefruit, partly inspired by "Ting," a well-known Jamaican soft drink based on grapefruit juice.

SERVES 4

FOR THE PANG & TING SAUCE
1 grapefruit
2 tablespoons sunflower oil
1 bunch scallions, thick green parts removed, whites finely chopped
3 garlic cloves, diced
1 teaspoon Kashmiri chili flakes
¾-inch (2-cm) piece fresh ginger
1 Scotch bonnet chile, seeded and coarsely chopped
¾ cup (7oz/200g) canned diced tomatoes
1 tablespoon tomato paste
⅓ cup (2¾oz/75g) firmly packed dark brown sugar
1 teaspoon white wine vinegar
1 teaspoon sea salt

FOR THE BUTTERFLIED HEN
1 tablespoon coriander seeds
2 teaspoons black peppercorns
¼ teaspoon cloves
½ cinnamon stick
3 allspice berries
¼ nutmeg, freshly grated
2 teaspoons thyme leaves
½ teaspoon dried oregano
2 teaspoons sea salt
2 Cornish game hens, backbones and wing tips removed
2 tablespoons sunflower oil

1. To make the sauce, using a sharp knife and working over a bowl to catch the juice, slice off the grapefruit skin and pith. Cut out the segments of half the grapefruit, leaving the membrane behind, and set aside. Squeeze the juice from the remaining half grapefruit and add to the bowl.

2. Put a large saucepan over medium heat, add the oil, and cook the scallions until soft. Add the garlic, Kashmiri flakes, ginger, and chile, stir, and sauté gently for 1 minute. Add the grapefruit, ¼ cup (2fl oz/50ml) of the juice, and the remaining sauce ingredients, turn up the heat, and bring to a simmer, then turn down the heat and simmer for 5 minutes, until the sauce has thickened slightly.

3. Remove from the heat and process in a food processor or with an immersion blender. Cover loosely and set aside. Preheat the oven to 350°F (180°C).

4. Grind the coriander seeds, peppercorns, cloves, cinnamon, and allspice, using a mortar and pestle, then add the nutmeg, thyme, oregano, and salt.

5. Put the Cornish game hens in a roasting pan, breast side up. Apply a little pressure to the birds with the palm of your hand until you hear a crack, then arrange them as flat as possible. Using a sharp knife, score the legs and breasts with three incisions on each.

6. Mix the seasoning blend with the oil to make a thick paste, then use it to coat the birds, massaging the paste all over the meat. Cover loosely with aluminum foil and roast for 35 minutes.

7. Remove from the oven, take off the foil, and pour the sauce all over the birds, then return to the oven and roast for another 20–25 minutes, until they're cooked; test by piercing the thickest part of a thigh with the tip of a sharp knife; the juices should run clear, not pink. Serve with buttered grilled corn-on-the-cob and some pepper-spiced rice.

CHICKEN MARRAKESH

This pan-fried chicken breast with spiced butter is a wonderful combination of warming flavors and pure, fresh spice. It's also a quick way to make a meal a little different while keeping things really simple and light. Spiced chicken, zingy mayonnaise, and crisp green salad ... what's not to like?

SERVES 4

4 chicken breasts, skin on
A little canola oil

FOR THE SPICED BUTTER
1¾ sticks (7oz/200g) unsalted butter, at room temperature
2 teaspoons ras el hanout (see page 266)
½ teaspoon lemon zest
1 tablespoon flat-leaf parsley leaves, finely chopped

1. Mix all the spiced butter ingredients together in a small bowl. If not using immediately, lay a square of plastic wrap on your work surface, put the butter mix at one end, then carefully roll it up into a log shape. Twist each end like a candy wrapper and put it into the refrigerator. When you need it, simply slice a thin disk of butter off the end, remove the plastic wrap, and get going.

2. Using a sharp knife, slice along the length of the thickest part of each breast to form a pocket, being careful not to slice right through.

3. Divide 7 tablespoons (3½oz/100g) of the spiced butter into four pieces (keep the remainder, wrapped in plastic wrap, in the refrigerator for up to four weeks). Spread one piece of butter into the pocket of each breast and secure with a toothpick.

4. Put a ridged grill pan, sauté pan, or skillet over medium heat. Rub a little oil over the skin of each breast and, when the pan is good and hot, put the chicken pieces into the pan, skin side down, and cook gently for about 5 minutes—don't move the chicken in the pan at this stage.

5. Turn the chicken pieces over, cover, and turn down the heat to low. Let cook in the vibrant-colored, buttery juices until the chicken is done; to test, pierce the thickest part with the tip of a sharp knife; the juices should run clear, not pink. This will take 5–8 minutes.

[*Continued*]

ALGIER AIOLI

2 fat garlic cloves, crushed
Sea salt
2 large egg yolks
1¼–2 cups (10–16fl oz/
    300–450ml) fruity olive oil
Juice of at least 1 lemon and
    zest of ½ lemon
1 teaspoon Garam Masala blend
    (see page 267)

1. While the chicken is cooking, make the aïoli and the vinaigrette. Crush the garlic with a little salt until it forms a paste. In a bowl, whisk the egg yolks and garlic paste together until thick.

2. Whisking continuously, pour in half the olive oil in a thin stream, then add a little of the lemon juice and some more oil. Continue beating, adding alternately more lemon juice and more oil until you have a thick mayonnaise.

3. Adjust the salt to taste and add the Garam Masala and lemon zest. Mix and set aside.

FOR THE VINAIGRETTE

1 garlic clove, halved
1½ tablespoons best-quality
    Dijon mustard
⅔ cup (5fl oz/150ml) grapeseed
    or sunflower oil
3 tablespoons fruity olive oil
1 teaspoon good-quality white
    wine vinegar
½ teaspoon sugar
Fine sea salt and finely ground
    black pepper

1. To make the vinaigrette, rub the inside of a large screw-top jar firmly with the cut edge of the garlic clove.

2. Add all the dressing ingredients, then pour in ¼ cup (2fl oz/50ml) boiling water (the water goes in last to prevent the jar from cracking).

3. Screw the lid on tightly and shake extremely vigorously until everything emulsifies—a minute or so should do it.

FOR THE GREEN SALAD

4 small butterhead lettuce
    hearts, such as Boston
1 large bunch of chives,
    tarragon and chervil

1. Divide the lettuce leaves among four plates. Spoon the vinaigrette generously over the leaves, then sprinkle the herbs on top.

2. Put the chicken breasts on the plates and serve with warmed flatbread and a ramekin of Algier Aioli.

POACHED CHICKEN WITH LEMONGRASS & HERBS

SERVES 4–6

FOR THE SEASONING

1 teaspoon white peppercorns

1 teaspoon coriander seeds

Seeds of 4 green cardamom pods

1 large cilantro sprig

1 large tarragon sprig

1 large chervil sprig

2½ tablespoons finely chopped fresh ginger

1 garlic clove, finely chopped

½ teaspoon sea salt

1 tablespoon light olive oil

FOR THE CHICKEN

1 oven-ready chicken (about 4lb/1.8kg)

½ cup (3½fl oz/100ml) Alsace Gewürztraminer or Riesling wine

2¼-inch (5.75-cm) piece of fresh ginger (about 3oz/85g), cut into three

1 lemongrass stalk, crushed and coarsely chopped

A few cilantro stems

Zest of 1 orange, pared into strips with a vegetable peeler

1 red chile, halved and seeded

1 leek, chopped into chunks

2 celery sticks, chopped into chunks

1 onion, halved

1 garlic bulb, halved horizontally

5 star anise

15 black peppercorns

Poaching is a wonderful and far too often overlooked cooking method, perfect for lovingly imparting delicate flavors to every type of ingredient, from the commonplace to the rare. Rant over—let's cook! This poaching method may seem a little controversial, but it produces the best, most delicate chicken. It's one of the first chicken recipes I ever made. It is excellent served with Pistachio & Rose Pilaf (see page 156) and some steamed greens.

1. First, grind the white pepper, coriander seeds, and cardamom seeds together, using a mortar and pestle. Then process or finely chop all the seasoning ingredients with the spices in a food processor so that you have a wonderful thickish paste. (If you don't have a food processor, chop the herbs finely and grate the ginger and garlic, then mix together in a small bowl.) Carefully insert this paste under the chicken's skin from the front and rear cavities right down into the legs. Try not to split the skin. This may take 15 minutes or so, but it makes the dish spectacular.

2. Dislocate the legs from the sockets, then put the chicken into a large saucepan or stockpot. Add the wine, ginger, lemongrass, cilantro stems, orange zest, chile, leek, celery, onion, garlic, star anise, and peppercorns. Pour in enough water to cover the chicken.

3. Cover the pan and bring to a boil. Cook for 5 minutes at a rolling boil, then turn off the heat and leave the chicken in the liquid until it's cool enough to handle—about 2 hours.

4. Remove the chicken from the stock, put on a large warmed serving plate, and strain the liquid into a clean pan, skimming off any excess fat. Discard the flavorings and vegetables. Bring the cooking liquid to a boil and reduce to 1¼ cups (10fl oz/300ml), then pour into a warmed sauce boat.

5. Carve the bird and serve, making sure that each guest has both dark and brown meats, pouring some of the sauce over the meat.

Sofa Chicken

Love this dish! Spiced, floured, and fried chicken, perfect for sofa, or couch, sloths—and a perennial favorite of my friends and family. I prefer using boned thigh meat because it's quicker to cook and easier to bite into. Whole thighs and drumsticks are great, too, but will take a little longer to cook through—7–10 minutes. You can skip the buttermilk-bath stage if you're in a hurry, but it does make an excellent and notable difference.

SERVES 4

1lb 2oz (500g) boned and skinned chicken thighs, cut into long lozenges, gristle and sinew removed
Peanut oil, for deep-frying

FOR THE BUTTERMILK BATH
1 cup (9fl oz/250ml) buttermilk
1 vanilla bean, split lengthwise
½ teaspoon Kashmiri chili flakes

FOR THE CRISP CRUMB
1¼ cups (5½ oz/150g) potato starch or cornstarch
1¾ cups (9oz/250g) instant polenta or medium cornmeal
Zest of ½ unwaxed lemon, grated
1 teaspoon sweet paprika
½ teaspoon smoked paprika
1 teaspoon cayenne pepper
¼ teaspoon chopped thyme leaves
½ teaspoon amchoor
1 teaspoon fine sea salt

FOR THE SPICED SALT
2 teaspoons black peppercorns
2 teaspoons coriander seeds
1 teaspoon fennel seeds
Seeds of 1 green cardamom pod
2 teaspoons sea salt

1. Put the buttermilk into a large bowl, scrape in the vanilla seeds, and add the vanilla bean and Kasmiri flakes. Add the chicken, cover, and put in the refrigerator for at least 6 hours or overnight.

2. When it's time to cook, put all the crisp crumb ingredients in a bowl and mix well. Lift the chicken out of the buttermilk bath and into the crumb bowl. Toss until well coated, then set aside on a wire rack.

3. Grind all the spices for the spiced salt, using a mortar and pestle.

4. Pour the peanut oil into an electric deep fryer set to 340°F (170°C). (Or fill a large saucepan one-third full of oil and put it over medium heat. After 4–5 minutes, drop a piece of white bread into the oil; if it takes 3 seconds to turn golden brown, it's the right heat for the chicken. If not, adjust the heat accordingly.)

5. Using kitchen tongs, pick up individual chicken pieces and gently lower them into the hot oil. Don't crowd the chicken—cook in two or three batches. Deep-fry for 4–6 minutes, depending on the thickness of the chicken, until crisp and golden; check by slicing into one of the thicker pieces; the juices should run clear, not pink.

6. Remove from the pan, sprinkle liberally with the spiced salt, and serve immediately. They go really well with Chile Preserves (see page 262) and a rich garlic mayo.

HYDERABADI CHICKEN WITH SPICED CASHEW BUTTER

When it comes to chicken, buy the best you can afford. To me, the breed and age of the chicken matter more than whether it's free-range or organic, but you must choose according to your own criteria. This recipe is somewhat of an adaptataion on a chicken curry, so whichever chicken you choose for it, enjoy!

SERVES 4

FOR THE SPICED CASHEW BUTTER

1⅓ cups (6oz/175g) cashew nuts
½ teaspoon black peppercorns
½ teaspoon cumin seeds
¼ teaspoon cloves
1 teaspoon powdered turmeric
½ teaspoon finely ground cassia
1 heaping teaspoon sea salt
2 tablespoons dried coconut
1 small handful curly parsley
    leaves, finely chopped
1 red Thai chile, seeded and
    finely diced
⅓ cup (1oz/30g) finely grated
    fresh ginger
½ teaspoon finely grated
    lemon zest

FOR THE CHICKEN

1 oven-ready chicken
    (about 3lb/1.4kg)
1 tablespoon canola oil
16 small shallots or pearl onions
12 whole garlic cloves, skin on
⅓ cup (5fl oz/150ml) chicken
    stock or broth
2 tablespoons crème fraîche or
    Greek yogurt
2 tablespoons (1oz/30g) unsalted
    butter, cubed and chilled

1. To make the cashew butter, put the cashew nuts into a saucepan, cover with water, and boil for 15 minutes. Drain, reserving 2 tablespoons of the cooking water. Put the nuts and reserved cooking water into a food processor or blender and process until smooth. Finely grind the whole spices, using a mortar and pestle. Add all the spices, salt, coconut, parsley, chile, ginger, and lemon zest to the nuts and pulse to form a thick paste. (Or chop the ingredients finely, then grind together, using a mortar and pestle). Reserve ½ cup (1¾oz/50g) of the cashew butter in a small bowl.

2. Wipe the chicken with paper towels and remove any excess fat. Put the chicken on a clean work surface. Carefully lift the skin of the bird away from the flesh, starting at the neck end, then gently push the cashew butter under the skin, using your fingers. Rub any remaining butter over the legs and breasts.

3. Tie the legs neatly to the body using kitchen string. Preheat the oven to 350°F (180°C). Put the oil in a large flameproof casserole or Dutch oven over medium–high heat. Add the shallots and garlic, and cook for 4–5 minutes to brown slightly. Remove from the heat. Add the stock or broth and the chicken. Cover with aluminum foil, then with the lid. Cook in the oven for 1 hour 20 minutes, or until the thigh meat juices run clear when pricked with the tip of a sharp knife. Remove the bird from the casserole, cover loosely with foil, and keep warm.

4. Skim off any excess fat from the juices. Put the casserole over medium–high heat and reduce the cooking liquid by half. Remove from the heat, add the crème fraîche or yogurt, and stir well to combine, then put back on the heat and continue to reduce until the sauce just coats the back of a spoon. Add the reserved cashew butter and the cubed butter and whisk to combine until glossy. Serve the chicken with the sauce and rice.

POT-ROASTED PHEASANT

I came up with this recipe when I was asked by Richard Corrigan to appear on his Channel 4 program, Cookery School. *I was showing the students how to cook with spices. This dish is my play on the classic pheasant-and-grape combination. Clementines make a beautiful fruity addition to the bird, while cardamom brings together the flavors of both. This recipe was classed as "super advanced" for the program, due to the number of elements and steps, but just take it easy when preparing it and you'll be fine.*

SERVES 4

3 clementines
1 teaspoon juniper berries
1 teaspoon cubeb pepper
1 teaspoon fennel
Seeds from 2 green cardamom
    pods
¼ teaspoon Sichuan pepper
1 star anise
1 teaspoon finely ground cassia
5½ tablespoons (2¾oz/75g)
    unsalted butter
2 oven-ready young hen
    pheasants, at room
    temperature
Sea salt and finely ground
    black pepper
10 thick slices dry-cured
    unsmoked bacon
1 tablespoon canola oil
3½oz (100g) pancetta, chopped
    into dice and blanched for
    about 3 minutes
6 small shallots, peeled
2 tablespoons Armagnac
    or Cognac
½ cup (3½fl oz/100ml) dry
    white wine
⅓ cup (2½fl oz/75ml) chicken
    stock or broth

1. Preheat the oven to 350°F (180°C). Using a vegetable peeler, remove the zest from the clementines in strips. Boil a small saucepan of water, add the zest strips, and boil for 1 minute to blanch them. Drain. Using a sharp knife, with a plate to catch the juice, slice off the top and bottom of a clementine, then slice off the pith. Cut out the segments, leaving the membrane behind. Squeeze the juice out of the membrane into a bowl and add the juice from the plate. Repeat with the remaining clementines. Set aside.

2. Grind all the spices together, using a mortar and pestle. Mix a quarter of the spice blend with the butter. Season the birds well inside and out with salt and black pepper, then cover generously with the spiced butter.

3. Lay the bacon slices over the breast meat, then truss to secure the bacon in place. Put a large flameproof casserole or Dutch oven over medium heat and pour in the oil. Brown the bacon-wrapped pheasants all over, then remove them from the casserole and set aside.

4. Put the pancetta and shallots into the casserole and cook until lightly browned. Remove from the heat and put the pheasants in the casserole, breast side down.

5. Pour the Armagnac into a small saucepan, heat until hot, then set it alight and pour it over the birds. When the flames have subsided, pour in the wine and stock or broth, sprinkle in the remaining spice blend, the clementine juice, and strips of clementine zest.

6. Cover the casserole with aluminum foil, then with its lid, and put on the middle shelf in the oven. Cook for 40 minutes.

[Continued]

2 tablespoons Mandarine Napoléon, Grand Marnier, or other orange-flavored liqueur

3 tablespoons (1½ oz/40g) unsalted butter, cubed and chilled

A drizzle best-quality cider vinegar or lemon juice

7. Remove the casserole from the oven. Remove the lid and foil (keep the foil), and turn the birds breast side up.

8. Return to the oven, uncovered, for another 10–20 minutes, then check to see if the birds are cooked; the legs should move easily when gently tugged. Remove the birds from the casserole, cover with the reserved foil, and set aside to rest for 10–12 minutes. Reduce the oven temperature to 325°F (160°C).

9. Using a slotted spoon, remove the pancetta and shallots from the casserole and keep warm. Remove and discard the zest.

10. Strain the cooking juices from the casserole, pour into a small bowl, skim off any excess fat, and set aside.

11. Put the casserole over medium heat, add the orange liqueur, and stir well to deglaze and loosen the browned cooking residue. Set the liqueur alight, making sure that you burn off all the alcohol.

12. Now pour the juices back into the casserole, bring up to a vigorous simmer, and reduce the sauce until it clings slightly to the back of a spoon. Add the cold, cubed butter and vinegar to taste, and whisk well. Check the seasoning, then set the sauce aside until you are ready to serve.

13. Meanwhile, remove the trussing string and the bacon from the birds. Put the bacon on a baking sheet and put it in the oven to crisp for about 5 minutes. Preheat the broiler.

14. Carve the birds—remove and cut up the legs, then neatly cut the breasts from the carcasses—and put them in a roasting pan. Flash the poultry pieces under the hot broiler for 30 seconds.

15. Pour the cooking juices from the "flashed" roasting pan through a strainer into the sauce. Finish the sauce by gently reheating it and adding the clementine segments. Only just warm it through to make sure you retain the integrity and freshness of the segments. Serve the pheasant pieces on warmed plates, with the crisp bacon, shallots, and pancetta, and a little of the sauce with a few clementine segments; serve the remaining sauce separately.

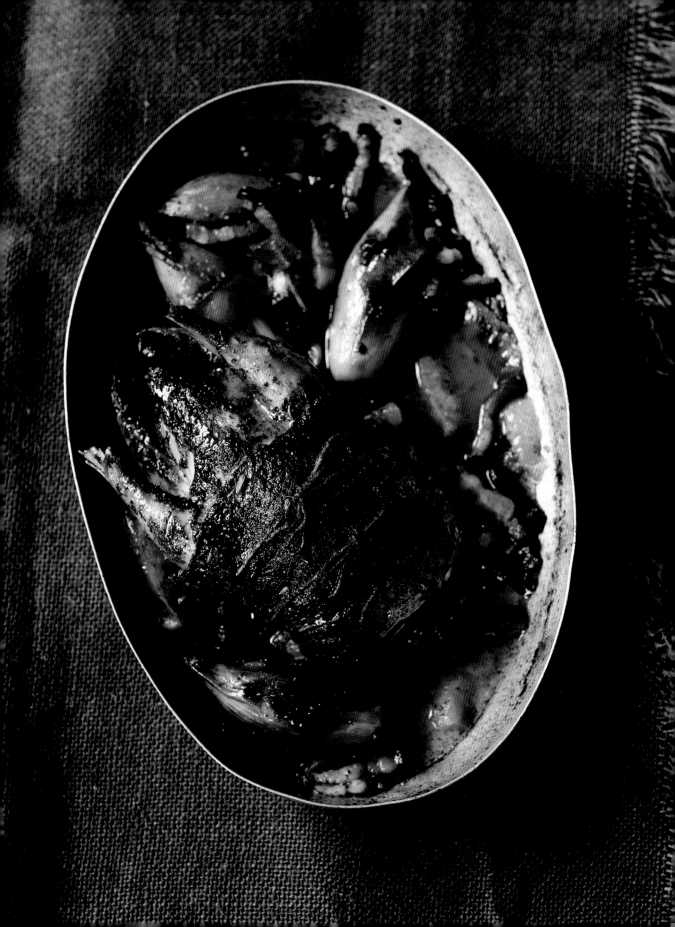

PERSIAN QUAIL

This is one of my favorite quick dishes—wonderful for entertaining or festive occasions. I love quail, and it goes so well with the Persian-style fesenjan *(pomegranate and walnut) sauce.*

FOR THE QUAIL

1 small pinch saffron threads
1 small handful pistachio nuts,
  coarsely chopped
1 small handful dried cherries
1 small handful golden raisins
1 tablespoon anardana, finely
  ground
2 tablespoons Grand Marnier or
  Cointreau
4 gratings nutmeg
1 tablespoon dried rose petals,
  chopped
4 oven-ready quail
2 tablespoons (1oz/30g) butter
A little light olive oil
½ butternut squash, peeled and
  cut into ¾-inch (2-cm) dice
1 tablespoon honey

FOR THE SAUCE

1 teaspoon black peppercorns
1 small piece blade mace
Seeds of 2 green cardamom pods
1 teaspoon ground cinnamon
1⅔ cups (7oz/200g) walnuts
½ teaspoon powdered turmeric
A splash light olive oil
2 banana shallots, finely diced
1 garlic clove, finely chopped
1 teaspoon sea salt
½ cup (3½fl oz/100ml)
  pomegranate juice
¼ cup (2fl oz/50ml)
  pomegranate molasses
1¼ cups (10fl oz/300ml)
  chicken stock or broth
Juice of 1 lime

1. Preheat the oven to 400°F (200°C). Soak the saffron in 2 tablespoons warm water in a large bowl, then stir in the nuts, cherries, golden raisins, anardana, liqueur, nutmeg, and rose petals to make the stuffing. Cover and set aside for 15 minutes. Fill the cavities of the birds with the stuffing, then truss the legs with kitchen string. Heat the butter and oil in a large skillet over medium heat until foaming, then add the birds and brown lightly on all sides, turning and basting as they cook. You may need to do this one bird at a time. Transfer the birds to a snug-fitting, deep roasting pan. Put the skillet to one side.

2. Cover the roasting pan tightly with aluminum foil, then roast the quail for 10–15 minutes—no more—just until the juices run clear when a thigh is pricked with the tip of a sharp knife. Remove from the oven, set aside, and keep warm.

3. To make the sauce, finely grind the peppercorns, mace, and cardamom, using a mortar and pestle, then add the cinnamon; set aside. Put the walnuts in a heavy skillet and lightly toast for 2–3 minutes. Transfer to a clean dish towel, gather up the corners, and rub vigorously to remove the skins. Put the nuts and turmeric into a food processor or blender and pulse to a coarse texture. (Or grind using a mortar and pestle.) Set aside.

4. Put the oil in a wide saucepan over medium heat. Add the shallots and sauté gently until soft and translucent. Add the garlic, the spice blend, walnuts, and the salt. Stir well, then add the pomegranate juice, molasses, and stock, stir again, and increase the heat. Once the sauce has begun to boil, turn down to a simmer and reduce to the thickness of heavy cream. Remove from the heat and add the lime juice. Stir and adjust the seasoning, if necessary, then set aside and keep warm.

5. Preheat the broiler. Heat a little more oil in the skillet over medium heat. Add the butternut squash and sauté for 8 minutes or until there's just a little give in the flesh. Add the honey, stir to coat, then put briefly under the broiler to brown. To serve, remove the string from the quail, add a spoonful of squash, and coat the meat generously with the sauce.

ROAST GUINEA FOWL

This dish helped me win a chef's version of Come Dine with Me *on Ireland's RTÉ channel's* Afternoon Show—*it was loads of fun. I then went home for Christmas and cooked it as a after-Christmas dish for 12 members of our family. With hindsight, it probably wasn't the best idea in terms of my workload, but it was really well received from a taste point of view. For that reason, I've since refined the recipe to cut out a little of the "fuss and bother." Enjoy it with lentils and my Clementine, Date & Chile Chutney (see page 258).*

SERVES 4

FOR THE SPICED BUTTER
Seeds of 5 black cardamom pods
1 teaspoon black peppercorns
1 teaspoon sea salt
2 tablespoons chopped tarragon leaves
1 teaspoon Grand Marnier or Cointreau (optional)
2¼ sticks (9oz/250g) unsalted butter, at room temperature

1. First, make the spiced butter. Finely grind the cardamom seeds and peppercorns, using a mortar and pestle. Put into a small bowl and add the salt, tarragon, liqueur (if using), and butter. Mix well.

2. Preheat the oven to 350°F (180°C). Remove the wishbones from the birds to make it easier to carve them (or you can ask your butcher to do this, if you prefer). Season the birds inside and out with a little salt, then gently lift the skin of each bird away from the flesh, starting at the neck end, and smear a quarter of the spiced butter between the meat and the skin. Try not to split the skin.

3. Lay the bacon slices over the breast meat, then tie the bacon in place with kitchen string.

4. Pour the oil into a large flameproof casserole or Dutch oven over medium heat. Lightly cook the birds all over until the bacon browns, then arrange them in the casserole, breast side down.

5. Pour in the wine and stock, cover with aluminum foil, then with the lid, and cook on a middle shelf in the oven for 25 minutes.

6. Remove from the oven and remove the lid and foil (keep the foil). Turn the birds breast side up.

7. Put the casserole back into the oven, uncovered, for 25–30 minutes. The exact cooking time depends on the size of the birds and how you like them cooked. Check to see if they're done by gently tugging the legs; they should move easily when the birds are ready.

FOR THE BIRDS

4 oven-ready young guinea fowl

Sea salt

16 thick slices bacon

1 teaspoon canola oil

**1 cup (7fl oz/200ml) dry
white wine**

**⅔ cup (5fl oz/150ml) chicken
stock or broth**

**3 tablespoons Armagnac or
Cognac**

**3½ tablespoons (1¾oz/50g)
unsalted butter, cubed and
chilled, plus a little extra at
room temperature**

**16 seedless grapes, preferably
peeled (but this isn't
absolutely necessary)**

8. Remove the birds from the casserole, set aside, and cover with the reserved foil. Increase the oven temperature to 425°F (220°C).

9. Strain the cooking juices through a strainer into a small bowl, skim off any excess fat, and set aside.

10. Pour the Armagnac into the casserole and gently heat it, then tip the casserole away from you slightly and carefully light the Armagnac with a match. Once the flames have died away, pour the cooking juices back into the casserole, bring up to a vigorous simmer, add the cold, cubed butter, whisk, and reduce for a moment.

11. Add the grapes and only just warm them through to make sure you retain the integrity and freshness of the fruit. Check the seasoning, adjust if necessary, then set aside.

12. Remove the trussing string and the bacon from the birds. Put the bacon on a baking sheet and put it in the oven for a couple of minutes to crisp, then take it out and set aside.

13. Carve the birds, first removing the legs, then neatly cut the breasts from the carcasses and put into a roasting pan. Cover with wax paper.

14. Put the roasting pan into the hot oven for 2 minutes, then cut up the legs, trim the breasts, and slice them on the diagonal; serve on warmed plates, with the crisp bacon and the grapes in their sauce.

Spiced Wood Pigeon, Artichoke, Beet & Endive Salad with Hazelnut Dressing

This salad is all about rich, bold, gamey notes of the pigeon, offset by the perfume of green cardamom, Sichuan pepper, and juniper. There are plenty of elements—including hot potato fritters, crisp leave,s and creamy dressing—but once the prep work is done, it's really more about presentation. I like pigeon cooked medium-rare. Try it—and don't be afraid of the pink!

SERVES 4

FOR THE ARTICHOKES
A splash light olive oil
4–6 globe artichoke hearts, each
    cut into 6 slices, through
    their poles
Juice of ½ orange
1 garlic clove, crushed
1 pinch sea salt
1 small thyme sprig

FOR THE BEETS
6–8 beets, unpeeled
Sea salt
½ teaspoon black peppercorns,
    finely ground
A splash canola oil

FOR THE PIGEON
5 juniper berries
½ star anise
1 teaspoon fennel seeds
Seeds of 4 green cardamom pods
½ teaspoon Sichuan pepper
2 teaspoons finely ground cassia
1 teaspoon smoked paprika
1 thyme sprig, leaves only

1. Preheat the oven to 350° (180°C). Put a heavy sauté pan over medium heat. Add a splash of oil, then gently sauté the artichoke slices for 2 minutes. Add the orange juice, garlic, salt, and thyme, and continue to sweat until just soft. Drain and set aside, discarding the garlic.

2. To prepare the beets, spread a thin layer of sea salt over the bottom of a small roasting pan, put the beets on top, and roast in the oven for 35–40 minutes, until they're just tender. Let cool. Peel and cut them in half through the poles, then cut each half into segments. Put them into a small bowl, add a touch of salt, the ground pepper, and a drizzle of canola oil. Set aside. Leave the oven on.

3. Finely grind the whole spices for the pigeon, using a mortar and pestle. Transfer all the spices to a bowl with the thyme and orange zest. Flatten each bacon slice with the back of a knife while gently stretching it, then slice in half lengthwise. Add the pigeon breasts to the spice mixture and roll them around until well coated, then wrap each breast in a piece of bacon, making sure the meat is fully covered.

4. Add a splash of olive oil to a sauté or skillet and gently sauté the pigeon breasts for 1–1½ minutes on each side, then remove and set aside on a large baking sheet.

5. To make the potato fritters, coarsely grate the potatoes into a bowl of cold water. Wash and rinse the potatoes throughly with running water, then drain well and put into a clean dish towel. Twist and squeeze the towel firmly to remove all the water.

Zest of ½ orange
4 slices dry-cured bacon
8 wood pigeon breasts

FOR THE POTATO FRITTERS

2 red-skinned or white round
    potatoes, peeled
1 teaspoon sea salt
1 teaspoon Quatre Épices blend
    (see page 266)
1 tablespoon light olive oil
2 tablespoons (1oz/30g)
    unsalted butter

FOR THE SALAD & DRESSING

¾ cup (3½oz/100g) fresh
    shelled hazelnuts
3 tablespoons canola oil
Seeds of 1 black cardamom pod,
    finely ground
1 teaspoon Dijon mustard
2 tablespoons crème fraîche
    or Greek yogurt, plus extra,
    if needed
½ teaspoon sea salt
1 small head white endive
1 small head radicchio
1 small piece fresh horseradish
    root, peeled

6. Transfer the potato to a bowl, season with the salt and Quatre Épices, and stir to combine. Divide the mixture into eight equal mounds.

7. Put the oil and butter in a nonstick skillet over medium heat. Put four potato mounds into the pan and gently press down with a spatula until they are about 3¼ inches (8cm) in diameter. Cook for 3–4 minutes on each, side until crisp and golden. Drain on paper towels and set aside. Repeat with the remaining four potato mounds.

8. For the salad, gently dry-roast half the nuts in a nonstick skillet over medium heat until they are just slightly browned, then set aside.

9. Drop the remaining nuts into a food processor or blender, add the canola oil, black cardamom seeds, mustard, crème fraîche or yogurt, and salt, and process to a smooth paste. (Alternatively, grind everything together well, using a mortar and pestle). Pass this paste through a strainer and add a little more crème fraîche or yogurt to achieve a pleasant dropping consistency.

10. Carefully separate the leaves of the endive and radicchio.

11. To serve, put the baking sheet with the wrapped pigeon breasts into the oven for 2–3 minutes, turning once, then remove, cover loosely with aluminum foil, and let rest for 3 minutes. Meanwhile, put the potato fritters into the oven to warm through for 4–5 minutes.

12. Arrange the salad greens, artichokes, and beets on four large warmed plates, then drizzle the salad with the dressing and sprinkle with the roasted nuts. Slice the pigeon breasts on the diagonal, arrange them attractively in the salad, then grate a little horseradish finely over each salad. Put two potato fritters next to the pigeon and serve.

DUCK, PORK & BEANS WITH SPICED CRUMB

On trips to France, I used to love buying jars of cassoulet packed full of beans, various meats, and herbs, almost set with duck fat. I came up with this recipe after a little trial and error, using spices to lift the earthy duck and beans and mute the saltiness of the pork. You'll notice I don't add any salt, simply because it doesn't need it with all that pork, but if you have a particularly salty palate, then be my guest!

SERVES 4

2¼ lb (1kg) salted pork belly
2 pig feet, split
3 duck legs
2 star anise
2 black cardamom pods
4 green cardamom pods
1 leek, halved
2 carrots, halved
½ head celery, cut into 3 chunks
1 onion, quartered
1 large bunch curly parsley,
    with stems
4-inch (10-cm) cassia stick
12 white peppercorns
4 cloves
6 pieces of beef bone marrow,
    2½–4 inches (6–10cm)
    long (ask your butcher to
    chop them)

1. Put the pork belly into a large flameproof casserole or Dutch oven, cover with cold water, and put over high heat. Bring to a boil, then reduce the heat and simmer gently for 8–10 minutes. Pour away the water, add the pig feet and duck legs, cover with cold water, and repeat. Meanwhile, lightly crush the anise and cardamom pods in a mortar and pestle. Set aside.

2. Pour away the water, put the meat into a colander under a faucet, and rinse well, then put the pork belly and pig feet back into the casserole. Add the leek, carrots, celery, onion, parsley, crushed anise, cardamom, and all the remaining spices, followed by the duck legs. Cover well with cold water, put over high heat, cover, and bring to a boil. Turn down to a gentle simmer and cook, partly covered, for 2½ hours or until the meats are really tender.

3. Remove from the heat, take out the meats, and let rest until cool enough to handle. Strain the vegetables through a colander over a bowl to retain the cooking liquid. Discard the vegetables and spices.

4. Once cooled, strip the pig feet meat and gelatinous skin from the bones. Shred the meat onto a plate. Keep the bright-looking pieces of fat and skin—but not any hairy parts or bony, gray fat—and dice them finely. Set aside on a separate plate from the shredded meat.

5. Cut away the rind from the pork belly and remove any dull-looking fat, keeping only the bright parts. Coarsely cube and shred the belly meat, and add it to the pig feet meat. Dice the retained fat and add it to the plate of pig feet fat.

FOR THE BEANS

½ star anise

Seeds of 2 green cardamom pods

3 cloves

2 (14½-oz/400-g) cans diced tomatoes

1 garlic bulb, halved horizontally

1 thyme sprig, leaves only

1 (15oz/425g) can navy or pinto beans, drained

FOR THE SPICED CRUMB

½ bunch curly parsley, coarsely chopped, stems and all

8 garlic cloves

2 tablespoons light olive oil

2¾ cups (4½oz/125g) coarse fresh bread crumbs

2 teaspoons Quatre Épices blend (see page 266)

2 tablespoons goose fat or olive oil

6. Finely grind the spices for the beans, using a mortar and pestle. Put the beans in a large saucepan, add the gelatinous skin of the pig feet, the diced fat, tomatoes, garlic, thyme leaves, and spices.

7. Add 1¾ cups (14fl oz/400ml) of the reserved meat cooking liquid, then put over medium heat, stir, and bring to a gentle simmer. Cook for 20–25 minutes, until it has reduced by one-third. Take off the heat and set aside.

8. Preheat the oven to 400°F (200°C). To make the crumb, put the parsley and garlic into a food processor and blend to a puree. Add the olive oil, pulse briefly, then pour the paste into a small bowl. (Alternatively use a mortar and pestle.) Add the bread crumbs, Quatre Épices, and goose fat to the bowl and mix everything together with your fingers.

9. Arrange the pork belly chunks and pig feet meat in a 12 × 8 × 3½-inch (30 × 20 × 9-cm) gratin dish, or a (10½ × 8½-inch (26 × 22-cm) oval Dutch oven.

10. Remove the skin from the duck legs, and cut them in two across the joints. Put them into the dish, then spoon over the beans. Gently sink the bone marrow into the beans and sprinkle the spiced crumb generously over everything.

11. Cook on the middle shelf of the oven for 20–30 minutes, until golden and bubbling. Serve while still bubbling, with plenty of Dijon mustard.

FISH

WHEN I THINK OF SPICING fiSH, MY THOUGHTS TURN fiRST TO ZINGY, UPLIFTING NOTES, PERFUMED HEAT, CITRUS FRESHNESS. But there's a host of spice possibilities to match the wealth of flavors and textures found in white fish, such as haddock, pollock, cod, and red snapper; oily fish, such as salmon, tuna, and mackerel; and smoked fish. Sweet, delicate sea-fresh white fish needs a light touch, with attention to the high notes, to heighten its flavor without overpowering. The darker, more pronounced flavors of the oily fish work well with the gnarled nuttiness of mustard seeds, the sweet-sourness of tamarind, the pungency of pepper.

For white fish I often use the perfumed notes of cardamom, nutmeg, star anise, long pepper. My Crisp Haddock Cobbler, with its rich sauce and biscuit topping, needs the slightly more robust but nonetheless fragrant spices in my Garam Masala. Ceviche has chile heat and a citrus bite, with cumin to help ground and pull back the acidic notes of the citrus fruits.

When it comes to oily fish, the gloves are off as far as subtlety goes! Tamarind, chile, mustard, and ginger perk up the Mackerel Skewers, creating a touch of the exotic and wonderful balance. In my Crammed Beach Fish, I use Garam Masala in the accompanying Aioli, preferring a fragrant ras el hanout blend and plenty of fresh herbs to help cut the richness of the fish.

In the Bengal Smoked Fish Brunch, I've combined smoked haddock, or Finnan Haddie, with the beautiful Bengali Panch Phoron blend. *Panch* translates from Hindi as "five" and *Phoron* as "flavor or spice"; it's the Indian five-spice blend, often used with fish and seafood. The nutty heat of the mustard seeds, subtle nutty pepperiness of kalonji, earthiness of cumin, bittersweet fenugreek, and sweet anise of the fennel seeds caress the smoky fish to flavor perfection.

Previous page: Aji lemon chiles have the most amazing pineapple-citrus flavor, a good level of heat and beautiful color.

PARSNIP & SALT COD CHOWDER

Salt cod (available from good fish dealers and online) and parsnips used to be considered poor man's food. I've devised this velvety smooth, creamy spiced soup to showcase both ingredients because, regardless of status, they work so well together.

SERVES 4–6

9oz (250g) salt cod fillet

FOR THE SPICE BLEND
1 teaspoon black peppercorns
5 cloves
2 teaspoons coriander seeds
1 teaspoon cumin seeds
Seeds of 3 green cardamom pods
1 teaspoon powdered turmeric
2 teaspoons finely ground cassia

FOR THE VEGETABLES
½ cup (3½fl oz/100ml) canola oil
3 tablespoons light olive oil
1 shallot, diced
½ garlic clove, crushed
2 Yukon Gold or red-skinned potatoes, peeled and diced
6–8 young parsnips (about 1½lb/700g), peeled and cut into ¼-inch (5-mm) slices
⅔ cup (5fl oz/150ml) whole milk, plus extra if needed
½ cup (3½fl oz/100ml) light cream

FOR THE GARNISH
3 tablespoons Greek yogurt
1 scallion, thinly sliced
3 plain poppadoms, cooked according to the package directions, cracked into interestingly shaped shards (optional) or plain unflavored tortilla chips

1. Soak the salt cod in cold water for 12 hours, changing the water once. Rinse the fish under cold running water. Put 2 cups (18floz/500ml) water into a saucepan over medium heat, bring to a boil, add the fish, and poach gently for 20–30 minutes, until cooked though.

2. Meanwhile, prepare the spice blend. Finely grind the peppercorns, cloves, coriander, cumin, and cardamom seeds, using a mortar and pestle. Add the turmeric and cassia. Set aside.

3. Using a slotted spoon, lift out the fish, then carefully remove the skin and bones and gently break apart into large flakes. Set aside. Strain the cooking liquid through a fine strainer, reserving 1⅔ cups (14fl oz/400ml).

4. Put the canola oil into a small saucepan and add one-third of the spice blend. Cook over medium heat for 2–3 minutes, until the oil is just warm. Remove from the heat and let cool. Strain through cheesecloth into a bowl (do not be tempted to squeeze the cloth). Set aside.

5. Put the olive oil into a large saucepan over medium heat. Add the shallot, garlic, potatoes, and parsnips, then partly cover and sauté gently, stirring from time to time, for 15 minutes, until they're just soft. Add the remaining spice blend and cook for another 1 minute. Add the reserved cooking liquid and 1⅔ cups (14fl oz/400ml) water, increase the heat, and bring to a boil. Reduce the heat and cook gently, covered, for 15–20 minutes, until the potatoes and parsnips are completely soft. Process in a food processor until really smooth, then pass through a fine strainer and pour back into the saucepan. Put the pan over medium heat, add the salt cod flakes, milk, and cream, and bring to a gentle simmer for 3–4 minutes to heat through.

6. Add the yogurt, stir well, then check the seasoning. Adjust the consistency, if necessary, by adding a little water or milk. Ladle the chowder into deep, warmed bowls. Drizzle with the spiced oil and sprinkle with scallion. Serve with a plate of poppadom shards or tortilla chips, if using, for your guests to add at will.

CRISP HADDOCK COBBLER

Soft-fleshed fish, perfumed cobbler biscuits, creamy sauce, and crispy, spiced topping—what's not to like? I've kept the flavors simple, turning the spotlight on the topping so that the beautiful, multilayered Garam Masala shines through and doesn't confuse. There's a generous amount of sauce, so you may need to put a baking pan under the baking dish to save your oven from bubbling spillages.

SERVES 4–6

2¼lb (1kg) haddock, pollock, or other white fish, skinned and cut into 1¼-inch (3-cm) dice
1¾ cups (¾ pint/425ml) whole milk
1 pinch sea salt
Ground black pepper

FOR THE SAUCE
2½ tablespoons (1¼oz/35g) unsalted butter, at room temperature
¼ cup (1oz/30g) all-purpose flour
½ cup (4fl oz/125ml) light cream
2 heaping teaspoons Dijon mustard
½ teaspoon sea salt
1 large handful curly parsley, no thick stems, finely chopped

1. Preheat the oven to 425°F (220°C). Put the fish into a saucepan and cover with the milk. Add the salt and black pepper to taste and put over medium heat. Bring up to a simmer, then poach gently for 5 minutes. Take off the heat, remove the fish pieces from the milk with a slotted spoon, and set aside to cool. Reserve the cooking liquid.

2. For the sauce, put a large saucepan over medium heat, add the butter, and let melt. Add the flour and whisk to form a roux, then cook for 30 seconds.

3. Pour 1⅔ cups (14fl oz/400ml) of the reserved cooking liquid and the cream into a small bowl, then pour it a little at a time into the pan, whisking all the time to combine well with the roux. Once all the liquid has been added, keep whisking and let the sauce cook until you see the first bubbles appear, then continue to cook for another 2 minutes.

4. Next, add the mustard and salt, and stir well to combine. Cook gently for 5 minutes, with only the odd bubble or two appearing, stirring occasionally. Add the parsley, stir, then cover the surface with wax paper and set aside.

5. Lay the fish in a 12 × 10 × 1¾-inch (30 × 25 × 4.5-cm) roasting pan or ovenproof dish. Pour in the sauce, coating the fish. Set aside to cool completely.

FOR THE TOPPING

1 cup (1¾oz/50g) fresh
    bread crumbs
1 tablespoon olive oil
⅓ cup (1oz/30g) finely grated
    fresh Parmesan cheese
½ teaspoon cayenne pepper

FOR THE COBBLER BISCUITS

1⅔ cups (7oz/200g) all-purpose
    flour
¼ cup (1oz/30g) cornstarch
1 tablespoon baking powder
½ teaspoon sea salt
2 teaspoons Garam Masala blend
    (see page 267)
1¼ sticks plus 1 tablespoon
    (5½oz/150g) unsalted butter,
    cubed and chilled
⅔ –¾ cup (5–6fl oz/150–175ml)
    whole milk

6. Put all the topping ingredients into a bowl and mix well. Set aside.

7. To make the cobbler biscuits, sift the flours and baking powder into a mixing bowl. Add the salt and Garam Masala and stir to combine. Rub the chilled butter into the flour with your fingertips until it looks like bread crumbs. Then using a fork to stir, pour in a little milk at a time until you have a batter with a thick dropping consistency.

8. Drop random blobs of the biscuit mixture over the fish, then put the pan or dish into a large roasting pan to catch any bubbling sauce that overflows as it cooks. Cook on a high shelf in the oven for 15 minutes or until the topping has risen.

9. Pull the pan out of the oven slightly, sprinkle the surface with the crumb topping, then put the pan onto a middle shelf and continue to bake for 12–15 minutes, until the crumbs are golden brown and the sauce bubbles up through the biscuits. Serve with some fresh, crisp leaves.

CEVICHE & CORN

I have loved ceviche, especially this Peruvian version, ever since my younger brother and his wife returned from their South American honeymoon and introduced me to this zingy classic—small pieces of delicate fish marinated with aji chiles, lime, and onion, served with corn. My brother now grows these chiles, so we can enjoy their lemony, pineapple-type perfume.

SERVES 4

1 red onion, finely sliced into rings
12oz (350g) sea bass fillet

FOR THE FENNEL SALAD
1 fennel bulb, with loads of
    green, feathery tops
Juice of ½ orange
Juice of ½ lemon
1 teaspoon sea salt
¼ teaspoon amchoor (optional)

FOR THE CEVICHE MIX
½ teaspoon each black
    peppercorns, white
    peppercorns, coriander seeds,
    cumin seeds
¼ teaspoon Scichuan pepper
1–2 gratings nutmeg
1 teaspoon sea salt
2 fresh aji lemon chiles
    (or 1 teaspoon aji paste
    or 1 Scotch bonnet chile),
    seeded and finely chopped
Juice of 3 limes and ½ orange

FOR THE CORN
7 tablespoons (3½oz/100g)
    unsalted butter
1 teaspoon cumin seeds
2 teaspoons ground black pepper
1 teaspoon red pepper flakes
1 teaspoon sea salt
2 corn cobs, halved

1. To make the salad, trim the ends of the fennel bulb, reserving the feathery tops. Shave the bulb thinly lengthwise on a mandoline slicer or use a sharp knife to slice it as thinly as you can. Put the shavings in a large glass bowl, add the orange and lemon juices, and sprinkle in the sea salt and amchoor powder, if using. Gently mix everything together, then cover with plastic wrap and chill in the refrigerator.

2. Put the red onion slices into a bowl of cold water for 5 minutes, then remove them, shake, and put onto paper towels to dry. Set aside.

3. To make the ceviche mix, finely grind the peppercorns, coriander and cumin seeds, and the Sichuan pepper, using a mortar and pestle, then mix in the nutmeg and salt. Finely chop the reserved fennel tops and add to the mix, together with the chiles.

4. Remove the skin and oily, dark flesh from the fish. Put the fish on a plate and coat with a generous layer of the ceviche mix. Let stand for 1 minute, then add the lime and orange juices and set aside for about 15 minutes.

5. To cook the corn, first preheat the broiler. Mix the butter with the spices and salt and spread over the corn. Put the corn into a broiler pan and broil for 10 minutes or until slightly charred all over.

6. To serve, put the corn on a serving plate and spoon the buttery juices from the broiler pan over it. Gently squeeze the fennel salad to remove the excess dressing, then put it onto a serving plate. Arrange the onion rings on a third plate. Slice the fish as thinly as possible, then gently scoop up the fish and put it on the onion. Serve with a shot glass of the ceviche marinade, the *leche de tigre* (tiger's milk) for those who dare!

SALMON, POTATO & FENNEL FISHCAKES WITH ORANGE, FENNEL & RED ONION SALAD

Earthy potatoes, sweet, moist salmon invigorated with hits of anise-perfumed fennel. Floral, sour capers, bites of fragrant crunch, celery, and shallot. These fishcakes have a fresh, palate-pleasing lightness, especially when served with a simple salad. Here, snap-crunchy fennel bulb combines with the cool, sweet acidity of ripe, juicy orange.

SERVES 4

FOR THE FISHCAKES

3–4 Yukon Gold or russet
 potatoes, unpeeled
A splash olive oil
¼ fennel bulb, finely chopped
½ celery stick, finely chopped
2 shallots, finely chopped
1 tablespoon fennel seeds,
 coarsely ground
2 teaspoons black peppercorns,
 coarsely ground
1 teaspoon sea salt
1½–1¾lb (750g) salmon fillet,
 skinned
2 scallions, finely sliced on the
 diagonal
3 feathery fennel tops, chopped
2 teaspoon baby capers, drained
1 large egg, lightly beaten, plus
 extra if needed
1 cup (1¾oz/50g) fresh bread
 crumbs, plus extra if needed

1. Preheat the oven to 375°F (190°C). Put the potatoes into a saucepan and cover generously with water. Bring to a boil and cook for 20 minutes or until tender. Drain and peel, then put back into the pan and mash with a potato masher. Meanwhile, heat 1 tablespoon oil in a skillet over medium heat and add the fennel, celery, and shallots. Cook for 8–10 minutes, until just soft but still a little crunchy. Set aside.

2. Put a square of wax paper, a little larger than the piece of fish, into a sturdy roasting pan. Give the paper square a random drizzle of olive oil, then sprinkle with half the fennel seeds, peppercorns, and salt. Lay the salmon on top of the spices.

3. Sprinkle the fish with a little more oil, then with the remaining salt and spices. Put the pan on the middle shelf of the oven and bake for 8 minutes. Remove the fish from the oven and set aside to cool to room temperature, then gently flake the fish into generous pieces and set aside.

4. In a large bowl, gently mix together the mashed potatoes, the cooked vegetables, scallions, fennel tops, capers, egg, and bread crumbs. Check the seasoning and adjust, if necessary. Add the salmon, being careful not to overwork the mixture. It should be just moist but not wet. If necessary, adjust the consistency with more egg or bread crumbs.

FOR COATING AND FRYING

3–4 tablespoons all-purpose flour
4 large eggs, lightly beaten with ¼ teaspoon sea salt
2 cups (7oz/200g) dried bread crumbs
Sunflower oil, for shlet-frying

5. Generously fill a 3¼–4-inch (8–10-cm)-diameter ring mold with one-eighth of the salmon mixture so that it's compact but not squashed. Turn it over and the cake should drop out. (Alternatively, use a greased teacup. Fill the cup halfway with salmon mixture, press it down gently, turn the cup over, and shake the cup; the fishcake should drop out. Tidy it up with a knife.) Repeat to make seven more fishcakes. Rest the fishcakes in the refrigerator for 30 minutes to firm up.

6. Dredge the fishcakes lightly in flour, then coat them in the beaten egg followed by the bread crumbs. Repeat the process, then rest the cakes in the refrigerator until needed.

7. When ready to serve, preheat the oven to 400°F (200°C). Pan-fry the fishcakes until lightly golden on both sides, then transfer to a baking sheet and cook in the oven for 5 minutes. Drain on paper towels.

FOR THE SALAD

1 fennel bulb, with plenty of green, feathery tops
2 red onions
2 oranges

FOR THE DRESSING

2 tablespoons balsamic vinegar
Sea salt and finely ground white pepper
⅓ cup (2½ fl oz/75ml) fruity olive oil

1. To make the salad, put some of the fennel tops to one side. Finely slice the fennel bulb lengthwise; this is best done using a mandoline slicer if you have one—just be really careful of your fingertips!

2. Put the slices of fennel into ice cold water until crisp. Slice the onions in the same way.

3. Using a small sharp knife, and a bowl to catch the juice, cut a thin slice from the top and bottom of an orange, then slice off its skin and all the pith. Cut the segments neatly away from the membrane. Remove any seeds and discard. Repeat with the other orange.

4. To make the dressing, dissolve a little salt in the vinegar, add a little ground pepper, 2 tablespoons of the reserved orange juice, and the olive oil, and whisk until it emulsifies. Taste and adjust the seasoning, if needed.

5. In a large bowl, toss all the salad ingredients together with the dressing, being careful not to damage the orange segments.

6. To serve, put a fishcake or two on each plate and gently pile the fennel salad alongside. Chop the reserved feathery fennel tops and sprinkle them over the top.

ROAST HERBED SALMON WITH CARDAMOM SAUCE

I use green cardamom in this recipe to cut through the rich fish and creamy sauce, while at the same time adding a gentle perfume to brighten up the whole, delicious experience.

SERVES 4

4 (6oz/175g) center-cut salmon
  fillets, thick and an even size
Dijon mustard, for brushing
Sea salt

FOR THE CRUST
A little light olive oil
¼ cup (1½oz/40g) finely diced
  shallots
1 garlic clove, finely diced
heaping ¾ cup (1½oz/40g)
  fresh bread crumbs
3 tablespoons grated fresh
  Parmesan cheese
2 tablespoons black peppercorns,
  finely ground
1 cup (1¾oz/50g) finely
  chopped mixture of soft
  herbs, such as parsley, chives,
  dill, and chervil

FOR THE SAUCE
6 green cardamom pods
½ cup (3½fl oz/100ml) heavy
  cream
1 cup (7fl oz/200ml) chicken
  stock or broth
3½ tablespoons (1¾oz/50g)
  unsalted butter, cubed
  and chilled
½ teaspoon white peppercorns,
  finely ground

1. Preheat the oven to 400°F (200°C). Put a little olive oil in a sauté pan over medium heat and cook the shallots for 3 minutes or until they become translucent. Add the garlic, bread crumbs, and a little more olive oil so that the crumbs are moist but not wet. Cook gently for 2 minutes, until golden brown. Remove from the heat, then transfer to a bowl to cool. Add the Parmesan, 1 teaspoon of the black pepper, and the herbs, and mix well.

2. Put the fish fillets on a plate, skin side down. Season with a pinch of salt and 1 teaspoon of the black pepper, brush with a little Dijon mustard, then apply the bread crumb crust until about ¼ inch (5mm) thick, gently pressing the edges with a spatula so that they're even, tidy, and tight. (Any leftover herb crust can be frozen for another day.)

3. Put a sheet of wax paper on a baking sheet. Brush it with a little olive oil, season with sea salt and 2 teaspoons of the black pepper, and put the fillets on it so that they are evenly spaced. Cook on the middle shelf of the oven for 8 minutes or until the crust is only just golden.

4. Meanwhile, prepare the sauce. Gently smash four of the cardamom pods. Put the cream and smashed cardamom pods into a small saucepan over medium heat and bring to a gentle simmer. Cook for 2 minutes, then take off the heat and let cool. Strain through a strainer. Remove the seeds from the other two pods and grind to a fine powder.

5. Pour the chicken stock or broth into a saucepan, bring to a boil, then turn down the heat and simmer to reduce by half. Add the strained cream and bring to a simmer. Whisking constantly, add the cold butter, and bring to a brisk boil. As the sauce starts to thicken, whisk in the white pepper and check the seasoning. Serve the salmon fillets on warmed plates, with the sauce drizzled around the fillets and sprinkled with the cardamom powder.

SEVEN-PEPPER TUNA WITH CHICKPEA CHIPS

This is a beautiful, and healthy, recipe. Tuna has a wonderful firm texture, the eggplant adds smokiness and a creamy texture, and the chickpea chips, influenced by southern French cuisine, are crunchy and add a subtle sweetness to the whole wonderful eating experience. Sashimi-grade tuna is best for this recipe; it should be bright red with a firm flesh. But you could use four tuna steaks, as long as they are thick so that they remain rare after searing.

SERVES 4

FOR THE CHICKPEA CHIPS

2¼ cups (7oz/200g) chickpea (besan) flour
2 teaspoons sea salt
1 teaspoon fenugreek seeds, finely ground
½ teaspoon fennel seeds, finely ground
½ teaspoon rosemary leaves, finely chopped
Sunflower oil, for deep-frying

FOR THE SMOKED EGGPLANT

2 firm eggplants
2 teaspoons coriander seeds
1 teaspoon cumin seeds
1 teaspoon black peppercorns
A splash light olive oil
2 garlic cloves, crushed
1 teaspoon Kashmiri chili flakes
1 teaspoon sea salt

1. Preheat the oven to 350°F (180°C). To make the chickpea chips, put all the ingredients, except the oil, in a bowl and add 1¼ cups (10fl oz/ 300ml) lukewarm water. Mix well, then put in the refrigerator and chill for 10 minutes.

2. Line an 8-inch (20-cm)-square baking pan with wax paper. Pour the batter evenly into the pan and bake for 20–25 minutes, until the mixture is cooked and set. Let cool, then remove from the pan and put it in the refrigerator to chill.

3. When cold, cut into chips about ½ inch (1cm) wide and 4 inches 10cm) long. Put back into the refrigerator until you are ready to fry them.

4. To make the smoked eggplant, insert a metal skewer through each eggplant so that you can turn them easily, prick them with a fork, then put them over the open flame of a gas stove or under a preheated hot broiler until charred. Cut each one in half, remove the flesh, and coarsely chop it. Discard the skins.

5. Finely grind the coriander and cumin seeds and peppercorns, using a mortar and pestle. Set aside.

6. Heat the olive oil in a skillet over medium heat. Add the garlic, all the spices, the salt, and chopped eggplants, and sauté gently until the mix is nicely soft, then mash gently and set aside to cool.

FOR THE PEPPER CRUST

2 teaspoons black peppercorns

1 teaspoon white peppercorns

½ teaspoon green peppercorns

½ teaspoon cubeb pepper

½ teaspoon Sichuan pepper

¼ teaspoon finely grated long pepper

¼ teaspoon finely ground allspice

1 teaspoon sea salt

FOR THE TUNA

1 tablespoon olive oil

1lb 2oz (500g) yellow-fin tuna loin, at room temperature

7. To make the pepper crust, coarsely grind the black, white, and green peppercorns with the cubeb and Sichuan peppers, using a mortar and pestle. Add the long pepper, allspice, and sea salt and mix well.

8. Rub the olive oil over the tuna, then roll it evenly, using a little pressure, in the ground pepper mix so that it has a nice crust all over.

9. Put a ridged grill pan over high heat until hot, then sear the tuna on all sides for 30–45 seconds on each side. Don't overcook the beautiful tuna, or it will turn gray, become solid, and taste like cardboard.

10. To fry the chickpea chips, heat the sunflower oil in an electric deep fryer set to 340°F (170°C). (Or fill a large saucepan one-third full of oil and put it over medium heat. After 4–5 minutes, drop a piece of white bread into the oil; if it takes 3 seconds to turn golden brown, it's the right heat. If not, adjust the heat accordingly.). Fry the chickpea chips for 2 minutes or until crispy. Drain on paper towels.

11. To serve, slice the tuna into four steaks. Serve with the hot chickpea chips and the cool smoked eggplant. My Sizzled Tomatoes (see page 182) also go well with this recipe.

LEMONGRASS & TAMARIND MACKEREL SKEWERS WITH TOMATO CHILI RELISH

I was given this idea by a friend of mine, a wonderful chef called Vivek Singh. It works perfectly on the barbecue, under a broiler, or in the oven and is guaranteed to bring a real "wow factor" to fresh mackerel.

SERVES 4

4 whole mackerel, scaled,
    gutted, and fins removed
4 long lemongrass stalks

FOR THE PASTE
5 dried Kashmiri chiles
2 teaspoons fennel seeds
1 heaping teaspoon powdered
    turmeric
1 teaspoon black mustard seeds
1 onion, coarsely chopped
4 garlic cloves
1-inch (2.5-cm) piece fresh
    ginger (about 1½oz 40g)
1 green chile
10 curry leaves, fresh or dried
2 tablespoons thick, black
    Indian tamarind paste
¼ cup (2fl oz/50ml) sunflower oil
1 teaspoon sea salt
1 teaspoon sugar

FOR THE RELISH
1 (14½-oz/400-g) can diced
    tomatoes
½ green Thai chile, seeded
    and diced
½ teaspoon sea salt
1 teaspoon sugar

1. Put the Kashmiri chiles for the paste into warm water to soak for 20 minutes while you prepare the fish. Using a sharp knife, carefully score both sides of each fish to create three short, diagonal cuts on each side. With the back of a heavy chef's knife, splat or bruise the lemongrass stalks slightly and insert one into the mouth of each fish, leaving about 2 inches (5cm) or so sticking out for presentation effect.

2. Drain the Kashmiri chiles and pat dry. Grind the fennel seeds, using a mortar and pestle. Add the turmeric and mustard seeds and mix well. Put these and the other paste ingredients into a food processor and process to a thick, fragrant paste. (If you don't have a food processor, grate the onion, garlic, and ginger, and chop the chiles and curry leaves finely. Then add the ingredients to a small bowl and stir well to combine.) Remove the paste from the bowl and divide into three equal parts. Set aside.

3. Use two-thirds of the paste to coat the fish on both sides. Set aside for 20 minutes. Preheat the oven to 350°F (180°C). Put the coated fish onto a baking sheet, put in the oven, and bake for 6 minutes. Turn the fish over, then bake for another 6–8 minutes, until cooked through.

4. To make the relish, put the remaining third of the spicy paste into a saucepan over medium heat, stirring frequently. As the paste begins to sizzle, let it to cook for 1 minute or so, stirring frequently, then add the tomatoes, chile, salt, and sugar, then stir again. Let it reduce to a soft dropping consistency, then set aside.

5. Serve each fish with a large dollop of the tomato relish on the side. A green salad and a baked potato make simple accompaniments.

CRAMMED BEACH FISH

These fish are not just stuffed, they are crammed full of flavor, texture, and pure spice in a wonderful, easy-to-make dish. The key to success is to use only the freshest of fish. The bread crumb stuffing has a touch of garlic and vibrant spices, with a little citrus fruit to add balance and freshness. Ideally, use Japanese panko bread crumbs, but other crisp dried bread crumbs will do at a pinch.

SERVES 4

8 sardines or 4 mackerel, cleaned and filleted (see Tip)

FOR THE STUFFING
¼ cup (2fl oz/50ml) olive oil, plus extra for grilling
2¾ cups (2¾oz/75g) baby spinach
⅓ cup (1¾oz/50g) finely chopped shallots
1 cup (2¾oz/75g) panko or regular dried bread crumbs
1 garlic clove, crushed
¼ teaspoon grated nutmeg
½ teaspoon finely ground star anise
Zest and juice of ½ orange
Sea salt and finely ground black pepper

FOR THE SPICED AIOLI
2 large egg yolks
2 fat garlic cloves, crushed
Sea salt
1¼–2 cups (10–16fl oz/ 300–450ml) fruity olive oil
Juice of at least 1 lemon
1 teaspoon Garam Masala blend (see page 267)
Zest of ½ lemon

1. First, prepare the stuffing. Put a small saucepan over medium heat, add 1 tablespoon olive oil, and the spinach. Cook for 30 seconds, then remove the pan from the heat, let the spinach cool, and chop it finely.

2. Combine the spinach and the remaining stuffing ingredients in a bowl and mix gently. Check and adjust the seasoning, then stuff the sardines evenly, being careful not to overfill the fish. Set aside.

3. Preheat the barbecue grill or broiler to medium–hot. Rub a little oil over the fish and grill or broil for 1 minute on each side. You want to char the skin nicely, without burning.

4. If you're using a barbecue grill, move the fish to a tray and put the tray on the rack. Cover the tray with a large lid and let cook and smoke for no more than 3 minutes—the flesh should be just cooked. If you are using a broiler, continue cooking until just cooked through. Serve on a large wooden board or tray, with the salad, tabbouleh, and aioli.

1. In a bowl, lightly whisk the egg yolks with the crushed garlic and a little salt until thick.

2. Pour in the olive oil in a thin stream, whisking continuously. Add a little of the lemon juice and some more oil, and continue beating, adding alternately more lemon juice and oil until you have a thick mayonnaise.

3. Adjust the salt to taste. Add the Garam Masala and the lemon zest, mix well, and set aside.

[*Continued*]

FOR THE TABBOULEH

2¾ cups (1lb 2oz/500g) couscous
1 tablespoon olive oil, plus extra
    to drizzle
2 red onions, finely chopped
½ garlic clove, crushed
¾ cup (7oz/200g) drained and
    rinsed, canned chickpeas
1 tablespoon ras el hanout
    (see page 266)
Juice of ½ orange
1 large handful each of flat-leaf
    parsley, cilantro, and mint,
    all finely chopped
Sea salt and finely ground
    black pepper

1. Put the couscous into a heatproof bowl. Heat 1 tablespoon oil in a heavy skillet over medium–low heat and cook the red onions and garlic gently until soft.

2. Add the drained chickpeas and the ras el hanout. Continue sautéing gently for 1 minute, then pour in the quantity of boiling water specified on the couscous package to make a delicious spicy stock. Immediately pour a boiling stock over the couscous and quickly fork through to mix.

3. Cover with plastic wrap and let steam for 10 minutes, then fluff up with a fork and add a generous drizzle of olive oil and the orange juice. Check and adjust the seasoning, if necessary.

4. Finally, when you're ready to serve, add the herbs.

FOR THE VINAIGRETTE

1 garlic clove, halved
1 heaping tablespoon Dijon
    mustard
⅔ cup (5fl oz/150ml) grapeseed
    or sunflower oil
3 tablespoons fruity olive oil
1 teaspoon good-quality white
    wine vinegar
½ teaspoon sugar
Fine sea salt and finely ground
    black pepper

1. To make the vinaigrette, rub the inside of a large screw-top jar firmly with the cut edge of the garlic clove.

2. Add all the vinaigrette ingredients, then pour in ¼ cup (2fl oz/50ml) boiling water (the water goes in last to prevent the jar from cracking).

3. Screw the lid on tightly and shake vigorously until it emulsifies— a minute or so should do it.

4. Put the lettuce leaves in a serving bowl. Spoon the dressing generously over the leaves, then sprinkle the herbs over the top.

FOR THE GARDEN SALAD

1 head butterhead lettuce
1 large bunch chives, tarragon,
    and chervil leaves

Tip

To fillet the fish, chop off the fish's head neatly and slightly on the diagonal, then put the fish on a board, belly side down, and press gently along the spine. Turn the fish so the belly side is facing up and gently ease the spine, with the ribs attached, away from the flesh. Snip it off with scissors just before the tail, leaving the tail in place.

BENGAL SMOKED FISH BRUNCH

Eastern and Western influences come together to make a perfect brunch or breakfast treat, inspired by kedgeree. Its heart is a generous slice of lightly poached smoked haddock, or Finnan Haddie, in a wilted salad of scallions and braised shiitake, all topped with the luxury of a slow-fried free-range duck egg. If you can't find smoked haddock, you can use smoked salmon.

SERVES 4

2 bunches scallions, trimmed
    and halved to about 3 inches
    (7.5cm) long
Sea salt
6 tablespoons (3oz/85g) unsalted
    butter
Light olive oil, for frying and
    greasing
7oz (200g) fresh shiitake
    mushrooms, sliced ¼ inch
    (5mm) thick
2 teaspoons Panch Phoron blend
    (see page 266)
1 garlic clove
2 lemon thyme sprigs, leaves only
4 (4½oz/125g) center-cut,
    naturally smoked haddock
    fillets, at room temperature
4 duck eggs

1. Put a saucepan over medium heat and add the scallions, 2 tablespoons water, a pinch of salt, and 1½ tablespoons (¾oz/20g) of the butter. Cook until they're just soft, then set aside.

2. Heat 1 tablespoon oil in a large, nonstick skillet, add the mushrooms, Panch Phoron, garlic, and thyme, and heat gently for 25 minutes or until the mushrooms soften slightly and (most importantly) give off some of their succulent juices. Add the wilted scallions. Stir well, but gently, then set aside to let the flavors to mingle. Keep warm.

3. Preheat the oven to 400°F (200°C). Lay a sheet of wax paper on a baking pan and lightly grease it. Put the haddock fillets on top, put a pat of butter on top of each, then put the pan in the oven for 7–10 minutes, until the fish is just cooked but still slightly translucent.

4. Put a large pat of butter (about 1 tablespoon) in each of two small nonstick skillets (or one large one), add a splash of light olive oil, and put over low heat. Carefully break two eggs into each pan, trying to keep the yolks intact. Season with a little sea salt, then gently cook the eggs until the whites are just set and the yolks are golden, rich, and runny—6–8 minutes.

5. Using a slotted spoon, divide the mushrooms and scallions among four warmed plates, and drizzle the succulent cooking juices evenly around them. Put a haddock fillet on top of each mound, followed by a fried duck egg. I like to spoon a little of the haddock cooking juices over the top. Enjoy with some crusty, buttered white sourdough toast.

Shellfish & Squid

SEA-FRESH SWEET flesh—with attitude! The crab's claws, the mussel's tightly shut shell, the lightning speed of a squid. I think of clean heat, delicate yet distinct perfume, astringent warmth, all the peppery flavors: black, cayenne, white, and Sichuan to get some real intrigue going. Freshness is important here—fresh pepper, freshly ground or cracked—as the high note perfume is what it's all about and is what works so well with citrus and chile.

Shellfish sometimes need coaxing out of their shells with earthy, floral, and peppery tones. My Crab Cakes use turmeric for earthiness, saffron and mace provide floral perfume, while white peppercorns, Sichuan, and cayenne pepper and ajwain bring peppery notes aplenty. The fresh chiles, shallots, and herbs add freshness and the pickle accompaniment contributes a sweet tang.

I adore squid and mussels, the sweet meat, soft flesh with just a touch of resistance as you bite into it, crying out for flavor. Mouclade is a traditional mussel dish from the Vendée region of France. In this region, mussels are harvested and cream produced—and in days gone by, spices were traded. My version uses a fragrant south Indian blend of spices. I spent a fantastic summer there on the Atlantic Coast, and I discovered that the perfect accompaniment to the mild curry spice, cream, and sweet mussel flesh is a glass of chilled Pineau des Charentes, another local speciality.

Squid, at first sight, appear docile beasts, but when they strike, they do so with speed and unnerving accuracy. The spicing for these cephalopods needs to reflect this side to their character, as well as bring delicate perfume. My Italian-inspired Old-School Squid Salad combines black pepper with nutmeg and Kashmiri chiles, spiked with lemony coriander, fresh mint, and saffron aioli.

Previous page: Kashmiri chiles offer subtle fruity flavor with a hint of smoky edge, gentle but definitive heat and ruddy red beauty.

CRAB CAKES WITH PICKLE

SERVES 6

FOR THE PICKLE
2 small onions, thinly sliced
¾ cup (5½oz/150g) sugar
1 teaspoon sea salt
1 teaspoon powdered turmeric
½ cup (3½fl oz/100ml) cider
    vinegar
1 large cucumber, thinly sliced

FOR THE CRAB CAKES
1 small pinch saffron threads
1 tablespoon lemon juice
1½ tablespoons (¾oz/20g)
    unsalted butter
1 small leek, finely diced
1 teaspoon white peppercorns
½ teaspoon Sichuan pepper
2 teaspoons coriander seeds
2lb (900g) fresh white crabmeat
1 tablespoon finely chopped
    tarragon leaves
1 small handful fresh chives,
    thinly sliced
Zest of ½ lemon
Scant ¼ teaspoon finely ground
    mace
½ teaspoon cayenne pepper
½ teaspoon carom seeds
1 green finger chile, seeded and
    finely diced
2 shallots, finely diced
2 teaspoons sea salt

FOR BINDING & FRYING
3 large eggs, lightly beaten
3 cups (5½oz/150g) fresh bread
    crumbs
1 pat unsalted butter
Sunflower oil, for frying

These cakes are light, meaty, and fresh-tasting, with no potato to make them heavy. The cucumber and turmeric pickle is simple, but it adds another flavor dimension.

1. In a large bowl, mix all the pickle ingredients together, except the cucumber, until the salt and sugar have dissolved, then fold in the cucumber slices. Cover the bowl with plastic wrap and set aside in the refrigerator for at least 4 hours.

2. For the crab cakes, put the saffron into a small bowl and add the lemon juice. Heat the butter in a skillet over medium heat and gently sauté the leek until just soft, but not browned, then remove from the heat. Add the saffron and lemon juice. Set aside to cool.

3. Line a baking sheet with wax paper. Finely grind the peppercorns, Sichuan pepper, and coriander seeds, using a mortar and pestle. Put all the crab cake ingredients, including the leek and saffron mixture, into a mixing bowl and gently fold to combine. Add the eggs for binding and fold to combine. Add the bread crumbs, a little at a time, until the mixture is just stiff enough to hold its shape. Form the mixture into golf-ball-size cakes, put each one on the lined pan, and gently press to flatten slightly. Preheat the oven to 325°F (170°C).

4. Put the butter and a little oil in a large skillet over medium heat. Lightly sauté the crab cakes on both sides, in batches. These have a delicate texture, so you'll need a gentle touch as you cook them. Set aside.

5. Pop the crab cakes onto a baking sheet and warm through in the oven for 5 minutes. Take the pickle from the refrigerator and give it a gentle stir. Serve the crab cakes immediately, with a forkful of the pickle.

BENGALI GRILLED SEAFOOD WITH CRISP OKRA

This makes a wonderful appetizer for an eligant dinner party. It's a showstopper, with its beautiful colors, textures, and spices. I first made it when I was (apparently) showing people "how to be fabulous" at home by making a dinner for a well-known Irish crystal company. Fab demos aside, this is a seafood dish that rocks!

SERVES 4 AS APPETIZER

FOR THE CHILI OIL DRESSING
2 tablespoons Kashmiri chili flakes
½ cup (3½fl oz/100ml) grapeseed oil
½ garlic bulb

1. Put the Kasmiri flakes into a bowl and pour over boiling water to cover. Wait for 5 minutes, then squeeze and pat dry with paper towels.

2. Put the softened Kasmiri flakes, oil, and garlic into a small saucepan and warm through over low heat for 5 minutes.

3. Let rest for at least 24 hours in the refrigerator to let the flavors develop, then strain through a fine strainer or cheesecloth.

---

8 raw jumbo shrimp, shell on, deveined
5½oz (150g) baby squid, cleaned and sliced, tentacles left whole
1 green Thai chile, seeded and coarsely chopped
2 teaspoons Panch Phoron blend (see page 266)
Generous splash grapeseed oil
10½oz (300g) fresh mussels, scrubbed and debearded
Sea salt and freshly ground black pepper

1. Put the shrimp and squid into a bowl with the chile and Panch Phoron blend, mix together, then toss together with the grapeseed oil. Let rest for 10 minutes to marinate.

2. Heat a ridged grill pan until hot, shake some of the oil off the shrimp, then put them onto the hot pan and sear for no more than 2–3 minutes on each side. Remove from the heat and set aside.

3. Discard any mussels that do not close when the shell is tapped. Put the mussels on the grill pan. They're ready when the shells open. Remove from the heat and set aside. Discard any mussels that remain closed.

4. Wipe the grill pan with paper towels, then grill the squid over high heat for no more than 30 seconds on each side. Remove from the heat and set aside.

5. Season the shellfish and squid with a little salt and black pepper to taste.

[*Continued*]

FOR THE CRISP OKRA

16 okra pods (about 7oz/200g)
3¼ cups (10½oz/300g) chickpea (besan) flour
2 teaspoons Panch Phoron blend (see page 266)
1 teaspoon amchoor (optional)
1 pinch sea salt
1 pinch freshly ground black pepper
1 cup (7fl oz/200ml) whole milk
About 5 cups (2 pints/1.2 liters) sunflower oil, for deep-frying

1. Trim the stems from the okra, then cut lengthwise into even slices.

2. Put the flour, Panch Phoron blend, amchoor powder, salt, and black pepper into a bowl and mix together. Pour the milk into another bowl, and dip the okra into it, then dredge through the flour mixture until lightly dusted, not gloopy.

3. Pour the sunflower oil into an electric deep fryer set to 340°F (170°C). (Alternatively, pour the oil into a large saucepan until one-third full and heat it over medium heat. After 4–5 minutes, drop a cube of white bread into the hot oil. If it takes 3 seconds to turn golden brown, it's the right heat. If not, adjust the heat accordingly.) Fry the okra, in small batches, for about 3 minutes, until crisp and golden, then drain on paper towels and set aside. This can be done up to 1 hour in advance.

FOR THE CORIANDER & POMEGRANATE DRESSING

1 pomegranate
3 tablespoons canola oil
2 tablespoons orange juice
Zest of ½ orange
1 dash Worcestershire sauce
1 large pinch Garam Masala blend (see page 267)
A splash mirin (sweet Japanese rice wine)
1 pinch sea salt
1 teaspoon coriander seeds, lightly crushed
2 mild fresh red chiles, halved, seeded and thinly sliced on the diagonal
2 scallions, thinly sliced on the diagonal

TO SERVE
Cilantro leaves
2 lemons, halved

1. For the pomegranate and coriander dressing, first cut the pomegranate in half and, holding it over a bowl to collect the seeds and juice, bang it until the seeds fall out. Pick out and discard any of the bitter white pith. Squeeze the halves to extract more of the juice. Mix all the ingredients together just before serving.

2. To serve, put two shrimp on each warmed plate, then add the squid and mussels around them. Drizzle the dressing generously over the squid and shellfish. Delicately (and decoratively) drop 1 teaspoon of the chili oil in "drops" onto each plate. Serve a small handful of the fried okra on top of the seafood or on the side. Sprinkle cilantro leaves over the seafood and serve with a lemon half on each plate.

Cajun Popcorn Shrimp with Hot Pepper Mayo

I used to snack on this delicacy when I worked the restaurant floor as a busboy for 51-51, a Cajun-Creole restaurant in London, back in the eighties. Here's my version.

SERVES 4 AS A SNACK

FOR THE HOT PEPPER MAYO
⅔ cup (5½oz/150g) best-quality
  mayonnaise
Juice of ½ lemon
½ teaspoon black peppercorns,
  finely ground
¼ teaspoon Sichuan pepper,
  finely ground
1 teaspoon cayenne pepper
9 gratings long pepper

FOR THE POPCORN SHRIMP
Sunflower oil, for deep-frying
ice cubes
1 large egg
2 cups (9oz/250g) all-purpose
  flour
1 teaspoon cayenne pepper
1 teaspoon sea salt
3¼lb (1.5kg) raw shrimp,
  shelled, deveined, and
  chopped into 1-inch
  (2.5-cm) chunks (aka
  the "popcorn shrimp")
Cornstarch, for dusting

1. Mix all the mayo ingredients together in a bowl, pour into a small serving dish, cover with plastic wrap, then set aside in the refrigerator.

2. Pour the sunflower oil for the popcorn shrimp into an electric deep fryer set to 340°F (170°C). (Alternatively, pour the oil into a large saucepan until one-third full and heat it over medium heat. After 4–5 minutes, drop a cube of white bread into the hot oil. If it takes 3 seconds to turn golden brown, it's the right heat for the shrimp. If not, adjust the heat accordingly.)

3. Take two mixing bowls, one slightly larger than the other. Put some ice cubes into the larger bowl and cover with cold water. Put the smaller bowl on top of the ice, nestling it into the iced water. In another small bowl, mix the egg with 1 cup (7fl oz/200ml) ice-cold water.

4. Add the flour, cayenne, and salt to the smaller bowl over the ice, mix well, then pour in the egg–water mix and only just combine the mixture with a fork. Don't worry at all about the few lumps; in fact, they'll help to form the crisp, cooked batter.

5. Put the shrimp pieces onto a plate, dust them in cornstarch, then dip them into the batter and coat well, letting any excess batter drain off. Gently lower them into the hot oil. Don't crowd the pan; cook in three or four batches, if necessary. Deep-fry for a few minutes, until crisp and golden, then drain on paper towels. Serve immediately in a large serving dish with the hot pepper mayo.

MOUCLADE

This fragrant French dish of steamed mussels is traditionally made with spices, cream, shallots, and a generous helping of parsley on top. It's perfect for a late-summer dinner, with crusty bread to mop up the juice. Moucle *is the name for "mussel" in the Vendée region of France. The spices, a reminder of the centuries-old spice trade between the port of La Rochelle and Asia, give this dish its unique flavor, fragrance, and inspiration. First make the sauce, then add the mussels to cook them.*

SERVES 4

FOR THE SAUCE

2 tablespoons unsalted butter
2 banana shallots, finely diced
1 garlic clove, crushed
2 heaping teaspoons Mouclade spice blend (see page 267)
1 tablespoon all-purpose flour
½ cup (4fl oz/125ml) light chicken stock or broth
½ cup (4fl oz/125ml) dry white wine or dry hard cider
⅔ cup (5fl oz/150ml) crème fraîche or Greek yogurt
Sea salt
½ teaspoon thyme leaves

FOR THE MUSSELS

3¼lb (1.5kg) mussels or clams, scrubbed and debearded
1–2 squeezes fresh lemon juice
1–2 grindings black pepper
1 small handful flat-leaf parsley, chopped

TO SERVE

sourdough bread
1 garlic clove, halved
butter for spreading
mixed bitter salad greens (dandelion, sorrel, parsley— whatever is on hand)

1. To make the sauce, put half the butter into a large, heavy saucepan. Put it over medium heat and when the butter has melted add the shallots and garlic and cook for 3 minutes or until just soft.

2. Add the Mouclade spice blend and the flour and cook for 2 minutes, stirring continuously.

3. Add the stock and wine, stir well, then turn up the heat and let simmer until the liquid has reduced by half. Add the crème fraîche or yogurt, salt to taste, the remaining butter, and the thyme leaves and stir.

4. Discard any mussels that do not close when the shell is tapped. Add the mussels to the pan and cook, uncovered, for 3–4 minutes. Their lovely juices will mix with the sauce, making it the same kind of consistency as vanilla custard. Discard any mussels that remain closed.

5. Add the lemon juice and black pepper to taste and, finally, a handful of parsley.

6. Slice the sourdough bread into thick wedges. Rub the cut edge of the garlic clove over the bread, then toast the bread under a hot broiler and spread generously with butter.

7. Fill a large warmed plate with the delicious saucy mussels, and serve immediately with the sourdough toast—and plenty of napkins or paper towels. Add a bitter, aromatic leaf salad of dandelion, mustard leaves, lovage, sorrel, parsley, cilantro, and a splash of vibrant color from nasturtium flowers.

OLD-SCHOOL SQUID SALAD

FOR THE GREMOLATA

½ cup (3½ fl oz/100ml) olive oil

3 fat garlic cloves, crushed

1 small handful flat-leaf parsley, finely chopped

Zest of 1 lemon

FOR THE SAFFRON AIOLI

1 russet potato, unpeeled

5 saffron threads

1 garlic clove

A little sea salt

1 large egg yolk

A splash fruity olive oil

Juice of 1 lemon

FOR THE SQUID

2 cups (18fl oz/500ml) sunflower oil, for deep-frying

¾ cup plus 1 tablespoon (3½ oz/100g) potato flour

2 teaspoons black peppercorns, finely ground

1 teaspoon coriander seeds, ground

2 teaspoons peperoncini or Kashmiri chili flakes

1–2 gratings nutmeg

½ teaspoon sea salt

14oz–1lb 2oz (400–500g) fresh squid, cleaned and thinly sliced, tentacles left whole

1 cup (7fl oz/200ml) whole milk

1 head radicchio

1 small handful mint leaves, chopped

1 red chile, seeded and diced

One of my first meals in an Italian restaurant in London was a salad like this—a taste of the sea from Liguria. Over time, I found that the best way to get crisp squid is to use potato flour for dredging. And as with every type of fish, try to buy the freshest possible squid from your fish dealer; it really does make a difference.

1. Combine all the gremolata ingredients in a bowl. Set aside for 30 minutes.

2. Meanwhile, for the aioli, put the potato into a saucepan and cover generously with water. Boil for 20 minutes or until tender. Drain and let rest until cool enough to handle, then peel and let rest until cool. Put the saffron into a small bowl and add 1 teaspoon warm water.

3. Chop the garlic with a pinch of salt until it forms a paste. In a small bowl, combine the potato, egg yolk, garlic paste, and saffron, gently working them into a smooth paste, then drizzle in the olive oil until the aioli has a lovely velvety texture. Add the lemon juice and sea salt to taste. Set aside.

4. To cook the squid, pour the sunflower oil into an electric deep fryer set to 350°F (180°C). (Alternatively, pour the oil into a large saucepan until one-third full and heat it over medium heat. After 4–5 minutes, drop a cube of white bread into the hot oil. If it takes 3 seconds to turn golden brown, it's the right heat. If not, adjust the heat accordingly.)

5. Mix the potato flour, spices, and salt in a bowl.

6. Dip the squid in the milk, gently shake off the excess, then coat in the seasoned flour mix. Deep-fry 6–7 squid pieces at a time for 3–4 minutes, until crisp and golden. Lift out, using a slotted spoon, and drain well on paper towels. Repeat until all the squid has been fried.

7. Arrange the radicchio on a large plate and dress the leaves with a generous drizzle of the gremolata. Sprinkle the crisp fried squid on top, followed by the mint and chile. Serve immediately.

Seafood Gumbo with "Dirty" Dumplings

The first restaurant I ever worked in as a busboy was when I moved to London at 18. It was called 51-51, a Cajun-Creole restaurant with a brigade made up mostly of chefs from Louisiana. There was one big, stocky guy called Yves, who was great. New Orleans was his home town and I couldn't always understand his thick, deep Southern accent, but he would occasionally show me how to cook a few dishes. "The secret is a dark roux, buddy—y'get it, see?" A real good guy, an excellent cook, and he made some really great food. Hopefully, this recipe would gain his approval and give you a taste of what gumbo is all about.

SERVES 4

(1lb 2oz (500g) large shrimp, deveined and shelled (retain the shells and heads)
Sunflower oil, for frying
1lb 2oz (500g) andouille or smoked sausage, cut into 2.5cm (1in) thick discs
10½oz (300g) okra, sliced into disks
5 tablespoons (2½oz/70g) unsalted butter
½ cup (2¼oz (65g) all-purpose flour
1 large onion, cut into ½-inch (1-cm) dice
3 garlic cloves, coarsely chopped
3 celery sticks, diced
4 scallions, finely sliced
1 green bell pepper, seeded and cut into 8 chunks
Sea salt
2 thyme sprigs, leaves only

1. Put the shrimp shells and heads into a large saucepan, pour in 6½ cups (2¾ pints/1.5 liters) water, then bring to a boil. Reduce the heat and simmer for 45 minutes, then remove from the heat and set aside. Strain the stock.

2. Add a splash of oil to a heavy sauté pan or skillet and cook the sausage, in batches, until light brown, then drain on paper towels.

3. Add a little more oil to the pan, then add the okra and cook gently over low heat, stirring frequently, for 20 minutes or until they're browned and somewhat dry-looking.

4. Meanwhile, to make the roux, melt the butter in a large saucepan over a medium–low heat, add the flour, and cook gently, whisking frequently, for 20–30 minutes, until it turns a dark caramel/milk chocolate color.

5. Add the onion to the roux and cook for 1 minute. Next, add the garlic, celery, scallions, green bell pepper, and salt to taste, stir well, and cook for 1 minute.

6. Add the shrimp stock to the saucepan, pouring it over the roux and vegetables. Stir well, then add the sausage and thyme leaves. Bring to a boil, then turn down the heat to a simmer. Add the cooked okra, and continue to cook, uncovered, at a gentle simmer for 1 hour.

9oz (250g) shelled fresh or
defrosted frozen crab claws,
or 1lb 2oz (500g) crab claws
in their shells
2 teaspoons black peppercorns,
finely ground
1 teaspoon cumin seeds, finely
ground
5 cloves, finely ground
½ teaspoon powdered turmeric
1 teaspoon hot paprika
1 teaspoon oregano leaves, or
½ teaspoon dried oregano
1 handful curly parsley, finely
chopped

FOR THE DIRTY DUMPLINGS

1 cup (9fl oz/250ml) whole milk
7oz (200g) stale baguette or
crusty bread, cut into ¾in
(2cm) dice
1 small handful curly parsley,
finely chopped
2 teaspoons black peppercorns,
coarsely ground
1 teaspoon cumin seeds, coarsely
ground
5 gratings nutmeg
½ level teaspoon cayenne pepper
1 thyme sprig, leaves only
1 pinch sea salt
1 large egg, lightly beaten
1 tablespoon all-purpose flour,
plus extra if needed
Unsalted butter, for frying

7. Add a little more stock, if necessary, to maintain a heavy cream consistency, then add the shrimp and crab claws and cook for another 5–10 minutes. Remove from the heat. Add the spices, oregano, and half the parsley, stir well but gently, then set aside and keep warm.

8. Meanwhile, boil the milk for the dumplings and set aside. Put the bread in a bowl. Add the milk and parsley and mix well to combine. Set aside for 15 minutes or until the milk is absorbed.

9. Add the spices, thyme, salt, and egg. Then add the flour, a little shake at a time, and mix well to achieve a sticky, not wet, texture. (Try not to use too much flour, or you'll run the risk of the dumplings becoming clumpy.)

10. Dampen your hands, then roll out 12–16 small dumplings between your palms.

11. Put the butter into a skillet over medium heat, then cook the dumplings until they're golden brown all over. Drain on paper towels.

12. Ladle the gumbo into warmed serving bowls, add the remaining chopped parsley, and put three or four dumplings into each bowl, then serve immediately.

EGGS & CHEESE

EGGS AND CHEESE, STAPLES OF EVERY HOUSEHOLD REFRIGERATOR, need light, subtle spicing. Their intrinsic flavors can so easily be diminished if the spices you choose are used with a heavy hand; with cheese and eggs, less is more.

Cheese needs spice notes to cut through fat and dense textures—such as nutmeg, peppers, mace—and to calm saltiness, such as peppers and chiles. But can spices that work perfectly with blue cheese work similarly well with hard cheese, soft cheese, pasteurized or raw, "sweet" cheeses, or those with more lactic bite? The answer is both yes and no. We're essentially pairing spice characteristics with the types of milk protein (casein), salt, and lactic tastes.

First I think about the type of milk used for the cheese: is it goat, sheep, or cow? Sheep milk cheese tends to be sweeter, so cardamom and cloves work well. Goat cheeses have a more pronounced and lactic flavor, so try cumin, nutmeg, and peppers. Cow milk cheeses vary wildly, but when cooking with hard, salty cheeses, turn to chile, clove, cubeb, and tamarind. These form your flavor foundation. To address the fat content of the cheese, use mace and nutmeg to accentuate or mask.

In my Cheese and Onion Flaky Puff Pie, I use a combination of green cardamom, black pepper, clove, and nutmeg to balance the mix of cows milk cheeses. Ardrahan and Comté are semihard, while Lancashire and Gruyère are hard, but all these cheeses have sweetness as well as lactic bite. Cardamom accentuates the sweetness, clove the natural fruitiness, nutmeg and pepper add definition.

When it comes to eggs, I try to use only organic or corn-fed and certainly free-range. Before cooking, try to start with eggs at room temperature. A cooked egg should have a glorious dark yellow yolk and sweet white surround. Egg's rich sweetness can be earthed with a little cumin, warmed with ginger, balanced with turmeric or clove, or lifted with green cardamom or nutmeg. I also love eggs with Garam Masala, cayenne, or chiles. So much depends on the other ingredients of the dish. My Lunch Box Frittata with spinach is simply spiced with nutmeg, which adds sweetness to astringent vegetables, and at the same time cuts the richness and cleans up the finish of creamy, buttery eggs.

Previous page: A subtle use of cloves can accent fruity tastes, add perfume and depth, yet also "clean up" a rich finish. But beware: Too much and the flavor's wrecked, bordering on the medicinal.

EGG & BACON PIE

This pie is perfect for late breakfasts, picnics, and food-on-the-run-type meals. My wife, Olive, once won a competition for hers; here's my version. When making the pastry, remember to work fast but with a light touch and keep everything as cool as possible; if the butter melts, the pastry will be tough. This makes a short, delicate dough: aim for dough that is slightly drier and more difficult to control than you might want. If it tears as you line the dish, simply patch it up. If the raw pastry is too wet, it will shrink from the sides of the dish as it cooks.

SERVES 6–8

FOR THE PASTRY DOUGH
¼ teaspoon cubeb peppercorns
3 cloves
Seeds of 1 green cardamom pod
½ teaspoon black peppercorns
1⅓ cups (6oz/175g) all-purpose
    flour
1 pinch fine sea salt
1 stick (4oz/115g) unsalted
    butter, cubed and chilled
1 large egg

FOR THE FILLING
5 extra-large eggs
1 tablespoon light olive oil
8 slices dry-cured bacon, zest
    removed, cut into strips about
    ¾ inch (2cm) wide
½ cup (4fl oz/125ml) whole
    milk, plus extra for brushing
½ cup (4fl oz/125ml)
    heavy cream
1 pinch sea salt
5 gratings nutmeg
1 small handful curly parsley,
    finely chopped

1. To make the pastry, finely grind the spices, using a mortar and pestle. Sift the flour, spices, and salt into a large mixing bowl (discarding any large pieces of spice) and rub in the butter using your fingertips until you have a bread crumblike texture. Lift the mix high above the bowl as you work to keep everything as aerated as possible.

2. Mix the egg with 1 tablespoon of cold water. Using a cold metal fork, add a little of the egg–water mixture to bring the dough together until it just begins to holds its shape. Cover in plastic wrap and put in the refrigerator for 25 minutes. Cut the dough in two. Roll out one half thinly and use it to line a 9½-inch (24cm) pie dish about 1¼ inches (3cm) deep. Roll out the other half so that it's ready to form a lid. Preheat the oven to 400°F (200°C). Put a baking sheet on a high shelf of the oven to preheat.

3. To make the filling, boil three of the eggs for 6 minutes, then immerse them in a bowl of cold water until cool. Peel and chop them into quarters. Heat the oil in a skillet and cook the bacon strips. Drain on paper towels and set aside.

4. Beat together the milk, cream, salt, and the remaining two eggs. Put the bacon and chopped boiled eggs into the lined pie dish, then pour in the milk mixture. Grate in the nutmeg and sprinkle with the parsley.

5. Dampen the edges of the pie and put the remaining dough on top. Trim to fit and press the lid to the bottom to seal. Make a hole in the center to let steam escape, then brush the top with a little milk. Put the pie on the heated baking sheet and bake for 10 minutes.

6. Turn down the heat to 350°F (180°C) and bake for 25–30 minutes, until the pastry is golden. Serve immediately, or let to cool completely and serve with Sizzled Tomatoes (see page 182).

Egg Curry

This is a dish my mother used to make for us as a treat—it evokes such good memories. I've spiced things up a little to include influences from southern India, adding coconut, fennel, and tamarind. Try to make sure the egg yolks are still a little runny.

SERVES 6

1 teaspoon cumin seeds
3 cloves
½ teaspoon finely ground mace
1 teaspoon black peppercorns
Seeds from 2 green cardamom
    pods
1 teaspoon fennel seeds
1 teaspoon powdered turmeric
1 teaspoon red pepper flakes
½ teaspoon finely ground cassia
1 handful slivered almonds
6 eggs
4½ tablespoons (2¼oz/60g)
    unsalted butter, ghee, or
    sunflower oil
2 onions, diced
3 fat garlic cloves, crushed
3 tablespoons grated fresh ginger
1 teaspoon sea salt
1 (14½-oz/400-g) can diced
    tomatoes
1¾ cups (14fl oz/400ml)
    coconut milk
1 handful cilantro, leaves only

FOR THE RAITA
1 cup (7fl oz/200ml) plain yogurt
½ cup (3½fl oz/100ml) crème
    fraîche or sour cream
2 teaspoons thick, black Indian
    tamarind paste
⅓ cup (1oz/30g) peeled and
    finely grated fresh ginger
Zest of 1 lime
1 small pinch finely
    ground cloves

1. Mix all the raita ingredients together in a small bowl and put it in the refrigerator.

2. Finely grind the first six spices, using a mortar and pestle, then add the turmeric, red pepper flakes, and cassia, and mix well. Dry-fry the almonds lightly in a skillet over medium heat; set aside.

3. Put the eggs into a saucepan of cold water, bring to a boil, and simmer gently for 4 minutes. Drain and refresh under cold running water for 3 minutes or so. Crack the eggshells and peel the eggs. Set the eggs aside on paper towels to dry.

4. Put a large, heavy saucepan, flameproof casserole, or Dutch oven over medium heat, add the butter, and heat for a moment. Add the onions, stir, and cook for a couple of minutes, then add the garlic and ginger, stir, and cook until the onions are soft.

5. Add the spice mix and salt, stir, then add the tomatoes. Stir again, turn down the heat slightly, and simmer gently for 1 minute or so.

6. Add the coconut milk, stir, turn up the heat, and bring to a boil, then let the mixture simmer gently for 1 minute before turning the heat back down to low and simmering, uncovered, until the sauce has the consistency of heavy cream and can coat the back of your stirring spoon with a glossy covering. This will take 10–15 minutes.

7. Turn off the heat. Cut the eggs in half lengthwise, put them onto warmed dinner plates, spoon over plenty of the beautiful sauce, then sprinkle with the fresh cilantro and toasted almonds.

8. Serve immediately with Pistachio & Rose Pilaf (see page 156) and a dollop of the raita on the side.

FULL IRISH BREAKFAST

Breakfast is renowned among chefs as one of the hardest sessions—particularly cooked breakfasts. With all the ingredients here, trying to get everything ready on a plate so it's all warm and freshly cooked is an art. I used to do the odd breakfast shift at Ballymaloe, and this recipe is one of the easier ones to get right. Good luck!

SERVES 4

4 teaspoons white peppercorns, finely ground
10 gratings nutmeg
Light olive oil, for frying
3 cups 7oz (200g) sliced closed-cap mushrooms (¾-inch/2-cm-thick slices)
Sea salt
1 lemon, halved
4 ripe tomatoes, halved horizontally
1 thyme sprig, leaves only
A little sugar (optional)
4 disks blood sausages, sliced 1½ inches (4cm) thick with a serrated knife
4 disks white sausages, such as boudin blanc, sliced 1½ inches (4cm) thick with a serrated knife
8 slices dry-cured bacon

1. Preheat the oven to 225°F (100°C). Preheat the broiler to medium. Mix the peppercorns with the nutmeg.

2. Put 1 tablespoon oil in a large, heavy sauté pan over high heat. Add just enough of the mushrooms to cover the bottom of the pan. Toss them around gently in the oil. Add a pinch of salt, a pinch of the spice mix, and a generous squeeze of lemon juice. As soon as the mushrooms become glossy and opaque, turn them out onto a large plate. Repeat until all the mushrooms are cooked. Set aside.

3. Put the tomatoes, cut side up, on a broiler pan, sprinkle with the thyme leaves, a pinch of salt, and a sprinkle of sugar, if you desire, and put under the broiler for 5–7 minutes, until they char slightly. Remove from the heat and set aside.

4. Wipe the sauté pan clean with paper towels and add 1 tablespoon oil. Cook the slices of blood sausages on both sides for 2–3 minutes, until browned and crisp. Transfer to a baking sheet, cover with aluminum foil, and put in the oven to keep warm. Fry the white sausages in the same way.

5. Wipe the pan again, then cook the bacon in a little oil on both sides to lightly crisp. Transfer it to the baking sheet with the sausages (but do not cover with the foil) and put the baking sheet back in the oven.

4 extra-large eggs
4 slices sourdough bread,
    1¼ inches (3cm) thick
½ garlic clove
Extra virgin olive oil, for
    drizzling
A pot of Chile Preserves
    (see page 262)

6. Add ⅓ cup (2½fl oz/75ml) oil to a second large, heavy skillet. Crack the eggs carefully into the oil and put over high heat. As soon as you hear the first spit and the eggs just start to undulate, turn off the heat, put on a lid, and let rest. After 4 minutes or so, check to see that the white has set; the yolk should still be golden yellow. If not, give the pan another short blast of heat. Using a spatula, cut the white around each yolk to separate the four fried eggs.

7. Meanwhile, toast the bread and rub the cut side of the garlic over one side of each slice. Turn up the broiler to high. Drizzle a little extra virgin olive oil onto the toasted bread. Arrange the toast, the sausages, bacon, a tomato half, and a spoonful of mushrooms on each of four plates. Put a plate (or two if they'll fit), under the broiler for 30–45 seconds, remove, and put an egg on the toast. Sprinkle it with a pinch of the spice mix, add a dollop of Chile Preserves by the bacon slices, and serve immediately.

Lunch Box Frittata

This fabulous omelet is packed full of flavors. It's superb hot or cold, and great as a snack, picnic item, or light dinner. Serve it with Sizzled Tomatoes (see page 182): the tomato dressing adds a wonderful tang that complements the rich combination of eggs and soft cheese.

SERVES 2

⅓ cup (2½ fl oz/75ml) olive oil
3 cups (3oz/85g) baby spinach
9oz (250g) large new potatoes, peeled and sliced into thin disks
2 large onions, thinly sliced
1 large pinch sea salt
6 eggs
½ nutmeg, freshly grated
4½oz (125g) Cashel Blue or other blue cheese
3 scallions, thinly sliced on the diagonal

1. Heat 1 tablespoon of the oil in a small skillet and quickly cook the spinach. Cool and press in a dish towel to remove the excess water. Set aside.

2. Heat the remaining oil in a large, heavy skillet over medium heat. Add the potatoes and cook for 3 minutes.

3. Add the onions, sprinkle with the salt, cover, and cook for 15 minutes or until soft, stirring from time to time.

4. Crack the eggs into a bowl. Sprinkle in the nutmeg and beat well.

5. Add the onion and potato mix to the beaten eggs and mix well. Crumble in the cheese, add the spinach and scallions, and stir gently to combine.

6. Pour the mixture back into the pan and cook over gentle heat until it begins to set. Shake the pan from time to time so that the omelet does not stick to the bottom.

7. Remove from the heat and turn the omelet over by putting a plate on top of the pan, then carefully turn the pan upside down so that the omelet lands on the plate. Slide it back into the pan and cook it for only another few minutes, until it looks firm but is still slightly moist inside.

8. Remove from the heat, rest for a few minutes, then slide it onto a large, clean serving plate.

EGGS AKOORI

This recipe was first shown to me by a Parsi man we were staying with on a visit to Goa. It's perfect on warm, buttery toast in the morning after a long night, and is a kind of Indian version of scrambled eggs, firmer set, with a kick of chile. It's totally up to you how softly set or firm you prefer your eggs, but whichever way you choose, this is simple and beautiful.

SERVES 4

8 large eggs

4½ tablespoons (2¼oz/60g) unsalted butter, cubed and chilled

2 onions: 1 chopped, 1 thinly sliced

3 tablespoons finely grated fresh ginger

½ teaspoon cumin seeds, finely ground

1 teaspoon powdered turmeric

2 red Thai chiles, seeded and chopped

2 ripe tomatoes, seeded and chopped

½ teaspoon sea salt

1 small handful cilantro leaves, chopped

1. Whisk the eggs in a bowl, then set aside.

2. Put a heavy, nonstick saucepan over medium–low heat and add half the butter. When it begins to foam gently, add the onions and gently sauté until soft. Try not to let them brown.

3. Add the ginger, spices, and chiles, give it a quick stir to combine, then add the tomatoes.

4. Add the sea salt to the bowl of eggs, give them another quick whisk, then add them to the pan along with the remaining butter and cook gently, stirring continuously to prevent the mixture from catching and to help form small, delicate clumps of soft, spiced egg.

5. Keep cooking until you're happy with the consistency, then remove from the heat, stir in the cilantro, and serve immediately on warmed plates with hot, buttered toast.

IRISH RAREBIT

This is a big shout-out to my adopted homeland and it's a really tasty way to use up scraps and pieces such as cold cuts of ham, or cooked pork, and cheese—with a fried egg on top.

SERVES 4

3 tablespoons (1½oz/45g)
  unsalted butter, at room
  temperature
⅓ cup (1½oz/45g) all-purpose
  flour
1¼ cups (10fl oz/300ml)
  Irish stout
½ cup (4fl oz/125ml)
  heavy cream
1⅓ cups (5½oz/150g) shredded
  sharp cheddar cheese
1 teaspoon English mustard
1 teaspoon black peppercorns,
  finely ground
Scant ¼ teaspoon finely ground
  mace
4 thick slices soda bread or
  sourdough
Light olive oil, for frying
4 eggs
14oz (400g) dry-cured ham
  or cooked pork, chopped
  or pulled
A little cayenne pepper

1. Put a large saucepan over medium heat. Add the butter, stir lightly with a small whisk, then when the butter has melted, add the flour. Whisk to form a roux and cook for 30 seconds.

2. Measure the stout and cream into a small bowl. Turn up the heat under the roux, then pour the liquid a little at a time into the pan, whisking all the time to combine well with the roux. Once all the liquid has been added, keep whisking until you see the first bubbles appear, then continue to cook for another 2 minutes.

3. Add the cheese, mustard, black pepper, and mace, and stir continuously to combine. Once the cheese has melted, continue to cook gently for 5 minutes, with only the odd bubble or two appearing, stirring occasionally. Set aside.

4. Toast the bread and let cool. Heat the olive oil in a large skillet and cook the eggs; the whites should be just set, the yolks still soft.

5. Meanwhile, preheat the broiler to its hottest setting. Arrange the ham or pork on the toast, place in a broiler pan, coat generously with the cheese sauce, and put under the broiler for 1–2 minutes, until the sauce bubbles and only just lightly scorches.

5. Put a slice of the toast on each of four warmed plates and top with a fried egg, then sprinkle with a pinch of cayenne pepper to serve.

CHEESE IN A BOX

*This is a beautifully simple, addictive dish that is perfect for the cold winter months.
I make it from October to April, when the French Vacherin Mont d'Or is available in Ireland.
It's a cow milk cheese from the Jura Mountains. The Swiss also produce this cheese. Take
a peek inside the box; the rind of the cheese should have a wavy surface with a wonderful
aroma of freshly rained-on undergrowth. If you can't find Vacherin Mont d'Or, you could
use Camembert—as long as it comes in a wooden box that you can put in the oven. This goes
perfectly with smoked ham and turmeric boiled potatoes, and the pickles help cut through the
richness and add crunch.*

SERVES 4

**1lb 2oz (500g) Vacherin Mont
d'Or or Camembert, in its
box, at room temperature**
**2¼lb (1kg) large new potatoes,
peeled, halved or quartered**
1 pinch sea salt
**1 heaping teaspoon powdered
turmeric**
1–2 pats unsalted butter
**½ teaspoon black peppercorns,
finely ground**
**A mix of pickled shallots or
onions and cornichons**
**1-lb 2-oz (500-g) piece lightly
smoked cooked ham**

1. Preheat the oven to 400°F (200°C). Put the cheese in its box on a
baking sheet, remove the lid, and gently slash the surface of the cheese
twice with a sharp knife, just scoring the rind so that you have two shallow
incisions about 2 inches (5cm) long.

2. Put the lid back on, then put the box into the oven for 15 minutes or
until the cheese is nicely runny and melted.

3. Meanwhile, put the potatoes into a large saucepan. Add the salt and
turmeric and cover with cold water. Boil the potatoes for 20 minutes or
until tender. Drain well, then transfer to a warmed serving dish, dab with
the butter, sprinkle with the ground pepper, and take them straight to the
table. Swiftly follow the potatoes with the pickles and your box of cheese
on a large warmed plate, keeping the lid on so that the cheese stays warm
and runny.

4. Carve the ham at the table. Spoon some lovely warm turmeric potatoes
onto warmed plates. Follow with a spoonful or so of the melted cheese,
with slices of ham and the pickles—glorious!

CHEESE & ONION FLAKY PUFF PIE

A delicious, simple pie that's best eaten slightly warm—any leftovers are great eaten at room temperature with Sizzled Tomatoes (see page 182).

SERVES 6

1 teaspoon black peppercorns
4 cloves
Seeds of 3 green cardamom pods
7 gratings nutmeg
2⅔ cups (10½oz/300g) shredded
    Ardrahan, Lancashire, or
    cheddar cheese
1 cup (3½oz/100g) shredded
    strong Gruyère or Comté
    cheese
3½ tablespoons (1¾oz/50g)
    unsalted butter
6 onions (about 1½lb/700g),
    coarsely sliced
3 garlic cloves, lightly crushed
    and left whole
1 sheet butter puff pastry
    (ready-to-bake is fine)
Flour, for dusting
1 large egg, lightly beaten
1 tablespoon whole milk

1. Finely grind the peppercorns, cloves, and cardamom seeds, using a mortar and pestle, then add the nutmeg and mix well.

2. Preheat the oven to 400°F (200°C). In a small bowl, mix the two cheeses together and set aside.

3. Put a heavy sauté pan over medium heat. Add the butter and let it melt, then add the onions and garlic and sauté gently until both are really soft and translucent, about 20 minutes. Add the spice mix, stir it through, then cook for 30 seconds. Remove from the heat and set aside to cool.

4. On a lightly floured work surface, roll out the pastry until thin, about 3⁄16 inch (2mm) thick. Cut the pastry in half and use one half to line a 9-inch (23-cm) pie plate, leting a little to hang over the edges.

5. Remove the cloves of garlic from the spiced onion, spread a layer of the onion over the bottom of the pie, then a layer of mixed cheeses and repeat to fill the pie generously.

6. Mix the egg with the milk and use this egg wash to brush around the edge of the pastry, then gently put on the other piece of pastry for the lid. Gently press to seal, then cut away any excess pastry and crimp the edges together.

7. Brush more egg wash over the top. Make a small hole in the center to let the steam escape, then put the pie on the middle shelf of the oven and bake for 20 minutes. Reduce the temperature to 350°F (180°C) and bake for another 20 minutes or so until the pastry is golden and the filling oozing. Let cool for 4 minutes, then slice into generous wedges and serve with English mustard and a bitter leaf salad, such as endive, dandelion, and mustard leaves.

MAC 'N' CHEESE

My mother used to roll this one out all the time when we were young—to the point that I didn't eat it for a while! I have, however, picked up the "Mac" mantle once again, and once again have fallen in love with it. Tempered clove adds a fruity note to the cheese, while the mace adds a truly delicious depth of flavor, fragrance, and tingly, clean finish.

SERVES 4–6

1 teaspoon sea salt
12oz (340g) dried macaroni
Splash of light olive oil

FOR THE SAUCE

1 tablespoon sunflower oil
9 cloves
3 tablespoons (1½oz/40g)
　　unsalted butter
⅓ cup plus 1 tablespoon
　　(1¾oz/50g) all-purpose flour
3¼ cups (1⅓ pints/775ml)
　　whole milk
½ cup (4fl oz/125ml) light cream
2 cups (9oz 250g) shredded
　　sharp cheddar cheese
2 teaspoons French mustard
2 teaspoons English mustard
1 teaspoon black peppercorns,
　　finely ground
Scant ¼ teaspoon finely
　　ground mace

FOR THE TOPPING

2 cups (3½oz/100g) fresh
　　bread crumbs
2 tablespoons olive oil
½ cup (1½oz/40g) finely grated
　　Parmesan cheese
½ teaspoon cayenne pepper
1 thyme sprig, leaves only
1 small handful flat-leaf parsley
　　leaves, finely chopped

1. Put 4¼ cups (1¾ pints/1 liter) water into a large saucepan and bring to a rolling boil. Add the salt and pasta, bring back up to a rolling boil, and cook for 11 minutes (or follow the package directions). Drain, rinse, and coat with a drizzle of light olive oil, then pour into a roasting pan or ovenproof dish about 12 × 10 inches (30 × 25cm) and 1¾ inches (4.5cm) deep. Set aside.

2. To make the sauce, put a large saucepan over high heat, pour in the oil, and, when smoking hot, carefully drop in the cloves—they will splutter and expand in size. Remove the pan from the heat, add the butter, stir lightly with a small whisk, then when the butter has melted, remove the cloves with a spoon and discard them, retaining all the butter and oil.

3. Put the pan back on the heat, turn the heat down to medium, add the flour, and whisk to form a roux, then cook for 30 seconds or so.

4. Measure the milk and cream into a small bowl, then pour it a little at a time into the pan, whisking all the time to combine well with the roux. Once all the liquid has been added, keep whisking until you see the first bubbles appear, then continue to cook for 2 minutes.

5. Add the cheese, mustards, ground pepper, and mace and stir continuously to combine. Once the cheese has melted, continue to cook gently for 5 minutes, with only the odd bubble or two appearing, stirring occasionally. Pour into the roasting pan, covering the macaroni. Set aside.

6. Preheat the oven to 375°F (190°C). Mix all the topping ingredients in a bowl, then sprinkle evenly over the macaroni and sauce. Put the roasting pan onto the middle shelf of the oven and cook for 15 minutes or until the crumbs turn golden brown and the sauce bubbles up through the topping.

GRAINS
& LEGUMES

GRAINS AND LEGUMES PROVIDE THE PERFECT BLANK CANVAS FOR DABS, SPLASHES, AND WHIRLS OF SPICE INTENSITY. Earthy, perfumed or pungent spices provide kicks of flavor as they nestle in soft, subtle grains.

Plainly cooked rice is a natural accompaniment to spicy food in many cultures, and for this I would always choose aged basmati rice: in India the best rice is aged for at least a year before use, which makes a huge difference to the flavor. However, in this chapter I'm featuring rice as a centerpiece, pairing it with floral perfumed saffron or fragrant garam masala. But for my Asafetida Risotto I've "gone against the grain" and created a dish to truly challenge the purists. The risotto gains depth from the subtly sulfurous asafetida, relying on an acidulated butter sauce, walnuts, and celery leaf to cut through glorious richness.

My passion for lentils and legumes started when I was young. I have fond memories of my mother and father organizing dinner parties. The day before, my father would fill large plastic bowls of water to soak chickpeas and various lentils. He'd go to his spice cupboard, pull out the various brightly colored cans, and arrange them on the counter. Next day, the magic would start. Peeling potatoes, pulling cauliflower florets, spilling frozen peas over the tiled floor. My father would start chopping, frying, and hunting for the "large enough" pots. My mother cleaning up after my father, smiling, scolding, laughing. Then the aromas, the glorious aromas.

My Tarka Dhal tempers the spices in hot oil to round the flavor and create a down-to-earth flavor sympathetic to the creamy-earthy little moong dahl (split mung beans). I use channa dahl (split peas) for its al dente texture, its earthy-sweet, pealike taste, and to act as the foil to the sweet aged basmati rice and the fragrant spice lift of Garam Masala in my Pistachio and Rose Pilaf.

Chickpeas have a delicate bite and sweet earthy flavor. The salad of Chickpea, Nectarine, and Feta is a celebration of summer flavors. Intended to burst with "sunshine," I've made a dressing incorporating my floral, fragrant Garam Masala with orange, mirin, and canola. The mix of vibrant flavors gives a different taste to every satisfying bite.

Previous page: Vibrant, earthy turmeric needs a light touch to showcase its gingery clean warmth.

BERBER COUSCOUS

Tagine, a type of stew, and couscous dishes have their roots planted firmly in the indigenous Berber people of North Africa. These proud people uphold culinary traditions observed for thousands of years: honey, sheep milk, goat cheese and butter, perfumed spices, barley, game, and meats. Bedouins brought dates and different grains to the region; the Moors introduced olives, herbs, and complex, flavored dishes; Jewish sects added salting methods; and the French gave everything general finesse. And now I'm adding my own twist!

Couscous is a much-revered product—a labor of love prepared from wheat, millet, or barley flours. Traditionally, Berber women took sacks of wheat to be ground into semolina and laboriously formed the now-familiar small balls, rolling the moistened flour between the palms of their hands. As with pasta, there are different types or sizes of couscous for different methods of cooking: mhammsa is ⅛ inch (3mm), keskou ¹⁄₁₆ inch (2mm), and ultrafine seffa is a mere ¹⁄₃₂ inch (1mm). For this recipe, I'm not suggesting making your own couscous, but look for the fine or ultrafine, precooked types. These make a lighter dish and you'll really notice a difference.

I've included the traditional Moroccan tfaia topping of spicy caramelized onions and golden raisins, adding another layer of flavor to this fragrant dish.

SERVES 4

FOR THE MEAT OR BARLEY
2 teaspoons cumin seeds
1 teaspoon coriander seeds
7 cloves
4 teaspoons Kashmiri chili flakes
1lb 2oz (500g) top sirloin steak, chopped into bite-size chunks, or 1¼ cups (9oz/250g) barley mixed with 2½ cups (1 pint/600ml) water
1 large onion (about 350g/12oz), chopped into chunky dice
1 teaspoon sea salt
At least 3 cups (26fl oz/750ml) good-quality dark chicken stock or broth

1. Finely grind the cumin seeds, coriander, and cloves, using a mortar and pestle, then add the Kasmiri flakes and mix well.

2. Put the beef chunks into a flameproof casserole or Dutch oven over medium–high heat. Add the onion, spices, salt, and enough stock or broth to cover the meat by 1¼ inches (3cm). (Alternatively put the barley, onion, spices, salt, and stock or broth into the casserole or Dutch oven.)

3. Bring to a boil, then turn down the heat to a gentle simmer, put the lid half on, and let to cook for 1½–2 hours, until the meat is tender. Don't let the pan dry out. (If using barley, it should need only 35–40 minutes, until the grains are tender.)

[*Continued*]

FOR THE COUSCOUS
3 cups (1lb 2oz/500g) fine or
  ultrafine couscous
1 pinch sea salt
2 tablespoons olive oil
2 teaspoon unsalted butter, diced

FOR THE TFAIA
10 saffron threads
½ cup (2¾oz/75g)
  golden raisins
1 tablespoon olive oil
2 tablespoons (1oz/30g)
  unsalted butter
3 large onions, thinly sliced
1 teaspoon sea salt
1 teaspoon black peppercorns,
  finely ground
1 heaping teaspoon finely
  ground cinnamon
2 teaspoons powdered ginger
1–2 gratings nutmeg
2 tablespoons honey

4. Meanwhile, preheat the oven to 350°F (180°C) and make the couscous. Pour the couscous into a heatproof bowl or ovenproof dish, stir the salt into 2 cups (18fl oz/500ml) warm water, and pour into the couscous. Let stand for 10 minutes. Or prepare according to the package directions.

5. Pour the oil over the couscous and, using your hands, gently mix the ingredients together, like making soda bread: gently, gently.

6. Sprinkle the butter over the surface, cover tightly with aluminum foil, and put the dish into the oven for 10–12 minutes. Take out and keep warm, replacing the foil with a dish towel. Set aside.

7. For the tfaia, soak the saffron in ¼ cups (2fl oz/50ml) warm water for at least 15 minutes. Soak the golden raisins in 3 tablespoons warm water for 10 minutes, then drain them. Set aside.

8. Put the oil and butter in a large, heavy skillet over medium heat. Let the butter melt, then add the onions and salt and sauté gently for 5 minutes.

9. Turn down the heat slightly, add the spices, adding nutmeg to taste, the saffron threads and their soaking water, and the honey, then stir. Cover and cook gently for 15 minutes or until the onions are soft and "melted."

10. Remove the lid and add the drained golden raisins, stir them through, and continue to cook for another 10 minutes, uncovered. Take off the heat and set aside.

11. Spoon all the couscous into a large serving dish, then make a small well in the middle. Strain the meat (or barley) and onions, reserving the juices in a small bowl or small bowl, and put the meat and onion (or spiced barley and onion) into the well, top with the tfaia, and serve immediately, with the meat juices served separately.

PAELLA TÚNEL

There are many versions of paella, but here I take it back to its roots, add a spice or two, and cook a dish that recalls the land workers of the Albufera, the freshwater lagoon on the Valencia coast, the true home of paella. More than 1,000 years ago, the Moors first cultivated rice in this Mediterranean Spanish region, and the famous Spanish dish arose from there. There's no "official" recipe, but rice is the star ingredient, so if you can find them, use one of the three main Valencian varieties: Bahía, Senia, or Bomba. The starch content ("white pearl") is what it's all about: the rice shouldn't be fluffy, but must have some bite while soaking up the glorious cooking juices. Túnel is a Mallorcan herb liqueur with hints of anise and juniper—use pastis if you can't find it. Lima beans are part of a traditional paella; you need to soak them overnight before putting this dish together.

SERVES 4–6

⅔ cup (5½oz/150g) dried lima beans or garrafón beans
12–15 saffron threads
6 chicken thighs, bone-in, trimmed of excess skin, chopped in half across the bone
1 wild rabbit, divided into small cuts; ask your butcher (optional, but worth it)
1 tablespoon coarse sea salt
9oz (250g) large flat green beans (ideally flat runner beans; if not, use snow peas; about 2½ cups prepared)
Several splashes olive oil
4 garlic cloves, lightly crushed
2 large onions, chopped
2 green bell peppers, quartered, seeded, and diced

1. Soak the dried lima beans overnight in 2 cups (18fl oz/500ml) cold water. The next day, drain and set aside. Soak the saffron threads in ¼ cup (2fl oz/50ml) warm water.

2. To make the spice blend, finely grind the peppercorns, cumin, and coriander seeds and star anise, using a mortar and pestle, then add the paprika, turmeric, and red pepper flakes. Set aside.

3. Lay out the chicken and rabbit pieces, if using, and sprinkle with the salt, then massage it briefly into the meat. Put the green beans into a saucepan of boiling water and boil for 1 minute to blanch them, then refresh in a bowl of ice cold water, drain, slice, and set aside.

4. Put an 18-inch (46cm)-diameter deep skillet (better still, a paella pan) over medium heat, add 2 large splashes of oil, then add the chicken thighs, scraping all the salt into the pan, and cook for 3–4 minutes, until lightly browned, turning them over as they cook.

5. Add the garlic, onions, green bell peppers, and thyme and toss or stir it all around. Add the rabbit pieces and another splash of olive oil and continue to cook for another 5 minutes.

[*Continued*]

2 small thyme sprigs, leaves only
1 fresh red finger chile, seeded
    and coarsely diced
1 (14½oz/400g) can diced
    tomatoes, or in summer,
    use the ripest plum or roma
    tomatoes and coarsely grate
1 rosemary sprig (about 3
    inches/7.5cm), leaves only
1 cup (7oz/200g) paella rice
5½oz (150g) fresh mussels,
    scrubbed and debearded
5½oz (150g) fresh clams,
    scrubbed
12 large jumbo shrimp, shell on,
    deveined
Zest of ½ lemon
3 lemons, halved, to garnish

FOR THE SPICE BLEND

2 teaspoons black peppercorns
½ teaspoon cumin seeds
1 teaspoon coriander seeds
1 star anise
2 teaspoons sweet Spanish
    pimentón paprika
1 teaspoon powdered turmeric
2 teaspoons dried red
    pepper flakes

FOR THE REDUCTION

¼ cup (2fl oz/50ml) white
    wine vinegar
½ cup (3½fl oz/100ml) Túnel
    de Mallorca, a French pastis,
    or Pernod

6. When the meat is a nutty brown, add the chile, stir, then add the tomatoes, green beans, and soaked lima beans. Turn down the heat a little and cook for another 8–10 minutes.

7. Next, add the spice blend and stir, then pour in 4¼ cups (1¾ pints/ 1 liter) warm water, add the rosemary, and finally add the saffron and its soaking water. Turn up the heat to high, bring to a strong, rolling boil, then gently pour in the rice. Jiggle and shake the pan to distribute things evenly and cook for 1 minute.

8. Lower the heat to medium, stir gently to combine the ingredients, then let simmer gently for 25–35 minutes.

9. Meanwhile, to make the reduction, put the white wine vinegar and the Túnel, pastis, or Pernod into a small, nonstick saucepan and stir over medium–high heat until reduced to the consistency of honey. Set aside.

10. Discard any mussels or clams that do not close when the shell is tapped. When the rice is nearly cooked, add the shrimp, mussels, and clams. Cover and cook gently for 3–5 minutes, until the seafood is just cooked and the rice is soft but still with a little bite. Discard any mussels or clams that remain closed.

11. Turn off the heat and sprinkle with the lemon zest. Take the paella to the table, put it on a trivet, and cover with a clean dish towel to rest for 3–4 minutes.

12. Remove the dish towel, drizzle the Túnel reduction over the rice, and serve on warmed plates with lemon halves and finger bowls at the ready.

ASAFETIDA RISOTTO WITH WALNUTS & CELERY LEAF

I think risottos are one of the ultimate comfort dishes, and I love to serve this one with a crisp green salad on the side. When you're cooking risotto, remember: only add liquid that's been heated to a gentle simmer; don't flood the rice with stock; and always be generous with the amount of stock you start with, because some rice varieties absorb more than you might expect.

SERVES 4–6

FOR THE ACIDULATED BUTTER

⅔ cup (3½oz/100g) finely chopped shallots

½ cup (3½fl oz/100ml) white wine vinegar

1 stick (4½oz/125g) unsalted butter, cubed and chilled

FOR THE RISOTTO

4¼–5 cups (1¾–2 pints/ 1–1.2 liters) hot light chicken stock or broth

A generous splash light olive oil

2 tablespoons (1oz/30g) unsalted butter

½ cup (1¾oz/50g) chopped celery leaves (¼-inch/5mm pieces), plus 1 tablespoon whole leaves to garnish

⅓ cup (1¾oz/50g) finely chopped shallots

½ garlic clove, finely chopped

1⅓ cups (9oz/250g) Arborio or risotto rice

¼ teaspoon asafetida resin

3½ tablespoons (1¾oz/50g) acidulated butter (see above)

1 cup (2¾oz/75g) freshly grated Parmesan cheese

A splash walnut oil

1. Make the acidulated butter well in advance, because it needs to freeze. Put the shallots and vinegar into a small saucepan and simmer gently until the vinegar has almost reduced by half, then remove the pan from the heat. Add the cubed butter, whisking, to form a smooth sauce—a beurre blanc—then pour into an ice cube tray. Let cool, then store in your freezer. The cubes make handy-size portions to work with.

2. Now for the risotto. Keep the stock or broth simmering in a saucepan over low heat. Put a sauté pan over medium heat, splash in a little olive oil, and add the butter. When the butter just begins to foam, add the celery leaves, shallots, and garlic, and sauté gently for a couple of minutes. Add the rice and stir to coat it in the buttery oil and vegetables. Stir continuously for 3–5 minutes, until you hear the rice "cracking." This means that the rice is releasing its starch.

3. Add the asafetida and continue cooking for a minute or so. Add a ladle of the hot stock, then carry on stirring and continuously adding just enough stock to keep the mixture moist. The rice will take 15–20 minutes to cook, depending on the variety and age of rice you're using.

4. When the rice has softened slightly but still has a little bite, add the acidulated butter, Parmesan, walnut oil, and a little more stock so that it has a slack, but not sloppy, consistency. Stir, remove from the heat, and cover the pan three-quarters with its lid for 2–3 minutes to relax the rice and let it absorb the extra stock.

5. Time to serve! The risotto should have a "molten" consistency now, so serve it on warmed plates, flatten it with the back of the spoon, then sprinkle with celery leaves to garnish.

PISTACHIO & ROSE PILAF

I came up with this gloriously fragrant version of pilaf rice because I wanted something light, perfumed, and interesting to serve as an accompaniment to curry dishes. Actually, this works wonderfully well with any saucy dish. I love the layers upon layers of perfume, natural sweetness, and vibrant colors.

SERVES 4–6

¼ butternut squash, peeled, seeded, and diced into 1-inch (2.5-cm) chunks

A splash canola oil

2 tablespoons (1oz/30g) unsalted butter

½ onion, finely diced

2 cups (13oz/375g) best-quality aged basmati rice, rinsed throughly and drained

½ cup (3½oz/100g) channa dhal (split peas)

5 cups (2 pints/1.2 liters) vegetable stock or broth or hot water

1 teaspoon powdered turmeric

2 teaspoon Garam Masala blend (see page 267), plus a little extra to serve

1 heaping teaspoon sea salt

1 handful bright green pistachio nuts, lightly crushed

2 tablespoons dried rose petals, coarsely chopped

1 large handful each cilantro leaves, flat-leaf parsley, and chives, finely chopped

1. Preheat the oven to 350°F (180°C). Put the squash into a roasting pan with the oil, and roast it in the oven for 20–25 minutes, until just soft and a little browned. Set aside.

2. Melt the butter, or a splash of oil, in a flameproof casserole or Dutch oven over gentle heat, then add the onion and sweat for 5 minutes or until it is soft.

3. Add the rice and channa dhal, then stir for a minute or two, coating all the grains with the melted butter.

4. Next, pour the stock, broth, or water into the casserole, sprinkle in the turmeric and Garam Masala, and give it a quick but gentle stir.

5. Cover the casserole with a tight-fitting lid or aluminum foil and put on a middle shelf in the oven. After 10–15 minutes, check to see if all the liquid has been absorbed. If there's still some liquid remaining, return the covered casserole to the oven and give it another few minutes, until all the liquid has been absorbed but the rice is still moist and glossy.

6. Remove from the oven, take off the lid, or gingerly rip off the foil, add the salt, and fluff gently with a fork. Stir through the butternut squash, pistachio nuts, and rose petals, sprinkle with the herbs and a little more Garam Masala, and serve immediately.

Vanilla & Long Pepper Oatmeal with Sugared Banana, Cardamom & Lime

I eat oatmeal every morning, rain or shine. Not always with cardamom syrup and bananas, I must confess. Vanilla in oatmeal is nothing new, but the addition of long pepper here offsets its creaminess, backing it up with heat, and the whole dish is wonderfully fragrant. Recently I've started to use unsweetened almond milk in place of cow milk; it adds a delicious toasted nutty flavor to my morning oatmeal.

SERVES 4

FOR THE OATMEAL
1 vanilla bean, split lengthwise
2 cups (7oz/200g) jumbo rolled oats
2½ cups (1 pint/600ml) whole milk
2½ cups (1 pint/600ml) water
½ long pepper spike, grated
1 teaspoon vanilla extract

FOR THE CARDAMOM–LIME SYRUP
6 green cardamom pods
3½ cups (1½lb/700g) sugar
Zest and juice of 2 limes

FOR THE BANANAS
2 short, sweet, only-just-ripe bananas
Confectioners' sugar, sifted

1. Scrape out the seeds from the vanilla bean. Put the bean and seeds into a large, heavy saucepan and add all the remaining oatmeal ingredients. Ideally, the ingredients should come no more than one-third of the way up the pan.

2. Put the pan over medium heat, stir the mixture well, and cook until it just begins to boil. Keep stirring from time to time.

3. When you see the oats gently boiling, turn the heat down to low so that it is only just simmering. Cook for 30–40 minutes, stirring frequently, until the starchy flavor has disappeared and the oatmeal has taken on an unctuous, whipped cream texture.

4. While the oatmeal is cooking, make the syrup. Put the cardamom pods on a cutting board and give them a firm, decisive, controlled bang with the bottom of a saucepan. This will slightly open up the pods to expose their fragrant seeds.

5. Put the sugar, 1¼ cups (10fl oz/300ml) cold water, and the smashed cardamom pods into a saucepan over medium heat and give everything a gentle stir. Make sure there are no sugar crystals up the side of the pan, because these will burn and cause problems. Don't be tempted to stir, but from time to time swirl the pan around. Once you're sure all the sugar has dissolved, let the syrup simmer for 2 minutes.

6. Remove the pan from the heat, and add the lime zest and juice. Stir well, then set aside.

7. Peel the bananas, then slice them on the diagonal about ⅛ inch (3mm) thick. Put the banana slices on a dinner plate and dredge with confectioners' sugar.

8. If you have a chef's blowtorch, this is the perfect time to use it. Simply flame the bananas until the sugar just starts to catch and brown to a light caramel. If you don't have a blowtorch, set the broiler to its highest setting, put the banana slices on a broiler pan, and put the pan close to the flames. Watching carefully, heat the bananas until the sugar just begins to brown.

9. To serve, remove the vanilla bean from the oatmeal, scrape any oatmeal from the bean back into the pan, and give it a good stir. Spoon generous servings into your favorite breakfast bowls, place 3 or 5 banana slices in a star shape in the center of each bowl, then spoon a little syrup over the bananas. (Or simply serve the oatmeal and let everyone help themselves to bananas and syrup.)

Red Lentil Dhal with Tomato, Coconut & Lime

This dish is inspired by the Malay cooking style of the south Malabari Indians. Fragrant cinnamon and cloves combine with red lentils, creamy coconut, a zesty kick of fresh lime, and chile. It's a wonderful recipe, one of the originals we've been serving at farmers' markets for years: a vegetarian bowl of absolute comforting delight.

SERVES 8

2½ cups (1lb 2oz/500g) dried red lentils
1 small handful cashew nuts
2 teaspoons black peppercorns
1 teaspoon cumin seeds
1 teaspoon coriander seeds
½ teaspoon cloves
½ teaspoon finely ground cinnamon
1 teaspoon powdered turmeric
4½ tablespoons (2¼oz/60g) unsalted butter or 3 tablespoons vegetable oil
2 cups onions, cut into large dice
2 red onions, diced
6 garlic cloves, finely chopped
1 red chile, seeded and finely chopped
1⅓ cups (4½oz/125g) grated fresh ginger
2 (14½oz/400g) cans diced tomatoes
1 tablespoon sugar
2 teaspoons sea salt
1¾ cups (14fl oz/400ml) coconut milk
2½ cups (1 pint/600ml) vegetable stock or broth or water
Juice of 1 lime
Cilantro leaves, chopped
1 small handful coconut flakes

1. Soak the lentils in enough water to cover for 10 minutes. Put the cashew nuts in a dry skillet and toast over medium heat for 5 minutes, or until lightly golden, tossing the pan frequently. Chop coarsely and set aside.

2. Finely grind the peppercorns, cumin and coriander seeds, and cloves, using a mortar and pestle, then mix in the cinnamon and turmeric. Set aside.

3. Heat the butter in a large flameproof casserole or saucepan over a medium heat. Add the white and red onions, the garlic, chile, and ginger, and cook gently for 5 minutes or until softened.

4. Add the spice mix and cook gently for another couple minutes.

5. Add the tomatoes, sugar, salt, and coconut milk, and simmer for 5–10 minutes, stirring occasionally.

6. Rinse the lentils well and add to the casserole. Simmer, adding the stock, broth, or water a little at a time as it's absorbed. Stir occasionally to prevent it from sticking. Cook over medium heat for 15–20 minutes, until soft.

7. Stir in the lime juice, sprinkle with fresh cilantro, coconut shavings, and the cashew nuts, and serve immediately with fragrant basmati rice or Indian flatbreads.

TARKA DHAL

Here's the way my father taught me to make tarka dhal. It's really simple and tastes wonderful. You'll need to have a skimmer on hand, because the turmeric and lentils produce a foam that needs skimming off the surface from time to time as they cook. This is just the impurities and excess starch coming to the surface. Remember to work quickly at the "tarka" stage to avoid burning the spices.

SERVES 6–8

1¼ cups (9oz/250g)
   moong dhal, red lentils, or
   your favorite type of lentil,
   rinsed well
About 2 cups (18fl oz/500ml)
   vegetable stock or broth
   or water
1 teaspoon powdered turmeric
1 (14½-oz/400-g) can diced
   tomatoes
Sea salt
¼ cup (2fl oz/50ml)
   sunflower oil
2 teaspoon coriander seeds
1 teaspoon cumin seeds
4 garlic cloves, finely chopped
1 red Thai chile, seeded and
   chopped, or 1 teaspoon red
   pepper flakes (optional,
   and according to your heat
   tolerance)
Cilantro leaves, finely chopped

1. Put the dhal into a saucepan and add the vegetable stock, broth, or water to cover. Add the turmeric.

2. Bring to a boil, cover halfway with a lid, then turn down the heat. Simmer gently until the lentils are just about tender enough to eat: 10–15 minutes if using moong dhal.

3. Add the tomatoes and salt to taste. Stir and let simmer gently for another 2–3 minutes. Turn off the heat, cover, and set the saucepan to one side.

4. Now you're ready for the "tarka" stage. Add the oil to a sauté pan or deep skillet and put it over high heat until the oil starts to smoke.

5. Add the coriander and cumin seeds. Take the pan off the heat and swirl the seeds around in the pan, then immediately add the garlic and chile, if using. Keeping a firm grip on the pan's handle, swirl all the spices around in the oil, taking the pan off and on the heat as you do so to prevent the garlic and spices from burning. You need to keep just enough heat to cook everything.

6. When the spices and garlic are a light brown, nutty color (this should only take about 1 minute maximum), turn off the heat and pour the hot oil and spices into the lentil saucepan. Immediately replace the lid. Be sure to stand well back! Be prepared for plenty of steam and sizzling, hissing sounds as you add the hot oil to the lentils. Gently swirl the lentil pan to combine all the flavors.

7. Leave the pan for a couple of minutes before lifting the lid. Savor the gorgeous spicy aromas as you sprinkle with the fresh cilantro. Serve immediately with aged basmati rice and a sliced onion and tomato salad.

SPICY CHICKPEAS ON TOAST

This is based on one of father's recipes. When my mother was in hospital having my younger brother, if we weren't given rice pudding and preserves at each meal, then he'd conjure up his favorite chickpea chana masala. This is my version of beans on toast: quick, tasty, good for you, and happy memories for me!

SERVES 4 AS A SNACK OR LIGHT DINNER

2 tablespoons (1oz/25g) ghee (clarified butter), unsalted butter, or a couple of splashes vegetable oil

1 large onion, chopped into ¾-inch (2-cm) dice

⅔ cup (2¼oz/60g) grated fresh ginger

5 garlic cloves: 4 finely chopped, 1 halved

3 teaspoon coriander seeds

1½ teaspoons cumin seeds

2 teaspoons black peppercorns

2 teaspoons powdered turmeric

1 teaspoon sea salt

1 (15-oz/425-g) can chickpeas, drained and rinsed

1 (14½-oz/400-g) can diced tomatoes

4 slices sourdough bread

Butter, for spreading

2–3 teaspoons Garam Masala blend (see page 267) (optional)

Cilantro leaves, coarsely chopped

2 teaspoon thick, black Indian tamarind paste

1. Put the ghee into a heavy saucepan over medium heat. Add the onion, ginger, and chopped garlic, and cook gently over low heat until the onions have softened and the garlic gives off its gorgeous fragrance. Try not to brown the garlic; this will give it and the end dish a bitter flavor.

2. Finely grind the coriander and cumin seeds and peppercorns, using a mortar and pestle. Add all the spices to the pan and add the salt, then stir for a couple of minutes to combine all the flavors. It may look dry at this stage, but don't worry; it's all fine.

3. Pour the chickpeas and diced tomatoes into the pan and add ¼ cup (2fl oz/50ml) water, then turn up the heat and gently stir. Heat the mixture until it just starts to boil, then turn the heat down and simmer gently for 15 minutes.

4. Toast the bread, then rub with the cut edges of the halved garlic clove. Spread generously with butter and put on warmed plates. Spoon on the chickpeas, sprinkle with the Garam Masala, if using, and the fresh cilantro. Drizzle each slice with ½ teaspoon tamarind paste and serve immediately.

CHICKPEA SALAD WITH NECTARINE, FETA & MINT

The combination of fresh, invigorating garden mint, sweet, juicy nectarines, soft-bite nutty chickpeas, and gently salty feta cheese is brought beautifully together with my clean-finishing, vibrant summer dressing—this is one to savor. This surprisingly quick salad goes with any meal, from sausages to steak, from fish to juicy chicken thighs. Its freshness is the key. So grab a glass of your favorite tipple, picnic rugs, friends, family, and enjoy a pure taste of summer.

SERVES 4–6

½ red onion, sliced very thinly
Juice of 2 limes
2 ripe nectarines
3 (15-oz/425-g) cans chickpeas,
    drained and rinsed
(1½oz/40g) feta cheese, diced
    into ½-inch (1-cm) cubes
1 handful arugula leaves, torn
1 large handful mint leaves, very
    thinly sliced

FOR THE DRESSING

⅓ cup (2½fl oz/75ml) canola oil
3 tablespoons fresh orange juice
1 teaspoon orange zest
1 teaspoon Worcestershire sauce
1 heaping teaspoon Garam
    Masala blend (see page 267)
2 teaspoons mirin (sweet
    Japanese rice wine)
1 teaspoon white wine vinegar
½ teaspoon sea salt
4½oz (125g) soft goat cheese

1. Put the sliced onion in a bowl and add the lime juice. Set aside for at least 30 minutes.

2. Skin the nectarines by scoring a cross into the bottom of each fruit and popping it into boiling water for 1 minute; carefully remove it and peel away the skin.

3. Put the nectarines onto a cutting board and cut each into quarters, slicing down around the pit. Then chop into small, even pieces.

4. Mix all the dressing ingredients, except the goat cheese, together in a small bowl, then stir in the goat cheese until well combined. Set aside.

5. Lift the onion slices out of the lime juice. Holding them in one hand over the sink, squeeze out the liquid with a firm but gentle grip, and put them in a large mixing bowl. Add the chickpeas and dressing, and mix well so that they are all nicely coated.

6. Add the feta cheese, nectarine pieces, arugula, and mint, and gently and carefully fold together just to combine. Chill before serving for an extra-refreshing effect.

Winter Vegetables

BRASSICAS (MEMBERS OF THE CABBAGE FAMILY), TUBERS, SQUASH, ALLIUMS (THE ONION FAMILY), AND MUSHROOMS ARE THE HEARTY HEAVYWEIGHTS OF THE VEGETABLE WORLD. When cooking and spicing this group it's good to play with warmth and perfume: warmth of ginger, pepper, chiles; perfume of cubeb, cardamom, mace, and saffron. Fragrant Garam Masala, a touch of amchoor or asafetida, or a pinch of chile give a kick to creamy winter soups and casseroles.

I adore cabbage of all types, with their beautiful textured leaves: my favorites, savoy and January King, have just the right combination of sweetness and astringency, perfect with pepper, chile, cumin, coriander, cubeb, turmeric, and ginger. My Celebration Lentil Cabbage includes green cardamom and mace to lift and brighten the lentils, while Kashmiri chiles help marry the rich béchamel sauce to astringent cabbage.

I moved to Ireland not being terribly passionate about potatoes. However, my wife Olive, like most inhabitants of the Emerald Isle, is a stalwart supporter of floury potatoes: we have Golden Wonders and Kerr's Pinks. For my Vada Pav (potato rolls) and Aloo Tikki (potato fritters) I use Maris Pipers, but any floury potatoes, such as Yukon Gold or russets, are perfect. Potatoes provide a blank canvas for spicing: define buttery mashed potatoes with nutmeg and white pepper; lift roasted potatoes with coriander and cumin; when frying, throw in a little chile and Sichuan pepper; liven up boiled potatoes with green cardamom, vanilla, and a grating of long pepper.

Squash and alliums can share many of the same spice notes: ginger, coriander, fennel, clove, turmeric, and white pepper, to bring out natural sweetness, add background heat, and balance sulfurous and bitter notes. At the age of 13, I had a revelation involving the humble onion. It was Saturday or Sunday evening, the TV was on, it may have been Keith Floyd, or Delia Smith. Anyway, they put a large onion into the oven with a little olive oil and pinch of salt and simply roasted it. That was it. I couldn't believe the simplicity. So I tootled off to the kitchen and did the same. About three-quarters of an hour later, hey presto, I produced a wonderfully soft, sweet, and deliciously pungent dinner with crusty bread. And that's the inspiration for my Allium Crisp.

Previous page: Caramel to the nose, tangy to the tongue, dried mango powder (amchoor) creates a satisfying, subtle, sweet–sour contrast to winter vegetables.

JERUSALEM ARTICHOKE SOUP

I first made a basic version of this recipe many years ago as part of my Ballymaloe Cookery School exam. I chose it for its comfort factor, earthy flavor, and the health-giving natural fiber (inulin) content of the artichokes.

SERVES 4

2 tablespoons (1oz/30g) butter
2 large onions, coarsely chopped
1 teaspoon sea salt
2 Yukon Gold, red-skinned, or
    white round potatoes, peeled
    and coarsely chopped
4 cups (1¼ lb/600g) peeled
    and coarsely chopped
    Jerusalem artichokes
2 cups (18fl oz/500ml) chicken
    stock or broth
1¼ cups (10½ fl oz/300ml)
    whole milk, plus extra
    if needed
1 teaspoon black peppercorns
1 teaspoon cumin seeds
2 teaspoons fennel seeds
1 teaspoon Kashmiri chili flakes
4 slices sourdough bread, cut
    into ¾-inch (2-cm) dice
¼ cup (2fl oz/50ml) light
    olive oil
¼ cup (2fl oz/50ml) sour cream
1 small bunch chives,
    thinly sliced

1. Put a large saucepan over medium heat. Add the butter, let melt, then add the onions and salt, and sauté gently for 5 minutes or until the onions are soft, stirring frequently.

2. Add the potatoes and artichokes, stir well, and cover with a piece of wax paper. Turn down the heat slightly, cover, and cook gently for 20 minutes, stirring occasionally.

3. Add the stock or broth and milk, turn up the heat, and cook at a gentle simmer for 15–20 minutes, until the potatoes and artichokes are completely soft.

4. Remove from the heat and process with an immersion blender or in a food processor to a smooth consistency. Add a little more milk, if needed, then adjust the seasoning and set aside.

5. Meanwhile, preheat the oven to 400°F (200°C) and put a roasting pan into the oven. Finely grind the peppercorns, cumin, and fennel seeds, using a mortar and pestle, then add the Kasmiri flakes. Put the diced bread into a bowl. Mix the spices with the oil and pour the mixture over the bread.

6. Stir well and transfer to the heated roasting pan in an even layer. Put the pan into the oven and roast the bread for about 10 minutes, turning it over from time to time until it's golden all over. Remove from the oven, transfer the bread to paper towels to drain, then set aside and let to cool.

7. Ladle generous amounts of the soup into warmed bowls, drizzle each bowl with 1 tablespoon sour cream, sprinkle with a handful of the spiced bread, then add the chives and serve immediately.

CREAM OF YOUNG PUMPKIN SOUP

The wonderfully fruity, almost smoky flavor and delicate heat of the Kashmiri chile work so well with the taste of new-season pumpkin. The pumpkin seeds and croutons add crunch and texture to this unctuous soup—something to bite into is somehow always more satisfying than merely a slurp or two.

SERVES 4

7 tablespoons (3½oz/100g) unsalted butter
1 lb 2oz (500g) pumpkin, or ½ large butternut squash, peeled and cut into chunks
4 shallots, finely chopped
1 garlic clove, chopped
2 teaspoons Kashmiri chili flakes
2 teaspoons coriander seeds, finely ground
1 teaspoon powdered turmeric
4¼ cups (1¾ pints/1 liter) vegetable stock or broth
1 cup (7fl oz/200ml) heavy cream
1 teaspoon ground black pepper
⅓ cup (1oz/30g) freshly grated Parmesan cheese

FOR THE CROUTONS
3 tablespoons canola oil
1 handful stale bread, cut into small cubes
Sea salt and freshly ground black pepper

TO SERVE
1 small handful dried pumpkin seeds
1 small handful chives, finely chopped or snipped with scissors
1 teaspoon Kashmiri chili flakes

1. Put a large, heavy saucepan over medium–low heat, add the butter, and let melt. Add the pumpkin or squash chunks and shallots and cook gently in the butter, without browning, for 6–7 minutes, until the edges of the pumpkin are starting to soften.

2. Add the spices and cook for 1 minute. Add the stock or broth and simmer for 5 minutes.

3. Add the cream, black pepper, and cheese, then bring just to a boil and remove from the heat.

4. Pour the soup into a food processor or process with an emmersion blender to a smooth consistency. Set aside to keep warm.

5. To make the croutons, heat the oil and gently cook the bread cubes until they're golden brown, then season with salt and black pepper.

6. Dry-roast the pumpkin seeds in a nonstick saucepan over medium heat until just toasted.

7. Pour the soup into warmed bowls, then sprinkle the croutons, pumpkin seeds, chives, and Kashmiri flakes over the top and serve immediately.

WINTER LEAVES & SPICED SQUASH

SERVES 4 AS A SNACK OR
LIGHT DINNER

FOR THE DRIED FRUIT

1 tablespoon each diced dried
   apricots, pitted prunes, and
   figs, and golden raisins
2 tablespoons honey
⅓ cup (3fl oz/90ml) warm
   jasmine tea
About 12 saffron threads
1 teaspoon rose water

FOR THE SALAD

¼ teaspoon cubeb peppercorns
¼ teaspoon finely ground mace
¼ teaspoon amchoor
2 teaspoons finely ground cassia
½ teaspoon powdered ginger
2 tablespoons canola oil
½ butternut squash or 1lb
   (450g) other winter squash,
   peeled, seeded, and cut into
   small wedges
1 green Thai chile, seeded and
   finely chopped
1 teaspoon sea salt
2 small heads radicchio
2 small heads endive,
   ideally 1 green and 1 red
1 head frisée lettuce
3 handfuls watercress
2 fresh raw chestnuts

FOR THE DRESSING

1 tablespoon Dijon mustard
2 tablespoons honey
1 teaspoon red wine vinegar
½ teaspoon sea salt

This is a great-tasting salad that looks really splendid if you're able to find different varieties of winter leaves and squash. That way, you'll not only have an attractive visual selection, but one that excites the palate.

1. Preheat the oven to 375°F (190°C). Put all the ingredients for the dried fruit into a saucepan, put over medium heat, bring up to a boil, and cook for 2 minutes. Remove from the heat, set aside, and let steep for 45 minutes, stirring occasionally, until all the fruits soften and plump up, then drain.

2. Mix the spices for the salad together. Put the oil, squash, spice mix, chile, and salt into a bowl, and mix well. Transfer to a large ovenproof skillet or flameproof casserole and sauté for 1 minute over high heat. Toss the ingredients around in the pan, then put it into the oven and roast for 15–20 minutes, until just soft and charring around the edges. Set aside to cool to room temperature.

3. Put all the dressing ingredients in a screw-top jar and add 2 tablespoons boiling water. Shake well, then set aside.

4. Carefully separate the leaves of the salad vegetables and arrange on a large serving plate.

5. Put the squash pieces on the leaves, sprinkle the fruits over them, drizzle with the lukewarm dressing, and shave the chestnuts over the top, using a vegetable peeler. Serve immediately.

ENDIVE, WATERCRESS, & GRILLED SQUASH SALAD

This simple winter salad makes a beautiful appetizer or main dish. The spiced blood orange dressing incorporates wonderful, fragrant garam masala, which may sound bizarre but tastes excellent and has to be tried. This recipe makes more dressing than is needed for this salad, so you'll have some leftover to use with other salads. I love sheep cheese, but you could use goat or even a blue cheese at a push.

SERVES 4–6

FOR THE DRESSING

⅔ cup (5fl oz/150ml) canola oil
½ cup (3½fl oz/100ml) blood-orange juice (about 2 juicy oranges), strained
Zest of ½ blood orange
1 teaspoon Worcestershire sauce
2 teaspoons Garam Masala blend (see page 267)
1 tablespoon mirin (sweet Japanese rice wine)
1 tablespoon white wine vinegar
1 teaspoon sea salt

FOR THE SALAD

½ cup (1¾oz/50g) skinned hazelnuts
1 butternut squash, or 2lb (900g) other winter squash, cut in half lengthwise, seeded, and peeled
1 head green endive
½ head red endive, cut lengthwise
2 bunches (7oz/200g) fresh watercress, large stems removed (you can add them to a soup stock) or mâche
3½oz (100g) sheep cheese, crumbled into small lumps

1. Put all the dressing ingredients into a clean screw-top jar and shake well. Set aside.

2. Put the hazelnuts for the salad in a dry saucepan and toast over medium heat until lightly golden. Coarsely chop and set aside.

3. Put the squash, flat side down, on a cutting board and, using a sharp knife, carefully cut thin slices the length of the vegetable. You're aiming for them to be no more than ⅛ inch (3mm) thick.

4. Put a ridged grill pan over high heat until drops of water immediately sizzle and evaporate. (You can use a hot broiler or heavy skillet if you don't have a ridged grill pan.) Put a couple of squash slices on the pan and cook until they char on one side, then flip the slices over and char the other side. Repeat until all the slices are similarly toasted and suitably floppy. Set aside.

5. Chop the bottom off each endive head, then carefully peel away whole leaves, one at a time, until you have stripped off all the leaves.

6. Put the toasted squash slices, the watercress or mâche, and the endive leaves in a large mixing bowl. Shake the dressing and pour 2 tablespoons of it over the leaves.

7. Using your hands, carefully tumble the leaves around to coat in the dressing, then lift, gently shake off any excess dressing, and transfer to a large plate or salad bowl. Sprinkle with the cheese, then the chopped hazelnuts, and serve.

CAULIFLOWER CHEESE WITH SPICED MORNAY SAUCE

This is a wonderful accompaniment to roasted beef or lamb, or simply serve by itself as a comfort-food dinner.

SERVES 4–6

1 pinch sea salt
1 cauliflower, outer leaves
    removed and chopped into
    ¾-inch (2-cm) slices;
    florets separated into
    golf ball-size chunks

FOR THE MORNAY SAUCE
2 tablespoons (1oz/30g)
    unsalted butter
¼ cup (1oz/30g) all-purpose
    flour
1⅔ cups (14fl oz/400ml)
    whole milk
¼ cup (2fl oz/50ml) light cream
⅔ cup (2¾oz/75g) shredded
    sharp cheddar cheese, plus
    ⅓ cup (1¾oz/50g) shredded
    cheese for the topping
⅓ cup (1¾oz/50g) shredded
    Emmental or Swiss cheese
⅓ cup (1oz/30g) freshly grated
    Parmesan cheese
2 teaspoons French mustard
1 teaspoon English mustard
1 teaspoon black peppercorns,
    finely ground
¼ teaspoon Sichuan pepper,
    finely ground
¼ teaspoon cayenne pepper
Scant ¼ teaspoon finely
    ground mace

1. Pour enough cold water into a saucepan, big enough to hold the cauliflower, to come 1¼ inches (3cm) up the sides of the pan. Add the salt and cauliflower leaves, then put the florets on top.

2. Bring to a boil over medium heat, then turn down the heat, cover the pan, and simmer for 12–15 minutes, until the florets are just tender; when pierced with a knife, there will be just a little resistance.

3. Remove from the heat and drain. Put the cooked greens into a roasting pan and put the florets on top. Set aside.

4. Preheat the oven to 400°F (200°C). To make the sauce, put a large saucepan over medium heat. Add the butter, stir lightly with a small whisk, and when it has melted add the flour and whisk to form a roux. Cook for 30 seconds.

5. Pour the milk and cream into a small bowl, then pour it a little at a time into the pan, whisking all the time to combine well with the roux. Once all the liquid is added, keep whisking and let the sauce cook until you see the first bubbles appear, then continue to cook for 2 minutes.

6. Next add the cheeses, mustards, peppers, and mace, stirring continuously to combine. Once the cheese has melted, continue to cook gently for 5 minutes, with only the odd bubble or two appearing, stirring occasionally.

7. Pour all the sauce into the roasting pan, covering the cauliflower, then sprinkle with the extra shredded cheddar. Put on the middle shelf of the oven, and bake for 15–20 minutes or until the cheese melts and the sauce begins to scorch without burning. Serve immediately.

SHIITAKE & SAVOY UPSIDE-DOWN CAKE

Cabbage is one of my favorite ingredients. I wanted to create a vegetarian terrine; this idea came together over a couple of months of thought—and many a cabbage later! It's based on a very elegant-sounding technique, the "chartreuse," which basically means things wrapped up in cabbage. If the egg mixture leaks out a little, don't worry; it simply fills the cabbage-vein divots—giving the end product a slightly otherworldly, pretty hip appearance.

SERVES 4–6

1lb (450g) new potatoes, unpeeled
1 large savoy cabbage, leaves plucked off, hard centered veins cut out and discarded
½ teaspoon cubeb peppercorns
2 teaspoons white peppercorns
1 teaspoon cumin seeds
2 tablespoons (1oz/30g) unsalted butter
2 tablespoons olive oil
2 large onions, sliced
1 teaspoon Kashmiri chili flakes
4 garlic cloves, finely chopped
1 teaspoon sea salt
1¼ cups (10fl oz/300ml) heavy cream
6oz (175g) fresh shiitake mushrooms, halved
5 extra-large egg yolks (use the egg whites to make meringues, see page 206)
Sunflower oil, for greasing
Sea salt and freshly ground black pepper

1. In a saucepan, boil the potatoes in enough water to cover for 25 minutes or until soft. Then, holding the hot potatoes in a clean dish towel, peel them, then slice into disks about ¼ inch (5mm) thick.

2. Put the cabbage leaves into a saucepan of boiling salted water and boil for 1 minute to blanch them. Drain and put into a bowl of ice cold water. Let rest until completely cold. Drain and pat dry with paper towels.

3. Finely grind the cubebs, white peppercorns, and cumin seeds, using a mortar and pestle. Heat the butter and olive oil in a skillet. Add the onions and cook gently until soft. Add the spices, Kashmiri flakes, garlic, and salt, stir, and cook for 1 minute. Pour in the cream, turn up the heat, and bring to a boil, then simmer rapidly for 5 minutes. Add the mushrooms, stir, and pour the mixture into a heatproof bowl. Set aside to cool completely.

4. Preheat the oven to 350°F (180°C). Stir the egg yolks into the mushroom mixture, one at a time, and season with salt and ground pepper to taste. Add the potatoes and gently fold to combine everything together.

5. Lightly oil a 9 x 5 x 3-inch (23 x 10 x 7.5-cm) loaf pan and line its sides and bottom with the blanched cabbage leaves so that they overlap each other slightly and fall over the top. Reserve a couple of leaves to cover. Pour in the mushroom mixture and cover with the reserved leaves. Stand the pan in a roasting pan of hot water, cover with a sheet of moistened wax paper, and bake for 1 hour. Let cool in the pan for 10 minutes, then invert the pan onto a board. Cut the terrine into thick slices and serve immediately.

CELEBRATION LENTIL CABBAGE

SERVES 4

A little light olive oil
1 large onion, cut into ¼-inch
   (5-mm) dice
1 carrot, cut into ¼-inch
   (5-mm) dice
¼ head celery, cut into ⅜-inch
   (8-mm) slices, leaves
   reserved and finely sliced
   for garnish
3 Jerusalem artichokes,
   peeled and cut into ¼-inch
   (5-mm) slices
¼ small head celeriac, peeled
   and cut into ¼-inch
   (5-mm) dice
1 garlic clove, coarsely chopped
Seeds of 2 green cardamom pods
1 teaspoon black peppercorns
1 teaspoon cumin seeds
1¼ cups (9oz/250g) dried French
   Puy or green lentils, rinsed
¼ teaspoon finely ground mace
3 cups (26fl oz/750ml) vegetable
   stock or broth
3½ tablespoons (1¾oz/50g)
   butter, plus extra for greasing
1 teaspoon sea salt
2 small, tight green cabbages,
   halved through the root
2 teaspoon Kashmiri chili flakes
¼ cup (1oz/30g) all-purpose flour
1½ cups (12fl oz/350ml) milk
½ cup (3½fl oz/100ml)
   light cream
2 teaspoons horseradish cream
1¾oz (50g) hard sheep cheese
   or cow cheese, shredded

This dish can be made really quickly if the lentils are prepared in advance. The combination of nutty spiced lentils, bright cabbage, and the warmth of the spicy cream makes a wonderful vegetarian main dish.

1. Put a large saucepan over medium heat. Add a large slug of oil and the vegetables and garlic, then sauté gently for 5 minutes, stirring occasionally. Finely grind the whole spices, using a mortar and pestle.

2. Add the lentils and the spice mix and mace to the pan. Stir everything to coat in the oil, then add the vegetable stock or broth and 2 tablespoons (1oz/30g) of the butter, bring up to a boil, stir, cover, and simmer gently for 40 minutes or until the lentils have lost their bite. Stir in the salt and set aside.

3. Grease a large, shallow ovenproof dish, big enough to fit the cabbages snugly inside, and spoon in the warm lentils so that they're about ⅝ inch (1.5cm) thick over the bottom.

4. Put the cabbage halves in boiling salted water for 3 minutes to blanch them. Drain well, then lay them, evenly spaced, over the lentils in the dish, alternating top to bottom and gently pressing them into the lentils.

5. Preheat the broiler to medium. Put a large saucepan over medium heat, add the remaining butter, and stir lightly with a small whisk. When the butter has melted, add the Kasmiri flakes and flour, and whisk to combine. Cook for 30 seconds.

6. Pour the milk and cream into a small bowl, then pour it a little at a time into the pan, whisking all the time to combine well with the roux. Once all the liquid is in, add the horseradish. Keep whisking and let the sauce cook until you see the first bubbles appear, then continue to cook for 2 minutes.

7. Pour this spicy béchamel over the cabbage, sprinkle generously with shredded cheese, then put it under the broiler until the whole dish is piping hot and the sauce is a beautiful speckled golden brown. Remove from the broiler, sprinkle with the reserved celery leaves, and serve.

GRILLED CHILE CABBAGE

This chile and charred cabbage filled with spicy lamb is my lighter version of a chili dog. It's a great alternative for those days you don't want a carb overload. It can be a little messy to eat, but that's half the fun; just have a roll of paper towels on hand and you'll be fine!

SERVES 4

2 January King or savoy
    cabbages
3 tablespoons canola oil, plus
    extra for basting
3 onions (about 1lb 2oz/500g),
    thinly sliced, plus 1 small
    onion, finely chopped
3 garlic cloves, finely chopped
1 green finger chile, seeded and
    finely diced
½ teaspoon Kashmiri chili
    flakes
1 heaping teaspoon black
    peppercorns, finely ground
1 heaping teaspoon coriander
    seeds, finely ground
1 teaspoon powdered ginger
1 teaspoon powdered turmeric
1 heaping teaspoon sea salt
2¼lb (1kg) ground lamb
1 (14½-oz/400-g) can
    diced tomatoes
generous 1 cup (9oz/250g)
    crème fraîche or sour cream
1 cup (4½oz/125g) shredded
    cheddar cheese

1. Gently snap off six outer leaves from each cabbage, then cut out and discard the centered, woody veins. Put the leaves in a large saucepan of boiling salted water for 30–45 seconds to blanch them, then immediately put them in a bowl of ice cold water to cool completely.

2. Cut each cabbage in half through their poles, cut out the centered stem and discard, then slice the leaves thinly into ribbons. Set aside.

3. Put the oil a large saucepan over medium heat. Add the sliced onions and sauté gently until soft, then add the garlic, chile, and Kashmiri flakes, the spices, salt, and 2 small handfuls of the thinly sliced cabbage leaves. Sauté gently for 1 minute, until wilted.

4. Add the lamb and cook over medium heat, stirring, until the meat is only just no longer pink.

5. Add the tomatoes and mix well, then bring up to a boil and simmer over low heat for 20 minutes or until the meat is tender. Take the pan off the heat, add a generous ¾ cup (7oz/200g) of the crème fraîche or sour cream, and stir well. Put the pan back on the heat, bring back to a gentle simmer and cook for another 1 minute. Remove from the heat and set aside.

6. Preheat the broiler to high. Take the large cabbage leaves from the water, drain well, and pat dry with paper towels. Rub them with a little oil on both sides. Put them under the broiler and broil both sides briefly until just scorched. Repeat until all the leaves are done, then set aside.

7. In a small bowl, mix the cheese with the remaining crème fraîche and the chopped onions. Take a charred cabbage leaf, spoon on some of the lamb mixture, top with some of the cabbage ribbons, then the cheese mix. Put on the broiler pan and repeat until the pan is snugly full. Put under the heat, cook for 1 minute, until the cheese melts, then remove from the heat, gingerly roll up each leaf, and serve immediately.

ALOO TIKKI—POTATO FRITTERS WITH SIZZLED TOMATOES

My father often used to make us fried potato cakes when he got into the kitchen when our mother was out. They're a staple of any street-food vendor in northern India and a must-have whenever you're walking around the streets of Old Delhi in winter. This is my version— simple, effective, and totally delicious. If you have a splash guard, then I'd recommend using it here, because the tomato sauce really spits. A little messy, I grant you, but essential for the finished dish, so don't be tempted to turn down the heat—but do be careful not to burn it.

MAKES 8 PATTIES

4 Yukon Gold or russet potatoes
  (about 1lb 2 oz/500g), peeled
3–4 tablespoons sunflower oil
1 large onion, diced
⅓ cup (1oz/30g) finely grated
  fresh ginger
2 green chiles, seeded and finely
  chopped (use less if you
  don't want it too hot)
1 tablespoon Garam Masala
  blend (see page 267)
1 teaspoon powdered turmeric
2 teaspoons black mustard seeds
1 teaspoon sea salt
1 handful mint leaves, torn or
  chopped
1 small handful cilantro leaves,
  chopped

1. Put the potatoes into a saucepan and cover generously with water. Bring to a boil and boil for 20 minutes or until tender. Drain and lightly mash. Set aside.

2. Heat 1 tablespoon oil in a heavy skillet or sauté pan over medium heat. Add the onion and sauté gently for 3 minutes, then add the ginger and continue cooking until the onion is soft.

3. Add the chiles, the Garam Masala, turmeric, mustard seeds, and salt. Stir and cook for another 2 minutes, then turn off the heat, set aside, and let cool to lukewarm.

4. Add the herbs and mashed potatoes and mix throughly. Divide the potato mix into eight mounds, then form them into even balls.

5. Add a little more oil to the skillet over medium heat. When hot, add three or four balls. Gently press them down into flat but chunky patties and cook for about 10 minutes, until light brown on each side. Repeat until you've cooked all the potato fritters. Serve immediately with Sizzled Tomatoes (see page 182).

[*Continued*]

FOR THE SIZZLED TOMATOES

**3 tablespoons olive oil,
    plus a little extra**
1 garlic clove, thinly sliced
**1 (14½-oz/400-g) can whole
    roma or plum tomatoes,
    drained**
**1 pinch finely ground
    black pepper**
Sea salt

1. Put a large saucepan over medium–low heat. Add the olive oil and garlic slices and cook for a few minutes to soften without browning.

2. Add the tomatoes, ground pepper, and salt to taste, then turn up the heat and cook fiercely, stirring to make sure it doesn't burn.

3. The tomatoes will release all of their juices. When all the thin liquid has evaporated, add a splash more olive oil, adjust the seasoning, and serve hot.

VADA PAV—POTATO ROLLS

SERVES 6

FOR THE RELISHES

2 garlic bulbs, skin on

1 tablespoon light olive oil

3 tablespoons thick, black
    Indian tamarind paste

Juice of 1 lime

1 teaspoon sea salt

½ teaspoon cumin seeds,
    finely ground

½ teaspoon black peppercorns,
    finely ground

¼ teaspoon cayenne pepper

2½ tablespoons grated
    fresh ginger

A few tablespoons Chile, Cilantro
    & Lime Relish (see page 257)

FOR THE BATTER

5½ cups (1lb 2oz/500g)
    chickpea (besan) flour

Juice of 1 lime

1 teaspoon sea salt

FOR THE POTATO CAKES

4 Yukon gold or russet potatoes
    (about 1lb 2oz/500g), peeled

1 tablespoon light olive oil

1 large onion, diced

3½ tablespoons finely grated
    fresh ginger

1–2 green chiles, seeded and
    finely chopped

2 teaspoon black mustard seeds

1 teaspoon powdered turmeric

1 teaspoon sea salt

1 large handful cilantro leaves,
    torn or chopped

Sunflower oil, for deep-frying

6 soft rolls, cut almost in half,
    to serve

We were visiting cousins in Mumbai when they mentioned these potato rolls one night. The next morning they delivered about eight to us—fantastic! This is perfect street food; once thought of as a poor man's lunch, today the "Bombay Burger" is revered. It's traditionally served with three relishes: garlic, chile, and tamarind.

1. Preheat the oven to 350°F (180°C) and put the garlic in a small roasting pan. Roast for 30 minutes or until golden and softened. Cool, then pop the cloves out of their skins into a small bowl. Mix the roasted garlic with the oil and set aside. In another bowl, mix the tamarind paste, lime juice, salt, spices, and ginger and set aside.

2. Next, put the chickpea flour for the batter in a bowl and whisk in about 1¼ cups (10fl oz/300ml) cold water to make a batter that has a consistency a little thicker than heavy cream. Set aside.

3. Now for the cakes. Boil the potatoes for 20 minutes or until tender. Drain and coarsely mash, then set aside.

4. Heat the oil in heavy skillet or sauté pan over medium heat. Add the onion and sauté gently for 2–3 minutes, then add the ginger and continue cooking until the onion is soft. Add the chiles to taste, the mustard seeds, turmeric, and salt. Stir and cook for 2 minutes, then turn off the heat, set aside, and let cool until lukewarm.

5. Add the cilantro and mashed potatoes and mix throughly. Divide the potato mix into six mounds, then form each mound into a patty.

6. Pour the sunflower oil into an electric deep fryer set to 340°F (170°C). (Alternatively, pour the oil into a large saucepan until one-third full and heat it over medium heat. After 4–5 minutes, drop a cube of white bread into the hot oil. If it takes 3 seconds to turn golden brown, it's the right heat. If not, adjust the heat accordingly.) Dip each patty into the batter and coat well, drain off any excess batter, then gently lower into the hot oil. Don't crowd the pan; cook in two or three batches as required. Deep-fry until crisp and golden, then transfer to paper towels to drain.

7. Put a potato patty into a roll, coat with a little garlic relish, then serve with the tamarind and chile relishes.

ALLIUM CRISP

FOR THE SPICED BUTTER

2 teaspoons coriander seeds
2 teaspoons fennel seeds
2 teaspoons white peppercorns
3 cloves
1¼ sticks plus 1 tablespoon
    (5½oz/150g) unsalted butter,
    at room temperature
1 heaping teaspoon powdered
    ginger
1 teaspoon black onion
    (nigella) seeds
½ teaspoon powdered turmeric
Zest of ½ lemon
1 small handful parsley,
    leaves chopped
1 tablespoon brandy

FOR THE CRUMB TOPPING

3 cups (5½oz 150g) fresh
    bread crumbs
2 tablespoons olive oil
½ cup (1½oz/40g) finely grated
    fresh Parmesan cheese
½ teaspoon cayenne pepper
1 small handful chives, finely
    chopped

FOR THE ONIONS

4 onions, halved through the root,
    each half cut into 4 slices
4 red onions, halved through root,
    each half cut into 3 slices
5 banana shallots, halved
    through the root
2 leeks, cut on the diagonal into
    1½-inch (4-cm) pieces
Generous splash canola oil

Onions, shallots, and leeks—all members of the allium family—get together here in a spicy butter under a crumb topping. This is great as a side dish or a light dinner.

1. Preheat the oven to 375°F (190°C). Finely grind the whole spices for the spiced butter, using a mortar and pestle. In a small bowl, mix all the spiced butter ingredients together really well. Set aside.

2. In another small bowl, mix all the crumb ingredients. Set aside.

3. Put all the onions, shallots, and leeks, cut side up, into a large roasting pan or ovenproof dish, about 16 × 10 × 1¾ inches (40 × 25 × 4½cm), and splash a little of the oil over them. Put the pan on the middle shelf of the oven. Roast for 35–40 minutes, until just softening and becoming a little charred.

4. Remove the dish from the oven, give it a quick, gentle stir, dab the spiced butter all around it, then put it back in the oven for 5 minutes. Remove once more and sprinkle the crumb mixture evenly over the surface of the onions.

5. Put the dish back in the oven and cook for a final 5–10 minutes, or until the crumbs are golden brown and the butter begins to bubble up through the topping.

6. Let cool slightly and serve with crisp green salad greens.

BHARVA BAINGAN

This classic north Indian stuffed eggplant recipe was described to me in full by both a cousin and an aunt when I was last visiting India. Here's my version—taking equal influence from both sources, you understand! It's a delicious veggie accompaniment to a meal, or is great served simply with flatbread, chile, and cucumber raita.

SERVES 4 AS A SIDE DISH

2 onions
4 teaspoons cumin seeds
1 tablespoon coriander seeds
2 teaspoons fennel seeds
¼ teaspoon asafetida resin
Sea salt
⅓ cup (2½ fl oz/75ml)
    mustard oil
8–10 baby eggplants, halved
    along two-thirds of their
    length, but held together
    at the stem
1½ teaspoons amchoor

1. Grate the onions coarsely into a strainer over a bowl. Discard any juices in the bowl. Finely grind the cumin, coriander, and fennel seeds, using a mortar and pestle. In a bowl, mix the ground spices with the asafetida, grated onion, and salt to taste. Set aside.

2. Heat the oil in a large skillet over medium heat, add the eggplants, and sauté for 5–8 minutes.

3. Remove the pan from the heat and carefully stuff the eggplants, spooning the spiced onion mix into the cut slits. Let any excess fall into the pan. Lie them on their sides in the pan and return it to the heat. (Some of the stuffing will escape during cooking, but that's all part and package of this dish.)

4. Cover and cook for 12–15 minutes, turning the eggplants over halfway through, until the oil separates from the onion mix and the eggplants are beginning to collapse. Remove the lid, sprinkle with the amchoor and a pinch of salt, then turn up the heat and cook to finish off for 2 minutes. Serve immediately.

SUMMER VEGETABLES

SUMMER VEGETABLES ARE DELICATE CREATURES OF THE LIGHT. NATURE GETS ALL EXCITED AT THIS TIME OF YEAR and brings out an array of dazzling colors and amazing flavors. It's that feeling of abundance and rich color I'm trying to reflect throughout the recipes in this chapter, mingling subtle fresh flavors with a light touch. Star anise and saffron compete for aromatic dominance, yet combine elegantly and wonderfully; add cumin's earthy sweetness, black pepper's rounded heat, long pepper's off-the-wall perfume, clove's fruitiness for a twist; cayenne for intense red color and heat.

At the beginning of the season, fava beans are at their best, sweet and tender. My Fava Beans and Anchovy Eggs takes a classic mix of flavors as its starting point, but the spices I've used take it in another direction. The long pepper and clove add high-note sunshine sparkle to the grounding effect of turmeric, with a touch of cayenne added as a little "devilment."

One of my all-time summer favorite salads has to be the Niçoise. Soft-boiled eggs with yolks oozing, anchovies, green beans, olives, and a good coating of lemon dressing. I've rolled the tuna in coriander, Sichuan, and black pepper to add zesty zing to the firm flesh, added a lightly spiced saffron aioli and put it all into lightly charred olive bread for a slight bitter note and crisp texture.

In my Charentes Cold Plate, the black pepper-peach dressing with a splash of vodka, melon, and a touch of saffron all bring heady perfume and suggest the height of summer lunch decadence. Fresh black pepper adds both perfume and an underlying heat to the peach dressing; black ripe olives provide a salty hit, toasted almonds add sweet crunch.

Playing on physical sensations of hot and cold, my Heritage Soup uses green cardamom to accentuate the natural sweetness of zucchini and add a heady pine perfume that works so well with the denser, creamier, warm potato soup. I recommend you serve this with a glass of chilled Albariño, Picpoul de Pinet, or the much-maligned Muscadet.

Previous page: Star anise adds richness, perfume, and depth and can broaden out deep notes to provide a firm foundation to many dishes.

Fava Beans & Anchovy Eggs with Crisp Pancetta

A celebration of summer eating—so simple, yet so delicious. Accented with the flavors of lemon and chervil, it's the perfect summer lunch appetizer, best enjoyed in the open air.

SERVES 4

9 eggs
12 slices pancetta
1 cup (5½oz/150g) shelled fresh fava beans (about 3¼lb/1.5kg pods)
1 (1¾-oz/50-g) can Spanish Ortiz anchovy fillets in olive oil, drained and oil reserved
2 teaspoons best-quality mayonnaise
1 clove, finely ground
½ teaspoon powdered turmeric
7 gratings long pepper
½ teaspoon cayenne pepper, plus extra for dusting
1 small handful curly parsley leaves, finely chopped
12 chervil sprigs, plus chervil leaves to garnish
Sea salt

FOR THE LEMON DRESSING
3 tablespoons fruity olive oil
Juice of ½ lemon
1 pinch sea salt

1. Preheat the oven to 375°F (190°C). Put the eggs into a large saucepan of boiling water, bring back to a boil, and cook for 6 minutes. Drain and refill the pan with cold water. Drain and refill the pan again, then drain again. Peel off the shells and cut the eggs in half. They should have a soft center. Lay the pancetta on a baking sheet, cover with another baking sheet, and bake for 7–10 minutes, until crisp. Set aside.

2. Put the beans into a saucepan of boiling salted water for 1 minute to blanch them, then drain and plunge them into ice cold water. Peel off the outer skins and discard. Set the beans aside on a plate.

3. Put six of the egg halves and all the yolks in a bowl and crush them with a fork. Add a tiny drizzle of the anchovy oil, the mayonnaise, spices, and four anchovy fillets, then work everything together into a coarse paste.

4. Add the parsley, mix to combine well, then spoon into a pastry bag with a fluted tip. Put into the refrigerator.

5. Put all the lemon dressing ingredients into a screw-top jar and add 4 teaspoons cold water. Shake well, then set aside.

6. Take the 12 remaining egg halves, season with a little salt, then pipe the anchovy paste generously onto each egg half. Dust with a little cayenne pepper. Set aside.

7. In a small bowl, coat the fava beans with the dressing, then arrange them along the center of a long plate. Dress with chervil sprigs, then put the egg halves on the beans. Lean the pancetta crisps against the eggs and garnish generously with chervil leaves.

NIÇOISE PAN BAGNAT

Pan bagnat is a wonderful sandwich that encapsulates the spirit of the Côte d'Azur. It's all about classic Provençal flavors and textures, layered between olive oil bread. Salade Niçoise is one of my favorites; here it is, in a sandwich. Preparation is the key here: searing tuna, soft-boiling eggs, making aioli, etc. The king of all sandwiches, it takes a little time to construct—so take a deep breath and off we go.

MAKES 2–3 SANDWICHES

2 eggs

1 handful extra-fine green beans

2 teaspoons black peppercorns

½ teaspoon Sichuan pepper

2 teaspoons coriander seeds

5½ oz (150g) fresh yellowfin tuna loin

1 fresh ciabatta loaf

2 teaspoon pitted and coarsely chopped green olives

2 ripe plum or roma tomatoes, thinly sliced

1 small romaine lettuce, shredded

1 red onion, thinly sliced

1 small handful basil leaves

1 small bunch arugula

1 (1¾-oz/50-g) can Spanish Ortiz anchovy fillets in olive oil, drained and oil reserved

1. Put the eggs into a large saucepan of boiling water and boil for 3½ minutes. Drain and refill the pan with cold water. Drain and refill the pan again, then drain again. Peel off the shells and slice each egg into six.

2. Steam the green beans for 5 minutes or until just soft, then cool and cut in half. Coarsely grind the peppercorns and coriander seeds, using a mortar and pestle.

3. Put a ridged grill pan or heavy skillet over high heat. Transfer the coarsely ground spices to a plate, roll the tuna loin in the spices to coat it well all over, then put on the pan for 30–45 seconds on each side to sear the tuna rare. Slice thinly and set aside.

FOR THE LEMON DRESSING

2 garlic cloves
1 pinch sea salt
Juice of 1 lemon
⅓ cup (2½ fl oz/75ml) fruity olive oil
1 tablespoon anchovy oil from the pan (see above)
½ teaspoon black peppercorns, finely ground

FOR THE SAFFRON AIOLI

1 Yukon Gold or russet potato, unpeeled
4 saffron threads
1 garlic clove
1 pinch sea salt
1 large egg yolk
2–3 tablespoons fruity olive oil, or more if needed
Juice of 1 lemon

4. To make the dressing, chop the garlic with the salt until it forms a paste. In a small bowl, mix all the dressing ingredients with a fork to bring them together. Set aside.

5. To make the aioli, put the potato in a saucepan and cover generously with water. Boil for 20 minutes or until tender. Peel and cool. Meanwhile, put the saffron in a bowl and add 1 teaspoon warm water.

6. Chop the garlic with the salt until it forms a paste. In a small bowl, combine the potato, saffron and its soaking liquid, egg yolk, and garlic, gently working them into a smooth paste, using a fork. Drizzle in the olive oil while whisking with a fork until the aioli has a lovely velvety texture. Add the lemon juice and salt to taste. Set aside.

7. Preheat the broiler to hot or return the ridged grill pan to a high heat. Cut the bread in half horizontally and put under the broiler or on the pan to lightly toast or char the cut surfaces. Drizzle 2–3 teaspoons lemon dressing over the bottom half of the loaf to moisten it, then spread the chopped green olives on top, followed by the saffron aioli.

8. Now for the layers: First add the sliced tomatoes, then the lettuce, sliced eggs, and beans, and drizzle with a little more lemon dressing. Next, add the sliced seared tuna, then the sliced onion, basil leaves, arugula leaves, and finally a single line of anchovies.

9. Cover the sandwich with the top half of the loaf and press down gently. Put an upturned plate on top of the loaf and let rest for 10 minutes. Slice the loaf into two or three pieces and serve.

My Bologna Sandwiches

Modena, the home of Ferrari, is where I got the inspiration for this delicious finger sandwich. It's a superb combination of flavors and textures—crushed peas, mortadella, Bel Paese cheese, and anise mayo—and simple to construct. Perfect for afternoon gatherings or canapés.

SERVES 2 HUNGRY PEOPLE

1 tablespoon light olive oil

3 star anise, slightly cracked

2 teaspoons finely chopped
    shallots

½ cup (3oz/85g) thawed frozen
    or canned small young peas

2 teaspoons good-quality
    mayonnaise

1 teaspoon finely chopped
    tarragon leaves

8 slices good-quality white
    bread, sliced ⅜ inch
    (8mm) thick

4 wafer-thin slices mortadella or
    Italian cooked ham

½ teaspoon black peppercorns,
    finely ground

A little sea salt

4 Bel Paese portions, or any
    soft cheese

1. Put the oil into a small saucepan and sauté the star anise over gentle heat for 5 minutes.

2. Add the shallots and continue to cook for 3 minutes or until they're only just soft. Add 3 tablespoons water; the mixture will thicken and emulsify slightly. Remove the star anise, then add the peas and cook for 2 minutes or until soft.

3. Remove the pan from the heat and dip the bottom into a bowl of iced water. When the peas are completely cold, crush them with a fork, then add the mayonnaise and tarragon and gently mix them together.

4. Spread a thick layer of the pea mixture over four slices of the bread, then top with the mortadella or ham. Season the remaining four slices with ground pepper and just a sprinkle of sea salt, then spread on the Bel Paese and sandwich together with the ham-topped slices. Gently press the bread down, then cover and chill for 45 minutes, until the mixture is firm.

5. Using a serrated knife, remove the crusts and cut into thin rectangles or triangles, trying not to squeeze out the mixture as you work. Serve with a chilled glass of something you love; they're the perfect apéritif foil.

CHARENTE COLD PLATE

Refreshing, summery, and full of flavor, this is my "sunshine-on-a-plate."

SERVES 4

½ cup (3½oz/100g) sugar
2 peaches
½ teaspoon black peppercorns, finely ground
1 tablespoon vodka
1 small handful blanched almonds
⅓ cup (2¾oz/75g) dried French Puy or green lentils
12 saffron threads
Juice of ½ lemon
½ fennel bulb, thinly sliced, feathery tops reserved
1 large carrot, shaved into ribbons with a vegetable peeler
½ Charentais melon or cantaloupe, balled with a melon baller
7 pitted black ripe olives, finely chopped
1 small handful pine nuts
A generous splash best-quality fruity olive oil
1 large handful fresh mint leaves, some finely chopped, a few left whole

1. Put ⅓ cup (2½fl oz/75ml) water and the sugar into a saucepan, stir, and put over medium heat. Skin the peaches, one at a time, by scoring a cross into the bottom of each fruit and putting it into boiling water for 1 minute; carefully remove the peach and peel away the skin. Halve and pit the peaches and chop them coarsely, reserving any juices.

2. Once the sugar has dissolved, add the peach pieces, their juices, and the black pepper to the pan and let to simmer gently for 5–8 minutes.

3. Take off the heat, pour in the vodka, then transfer to a food processor or blender and process to a smooth paste. Let cool, then put the mixture into the refrigerator to chill completely.

4. Put the almonds into a small saucepan and dry-toast them over medium heat until golden. Let cool, then coarsely chop. Set aside.

5. Put the lentils into a small saucepan, cover well with cold water, and put over high heat. Bring to a boil, then turn down the heat and simmer gently for 15 minutes or until cooked but still with a little bite. Drain, rinse under cold water, then set aside to cool completely.

6. Put the saffron into a small bowl, add 2 tablespoons hot water, and set aside to steep for at least 15 minutes, then add the lemon juice and stir.

7. To assemble the plate, arrange the fennel, the feathery fennel tops, and the carrots on a large serving plate, then add the melon balls and drizzle generously with the peach puree. Sprinkle with the olives, pine nuts, and lentils, then spoon the saffron and its soaking water over the salad. Finish off with a splash or two of the olive oil, sprinkle with the mint, and serve immediately.

HERITAGE SOUP

SERVES 4–6

*Two soups in one bowl. The earthy, creamy potato soup
is served hot, the delicate zucchini and cardamom
soup is chilled, making a wonderful contrast of hot
and cold, creamy and dense, and light and fragrant.*

FOR THE POTATO SOUP

**5 new potatoes, peeled and cut
    into chunks**
**1¼ sticks plus 1 tablespoon
    (5½oz/150g) unsalted butter**
1 onion, cut into chunks
1 leek, white only, cut into chunks
**2½ cups (1 pint/600ml)
    whole milk**
**½ cup (3½fl oz/100ml)
    heavy cream**
1 teaspoon sea salt
**A little freshly ground
    white pepper**

1. Put the potatoes into a large saucepan over medium–low heat and add
the butter. Cover and cook them gently for 30 minutes, stirring frequently.

2. Add the onion and leek, then cover and cook gently for another
15 minutes. Add the milk and 1¼ cups (10fl oz/300ml) water, bring to
a gentle simmer, and let simmer gently, uncovered, for 25 minutes. Add
the cream, then pour the mixture into a food processor or blender and
process until smooth and creamy. Season with salt and ground pepper to
taste. Set aside.

FOR THE ZUCCHINI &
CARDAMOM SOUP

**1¼ sticks plus 1 tablespoon
    (5½oz/150g) unsalted
    butter, chilled**
4 small zucchini, thinly sliced
3 shallots, finely chopped
**Seeds of 6–8 green cardamom
    pods, finely ground**
**3 handfuls spinach, thick fibrous
    stems removed**
1 cup (7fl oz/200ml) buttermilk

1. Put a shallow saucepan over medium–low heat and add 7 tablespoons
(3½oz/100g) of the butter. Add the zucchini, shallots, and most of the
ground cardamom and cook gently for 10 minutes or until the vegetables
are really soft. Try not to brown the vegetables at all. Add the spinach
and let it wilt, then remove the pan from the heat and let cool completely.
Chill for at least 10 minutes.

2. Put everything into a food processor or blender and process, then add
the buttermilk, the remaining cold butter, and the remaining ground
cardamom. Process again until it's really smooth and glossy.

3. Cover and put it into the refrigerator until ready to serve.

TO SERVE

**Seeds of 2 green cardamom
    pods, finely ground**
8–12 chervil sprigs

1. Heat the potato soup until hot, but not boiling. Check the seasoning
and adjust it, if necessary. Meanwhile, whisk the zucchini soup or quickly
process it with an immersion blender to froth it—like a cappuccino.
Check the seasoning. Ladle the potato soup into warmed bowls, then
pour on the chilled zucchini soup. Garnish with a light dusting of green
cardamom and a couple of sprigs of fresh chervil—beautiful, simple, and
delicious! Serve with warm soda bread.

Just Raw Salad

A superb, fresh and strikingly beautiful salad to serve as an appetizer, main dish, or when you want to treat yourself or friends to a light snack bursting with vibrant flavors. Just be careful if you're using a mandoline slicer and avoid nipping your fingertips.

SERVES 2

2 heritage golden and candy-
    striped beets, peeled
3 carrots
7–8 radishes
1 fennel bulb, trimmed
1 star anise, finely ground
⅓ cup (2½ fl oz/75ml) extra
    virgin olive oil
2 tablespoons lemon juice
1 small dried red Thai chile,
    crumbled
½ teaspoon coarsely ground
    black pepper
Sea salt
1 fresh pomegranate, halved
1¾–3½ oz (50–100g) strong
    crumbly goat cheese
Generous bunch of flat-leaf
    parsley, finely chopped
1 small handful pea shoots,
    stems removed

1. Using a mandoline slicer or a sharp knife, being careful, very thinly slice the beets, carrots, radishes, and fennel, then put them all in a bowl.

2. Add the star anise, olive oil, and lemon juice, then sprinkle in the chile, black pepper, and salt to taste. Let the salad rest for 5 minutes, then toss everything together. Transfer to a serving plate.

3. Hold a pomegranate half in one hand just above a small bowl, cut side down. With your other hand, firmly and repeatedly strike the pomegranate with a wooden spoon to release the seeds and juice into the bowl.

4. Remove any white pith from the seeds, then sprinkle them over the salad, followed by the gorgeous red juices.

5. Now, just crumble the goat cheese over the top, sprinkle the parsley over that, and top with the pea shoots. Serve immediately.

BAKED EGGPLANTS WITH CRUMBLY GOAT CHEESE

Simple earthy flavors make this a great snack or addition to a picnic basket or a summer salad table.

SERVES 4

2 teaspoon cumin seeds

4 eggplants

2 tablespoons extra virgin olive oil, plus extra for drizzling

1 red finger chile, seeded and finely diced

Juice of 1 lemon

Olive oil, for broiling

1 teaspoon sea salt

1 small handful flat-leaf parsley, finely chopped

6oz (175g) crumbly local goat cheese, or Valençay St. Maure

1. Put the cumin seeds into a small saucepan and lightly dry-toast over medium heat to release their aroma. Lightly crush them in a mortar and pestle, and set aside.

2. Cut the eggplants in half lengthwise and gently score the exposed flesh to create a crisscross pattern on each half.

3. In a small bowl, mix the olive oil with the chile and lemon juice, then set aside.

4. Preheat the oven to 400°F (200°C). Put a ridged grill pan over high heat until it's hot. Rub a little olive oil on the exposed flesh of the eggplant halves, then put them, cut side down, in the ridged grill pan and cook for 3 minutes. Turn them over and cook their skins for another 1 minute.

5. Take the eggplants from the pan and put them into a large roasting pan or baking sheet, flesh side up. Put the roasting pan on a high shelf in the oven and cook the eggplants for 15 minutes. Take them out, drizzle them with half the chile-lemon juice mixture, then put them back into the oven and cook until they have collapsed and are soft.

6. Put the eggplants onto a warmed serving plate and drizzle with olive oil. Sprinkle evenly with the salt, the toasted cumin seeds, and parsley, then crumble the cheese on top. Serve immediately.

WINTER FRUIT

WINTER FRUITS, COMFORT AND SPICE. Fruit and nuts foraged from the countryside or fresh from farmers' markets, and their tropical cousins oranges, pomegranates, and passion fruits. Match their sweet notes with creamy floral vanilla or heady cinnamon, or lift the fruit with the sweet floral astringency of rose or saffron, the menthol perfume of green cardamom or aromatic star anise.

Plums and Miso Candied Pistachios is a fireside feast. Sticky umami pistachios, soft plum flesh, rich mascarpone warmed with black pepper and scented with rose and vanilla. Because food tends to be a little heavier at this time of year, this sweet treat stands out as a dish of indulgence with little guilt factor. In absolute contrast, I created the Chestnut Meringue, combining sweet, light meringue with a dense chestnut mousse, made brighter with green cardamom and rose, warmed and rounded out with cinnamon, and served with pears poached in a sugar syrup "spiced" with whiskey.

For winter fruit colors, I think of rusty reds, deep oranges, mellow yellows, and nutty browns. Main spice notes are perfumed and fruity, earthy, rich and floral. These characteristics work to enrich the depth of flavor and bring out both the sultry character and the unique richness winter fruits offer.

I based my Cornmeal Tea Cake on my friend Stefano's recipe; I love the simplicity of the method. For my version of this classic combination of north Italian ingredients (where they use polenta, very similar to a medium-to-coarse cornmeal), I add fruity notes of clementine and dried cherries, and plenty of perfumed oomph with the spicing: clove to back up the fruit, fennel for a comforting anise twist, black pepper for depth, and green cardamom for a high-end "ping." I pair the cake with a passion fruit mascarpone cream to focus attention on all the fruity flavors.

Previous page: The floral astringency of rose balances and contrasts with its sweet, heady perfume. Wonderful with windfall apples and blackberries, or use to lift the richness of cream and mascarpone to serve with fruity desserts.

Celeriac & Beets with Blood Orange & Walnut

This side dish works well with game or beef. It's zingy, textured, and earthy, with a healthy sprinkling of spice for good measure. You can prepare the vegetables and the dressing ahead; when you're ready to serve, put the vegetables back in the oven to heat up and follow step 4.

SERVES 4

3 beets (a mix of heritage
    varieties is great), peeled,
    halved though the poles, then
    each half cut into wedges
½ celeriac (about 9oz/250g), cut
    into 1-inch (2.5-cm) dice
Generous splash canola oil
2 teaspoons sea salt
2 blood oranges

FOR THE DRESSING
⅔ cup (2¾oz/75g) walnuts
2 tablespoons honey
⅓ cup (1oz/30g) peeled and
    finely grated fresh ginger
1 tablespoon white wine vinegar
Juice of ½ lemon
1 tablespoon silver tequila
1 star anise, finely ground
1 teaspoon black peppercorns,
    finely ground
2 teaspoons black cumin seeds
½ teaspoon carom seeds
7 gratings long pepper
½ teaspoon sea salt
1 large handful curly parsley,
    leaves finely chopped

1. Preheat the oven to 350°F (180°C). Put the beets, celeriac, oil, and salt into a roasting pan and mix to coat all the ingredients. Roast for 35–40 minutes, until the vegetables are just becoming soft without being too squishy.

2. Meanwhile, using a sharp knife, slice of the tops and bottoms of the oranges, then cut off the peel and pith. Cut 1 orange into ¾-inch (2-cm) disks, and for the second orange cut between the membrane into individual segments. Remove all the seeds but reserve the juice.

3. For the dressing, put the walnuts into a small saucepan and dry-toast over medium heat until lightly browned. Chop coarsely. Put the honey, ginger, vinegar, lemon juice, tequila, and ground and whole spices into a small saucepan. Put over medium heat, bring up to a boil, and simmer gently for 1 minute, stirring. Remove from the heat, add the salt and reserved orange juice, stir, then add the parsley and stir briefly to combine.

4. Remove the vegetables from the oven and immediately, but carefully, stir in the orange disks. Drizzle with the dressing, sprinkle the walnuts over the vegetables, and spread the orange segments over the top.

PLUMS & MISO CANDIED PISTACHIOS WITH ROSE VODKA SAUCE

This is a delicious combination of taste and texture and the most wonderful of light, fruity desserts. The miso pistachio nuts are something I came up with after a trip to meet my friend Ben at the Nordic Food Lab in Copenhagen. They add crunch, with a subtle umami twist. Try to find plums that are really ripe, juicy, and ready for eating. Using different varieties of plums makes presentation that much more intriguing.

SERVES 4

2 cups (9oz/250g) pistachio nuts

Sunflower oil, for greasing

1 tablespoon miso paste (sweet white is good, but any good-quality miso is fine)

¼ cup (2fl oz/50ml) honey

12 plums in a variety of colors, including red, purple, green, and/or yellow

At least 24 juicy blackberries

1 vanilla bean, split lengthwise

¾ cup (6oz/175g) mascarpone cheese

2 teaspoons rose water

1 teaspoon black peppercorns, finely ground

1 tablespoon vodka

⅓ cup (3oz/85g) firmly packed light brown sugar

1. Preheat the oven to 300°F (150°C). Put the pistachio nuts onto an oiled baking sheet and cook on the middle shelf of the oven for 10 minutes. Meanwhile, in a small bowl, mix the miso paste with 1 tablespoon water, stir, then add the honey and stir again to combine well.

2. Take the warm nuts from the oven and put them into the miso bowl, stir well, then put the mixture back onto the baking sheet. Return it to the oven and cook for 5–10 minutes, until the nuts start to brown slightly. Take them out, pour them onto a plate, and set aside to cool.

3. Preheat the broiler to high. Cut each plum in half, removing and discarding the pits. Put the plums, hollow side up, on a shallow baking sheet, then put a blackberry or two into each plum half.

4. Scrape out the seeds from the vanilla bean. In a bowl, mix together the mascarpone, rose water, pepper, vodka, and vanilla seeds. Carefully spoon the creamy mixture over the plums, sprinkle with the sugar, and put the baking sheet onto the top rack of your broiler. Broil for 15–20 minutes, until the plums just begin to collapse.

5. Spoon the plums and as much of the gorgeously gooey mascarpone mix as you desire onto a large, warmed serving plate, top generously with the miso pistachio nuts, and let everyone dig in!

CHESTNUT MERINGUE

With its saffron-poached pears, whiskey syrup, and whipped cream, this is a wonderfully indulgent winter treat. I love meringues, and this method is simple to get right. The mousse, fruit, and syrup make it something really special.

SERVES 4

FOR THE PEARS
3½ cups (1½lb/700g) demerara or other raw sugar
12 saffron threads
2 strips of lemon zest, pared with a veg peeler
6 Comice pears, peeled, cored, and each cut into 4 slices
¼ cup (2fl oz/50ml) whiskey

FOR THE MERINGUE
6 extra-large egg whites
1¾ cups (12oz/350g) superfine sugar

1. To cook the pears, put the sugar and 1¼ cups (10fl oz/300ml) water into a heavy saucepan. Stir once, then put over medium heat until the sugar has dissolved, swirling the pan from time to time, but do not stir. Add the saffron and lemon zest, and gently swirl the pan a little more.

2. Add the pears and cover with a piece of wax paper. Turn the heat down to a gentle constant simmer, and cook for 15–20 minutes, until the fruit softens and becomes translucent—just so that there's no resistance when you poke them with the tip of a sharp knife.

3. Remove the pears with a slotted spoon and put them onto a wire rack over a plate to collect the juices. Turn up the heat under the pan, reduce the syrup by half, and then pour in the whiskey. Swirl the pan to combine, and set aside.

4. To make the meringue, preheat the oven to 325°F (160°C). Line a baking sheet with a sheet of parchment paper. Put the egg whites and sugar into a clean, grease-free bowl and whisk to form smooth, stiff, glossy peaks—12–15 minutes with an electric handheld mixer.

5. Put a small dab of meringue mixture under the four corners of the parchment to stick it to the baking sheet. Take a large metal spoon and dollop the meringue onto the parchment paper to form a large doughnut-type shape about 8 inches (20cm) in diameter. Be a little creative with your meringue by shaping the edges of the ring into turretlike peaks.

6. Put it into the oven and bake for 10 minutes, then turn the oven down to 275°F (140°C) and continue to bake for another 50 minutes, then remove from the oven and set aside to cool completely.

FOR THE MOUSSE

2⅔ cups (14oz/400g) cooked and peeled chestnuts

¾ cup (6fl oz/175ml) whole milk, plus extra if needed

1 tiny pinch sea salt

2 extra-large egg yolks

¾ cup (6oz/175g) firmly packed light brown sugar

¼ cup (2¼oz/60g) crème fraîche or Greek yogurt

½ cup (3½fl oz/100ml) heavy cream, plus extra whipped cream to serve

1 teaspoon dried rose petals, finely chopped

Seeds of 3 green cardamom pods, finely ground

1 teaspoon finely ground cinnamon

7. For the mousse, put the chestnuts, milk, and salt into a saucepan. Put the saucepan over medium heat, partly cover, and bring to a gentle simmer. Simmer gently for 10 minutes or until the chestnuts are soft.

8. Put the chestnuts and hot milk into a blender or food processor and process to a smooth puree. You may need to add a little more milk so that you end up with a thick, but only just pliable, paste. Transfer to a bowl and put a sheet of plastic wrap on the paste's surface. Set aside to cool.

9. Meanwhile, put the egg yolks into a mixing bowl and, using an electric handheld mixer, whip until they become pale and fluffy. Set aside.

10. Put the brown sugar and ½ cup (4fl oz/125ml) water into a saucepan and stir throughly just once. Put the pan over medium heat and simmer gently to make a clear syrup. After 5 minutes, take a metal spoon, dip it into the sugar solution, then raise the spoon to about the same level as the rim of the pan, tilt the spoon, and let the syrup fall from the spoon back into the pan. Repeat until you see a gloopy drop fall from the spoon. It should no longer run freely but be more like molten preserves; this is the soft ball stage.

11. Remove the pan from the heat. Using your electric mixer, immediately pour the hot sugar syrup into the egg yolks, whisking constantly. Keep whisking for 5 minutes or until the mixture has cooled. Set aside.

12. Make sure the chestnut paste is at room temperature, then add it to the yolk mixture and mix in. Add the crème fraîche and mix again. Whip the cream to soft peaks, then fold the cream and spices into the chestnut mixture and mix throughly but gently to combine. Put the meringue on a large serving plate and spoon the mousse into the center, arrange the pear segments on the mousse, drizzle with the whiskey sauce, and serve with a little whipped cream.

CORNMEAL TEA CAKE

Although this is simple to make, it does take a little patience to cook and cool but it produces a totally satisfying, deep-crust crunch with an addictive, moist center and delicious cornmeal bite. I've used the spices here to brighten up the richness and add some oomph to the subtle, zesty clementine flavor.

MAKES ABOUT 20 SLICES

2 teaspoons fennel seeds

5 cloves

Seeds of 5 green cardamom pods

1 teaspoon coriander seeds

1 teaspoon black peppercorns

⅔ cup (3½oz/100g) dried
    cherries, halved

1⅔ cups (8oz/225g) cornmeal

1 cup (7oz/200g) demerara or
    other raw sugar

1 pinch sea salt

1⅓ cups (6oz/175g)
    all-purpose flour

1 teaspoon baking powder

1 teaspoon baking soda

½ cup (1¾oz/50g) walnuts,
    coarsely chopped

3 clementines

1 cup (9oz/250g) ricotta cheese

7 tablespoon (3½oz/100g)
    unsalted butter, melted,
    plus extra for greasing

1 large egg white

TO SERVE

¾ cup (7oz/200g) mascarpone
    cheese

Pulp and seeds of 2 passion
    fruits

1 teaspoon confectioners' sugar,
    sifted

1. Preheat the oven to 340°F (170°C). Lightly butter a 9 x 5 x 3-inch (23 x 10 x 7.5-cm) loaf pan, line it with wax paper, and butter it again.

2. Finely grind the spices, using a mortar and pestle. Add the cherries to the spices and mix to coat them throughly.

3. Put the cornmeal, sugar, and salt into a large bowl and mix together, then sift in the flour, baking powder, and baking soda. Add the walnuts, spices, and cherries, and mix well to combine. Grate the zest of the clementines into the same bowl and mix well.

4. Put the ricotta in a separate bowl, give it a quick whisk, then add 1 cup (9fl oz/250ml) water and the melted butter. Squeeze in the juice of two of the clementines. Whisk again.

5. Pour the wet ingredients into the dry ingredients, stirring with a wooden spoon or rubber spatula. Mix the batter well, stirring, and scraping the bottom and sides of the bowl until you have an unctuous mixture.

6. In a clean, grease-free bowl, whisk the egg white to stiff peaks. Carefully fold it into the batter, then pour the batter into your lined loaf pan. Put the loaf on a middle shelf of the oven and bake for 1 hour 20 minutes or until a toothpick inserted into the center comes out clean.

7. Remove the pan from the oven and put it on a wire rack. Let the loaf cool for 30 minutes, then turn it out of the pan to cool completely. Carefully tear away the wax paper. Store in a cake container for up to one week, or freeze for up to two months.

8. To serve, mix the mascarpone, passion-fruit pulp and seeds, and confectioners' sugar together in a bowl. Slice the cake and serve with a dollop of the passion fruit mascarpone or a thick layer of butter.

BLACKBERRY, APPLE & COMICE PEAR COMPOTE

This is an especially simple dessert. It's fruity, light, and packed full of generous flavors with virtually no guilt factor attached. As such, it makes the perfect New Year's Day dessert for when you might still be reeling from your enjoyment of Christmas meals and New Year's party excesses.

SERVES 4–6

3½ cups (1½lb/700g) demerara
    or other sugar
1 star anise, lightly crushed
2 green cardamom pods, crushed
3 cloves
4 black peppercorns, crushed
½ teaspoon Sichuan pepper
½ teaspoon dried rose petals,
    finely chopped
2 strips of lemon zest, pared
    with a vegetable peeler
2 crisp, sweet apples, such as
    Pippin, Pink Lady, Jonathan,
    or Golden Delicious, peeled,
    cored, and each cut into
    16 thin slices
4 pears, such as Comice, peeled,
    cored, and each cut into
    8 slices
1 cup (5½oz/150g) blackberries,
    fresh or thawed frozen
Thick cream (optional),
    to serve

1. Put the sugar and 1¼ cups (10fl oz/300ml) water into a heavy saucepan, stir to combine, then put over medium heat until the sugar has dissolved, swirling the pan from time to time but not stirring.

2. Add the spices and strips of lemon zest, and gently swirl the pan a little more.

3. Add the apples and pears and cover with a piece of wax paper. Turn the heat down to a gentle constant simmer, and cook for 10–15 minutes, until the fruit softens and becomes translucent—just so that there's no resistance when you poke them with the tip of a sharp knife.

4. Remove the fruit slices from the pan, using a slotted spoon, and put them on a plate to rest. Turn the heat up under the pan and reduce the syrup by half.

5. Next, carefully pour the syrup through a fine strainer, discard the spices and zest, then return the syrup to the pan and heat gently. When warm to the touch, add the blackberries, then return the cooked pears and apples to the syrup and warm through for no more than 30 seconds. Turn off the heat and transfer to a serving bowl.

6. Serve immediately with a couple of generous dollops of thick cream or my Slaked Passion-fruit Ice (see opposite) and dig in.

SLAKED PASSION-FRUIT ICE

I call this slaked ice, not sorbet, because I'm using milk—like a sherbet—instead of water. It's a really refreshing dessert. I came up with this idea when I wanted something a little lighter than ice cream. It's a kind of guilt-free version, with a little lactic hit and a beautiful floral punch.

SERVES 10–12

3 cups (26fl oz/750ml)
    whole milk
10 saffron threads
4 extra-large eggs, separated
2 cups (14oz/400g) superfine or
    granulated sugar
scant ½ cup (3½fl oz/100ml)
    strained lemon juice (from
    2 lemons)
Pulp of 10 passion fruits,
    rubbed through a strainer
    to remove the seeds

1. Put ⅓ cup (2½fl oz/75ml) of the milk and the saffron into a small saucepan. Put over medium heat until you see a gentle shimmer, then take off the heat and let steep and cool completely.

2. In a small bowl, lightly whisk the remaining milk with the cooled saffron milk, then add the egg yolks and whisk well. Add the sugar, lemon juice, and passion fruit pulp. Mix well, then set the bowl aside.

3. In a clean, grease-free bowl, whisk the egg whites to form stiff peaks, then add them to the bowl of fruit pulp and fold through to combine the mixture throughly.

4. Put the bowl into the freezer for 2 hours. Remove from the freezer, transfer the mixture to a food processor or blender, process, then pour and scrape the semifrozen mixture back into the bowl, smoothing it down with the back of a metal spoon.

5. Put the mixture back into the freezer for another 1 hour or so. Serve generous scoops with my Blackberry, Apple & Comice Pear Compote (see opposite).

SUMMER FRUIT

THIS CHAPTER IS CRAMMED WITH ALL MY SUMMER FRUIT FAVORITES:
figs, raspberries, peaches, cherries, and apricots. As these fruits ripen on the bush or tree, they produce wonderful natural sugars and their own distinctive perfumes. Beguiled by their beauty, we're rewarded with every sweet, sour, satisfying bite.

It's the combination of natural sugars and perfumes that make summer fruits so interesting to me—so many mixed and varied flavors. So the group of spices that I work with edge toward the more challenging, working in subtle opposition to the natural fruity notes; spices help my palate understand the complex beauty of these delicate fruits. After all, many spices are also fruits: the complex, almost citrus notes of allspice or equally complex long pepper (a flower spike packed with minuscule "fruit"), the twisted heat of cubeb, the sweet anise perfume of fennel, or richer notes of star anise. Summer fruit, fresh from the garden (or farmers' market or supermarket), can work well with soft green aromatic leaves of fresh herbs, lifting fruity flavors to another level. Combine the pungency of peppers, twists of anise perfume from fennel, add a touch of basil freshness, and you have the inspiration for my Apricot Crunches.

A recent wonderful olfactory experience in Pollença, Spain, is part of the inspiration for my Black Figs with Goat Cheese and Arugula salad. The sun was beaming down, I was running around shooting water pistols at my niece and nephew, and I stopped to take a much-needed rest under a fig tree in the yard. As the sun poured onto the thick, leafy canopy, the fruit gave up the most delicious, deep, heady perfume, similar to vanilla, but with a fruity, tobacco twist. The kind of fragrance you can almost taste. Then a wasp, probably also enjoying a similar experience, stung me and so moved me on!

I adore the light texture of a clafoutis, and my version, incorporating raspberries and light spicing, is a refreshing twist on the French classic. Star anise reflects and reinforces the deep fruity richness of raspberries. Nutmeg and green cardamom add diamond-bright sparkle and both work well with the orange aromas of Grand Marnier. Fresh black pepper is a personal indulgence, but I think it brings further depth and clarity, cutting through rich, buttery flavors.

Previous page: Long pepper brings perfumed notes of allspice, pepper, nutmeg, and cloves to all it touches, adding definition and clarity to the myriad of flavors in summer fruits.

APRICOT CRUNCHES

Great as a snack for a morning or afternoon coffee or tea break, or simply as a dessert, these crunches are simple to construct—and far too easy to devour. Serve them with homemade lemonade or a cup of fragrant Earl Grey tea.

SERVES 4

½ cup (3½oz/100g) superfine or
  granulated sugar
12 fresh apricots, halved and pits
  removed
1 teaspoon black peppercorns,
  coarsely ground
5–6 gratings long pepper
1 tablespoon vodka
1 French baguette, sliced
  in half lengthwise
1 teaspoon allspice berries
2 teaspoons fennel seeds
½ teaspoon cubeb pepper
1¾ cups (14oz/400g)
  mascarpone cheese
3 tablespoons whole milk
1 handful fresh basil leaves, torn

1. Put ⅓ cup (2½fl oz/75ml) water and the sugar into a saucepan, stir, and put over medium heat. Once the sugar has dissolved, add the apricot halves, black pepper, and long pepper, and simmer gently for 5–8 minutes or until the apricots are soft without breaking up too much.

2. Take off the heat, add the vodka, pour into a small bowl, and set aside to cool completely. Cover with plastic wrap and put in the refrigerator.

3. Preheat the oven to 400°F (200°C). Put the baguette halves on a baking sheet and put in the oven for 12–15 minutes, until lightly toasted. Remove and let cool completely.

4. Coarsely grind the spices, using a mortar and pestle. Mix the mascarpone, milk, and spice mix in a small bowl. Put in the refrigerator.

5. When it's time to serve, spread the baguette halves generously with spiced mascarpone, then add the apricots and basil. Slice each half into 10–12 diagonal pieces with a serrated knife and serve.

BLACK FIGS WITH GOAT CHEESE & ARUGULA

I absolutely love figs, fresh or dried, and so this dish is all about the figs. I first had a salad similar to this at a birthday barbecue back in the mid-nineties and totally loved it. I knew I'd be doing something with it one day, so—with a few tweak—here it is for you to enjoy. When buying figs, make sure they feel heavy, have a little "squish" to them, and don't smell sour. Only buy those that are fully ripe and with flesh that has a honeyed, ripe sweetness.

SERVES 4

8 ripe black figs, halved
3 tablespoons honey
4 teaspoons French pastis or
    Pernod (optional)
2 teaspoons fennel seeds,
    coarsely ground
1 teaspoon black peppercorns,
    coarsely ground
⅓ cup (1¾oz/50g)
    sunflower seeds
½ cup (3½fl oz/100ml)
    balsamic vinegar
10 cups (7oz/200g)
    arugula leaves
3½oz (100g) goat cheese,
    crumbled
Zest of ½ orange

1. Preheat the oven to 350°F (180°C). Put the figs, cut side up, onto a roasting pan and drizzle them as evenly as possible with 2 tablespoons of the honey and the pastis or Pernod, if using. Sprinkle with the ground fennel seeds and black pepper.

2. Put on a middle shelf in the oven for 10–12 minutes, until they start to collapse slightly. Put the sunflower seeds in a small saucepan and dry-toast over medium heat until lightly golden. Set aside.

3. Pour the balsamic vinegar into a small saucepan and put over medium heat. Bring up to a steady, rolling simmer and let reduce by half, then set aside and let cool.

4. When the figs are soft, take them out of the oven and delicately cut each half in half again. Set aside.

5. Sprinkle a large serving plate with the arugula leaves, then spread the figs and goat cheese over the leaves and grate the orange zest over the top. Drizzle with the remaining honey and the reduced balsamic vinegar, and top with the sunflower seeds before serving.

CHERRY BRIOCHE DESSERT

Indulgent only just comes somewhere near to describing this dessert's beauty. This is bread pudding with a delightful tweak of fresh cherry, fennel, pistachio cream—nothing too fancy, just a flavor combination that really works.

SERVES 4

2 tablespoons Grand Marnier, Cointreau, or kirsch (or a mix)

1 cup (5½oz/150g) pitted fresh cherries, lightly crushed so that they still hold most of their shape

⅓ cup (1¾oz/50g) dried or sour cherries

1 tablespoon sugar

1 teaspoon black peppercorns, finely ground

1¼ cups (10fl oz/300ml) whole milk

1¼ cups (10fl oz/300ml) heavy cream

1 vanilla bean, split lengthwise

6 large egg yolks (use the whites to make meringue, see page 206)

⅔ cup (4½oz/125g) demerara or other raw sugar

1 small pinch sea salt

7 tablespoons (3½oz/100g) unsalted butter, at room temperature

4 teaspoons fennel seeds, finely ground

12 slices brioche, about ½ inch (1cm) thick

¼ cup (3oz/85g) orange marmalade (with peel)

½ cup (2¾oz/75g) pistachio nuts, coarsely chopped

1. Pour your chosen alcohol into a small saucepan, put over gentle heat, and warm for 1 minute—don't let it simmer. Add both types of cherries, the sugar, and pepper, swirl the pan around, then set it aside to cool for 2 hours.

2. Pour the milk and cream into another saucepan over medium heat. Scrape out the seeds from the vanilla bean. Add the seeds and bean to the milky mixture. Heat gently until it just starts to simmer.

3. Meanwhile, put the egg yolks into a large heatproof bowl with the demerara sugar and salt, and whisk well.

4. Pour the hot milk mixture into the bowl, giving it all a vigorous whisk. Remove the vanilla bean from this custard mixture and set aside.

5. In a small bowl, mix the butter with the ground fennel seeds, then spread a little on the brioche slices, reserving a couple of teaspoons. Spread the buttered slices with the marmalade, then cut into triangles.

6. Lightly butter a large pie dish, at least 2-quart (3½-pint/2-liter) capacity, with the reserved spiced butter, then layer it neatly with the brioche triangles, spreading the cherries and their liquid on top.

7. Pour the warm custard over the slices and finish with a sprinkling of pistachio nuts, then carefully put the dish into the refrigerator to rest for 30 minutes.

8. Preheat the oven to 350°F (180°C). Put the dish on the middle shelf of the oven and bake for 25–35 minutes, until the dessert puffs up and the brioche is a glorious nutty brown. Serve warm with chilled cream.

BERRY SUMMER DESSERT

This is my favorite summer dessert. It's tangy, soft-textured and has just the right amount of sweetness, with the spices adding depth and clarity to the finish. We chose this as our wedding dessert. Using sponge makes a real difference; it's best to make your own, but you could use store-bought plain pound cake, cut into batons, at a push.

SERVES 8–10

FOR THE SPONGE CAKE

1 vanilla bean, split lengthwise
1 stick plus 1 tablespoon
    (4½oz/125g) unsalted butter
¾ cup plus 2 tablespoons
    (6oz/175g) superfine or
    granulated sugar
1⅓ cups (6oz/175g)
    all-purpose flour
1 teaspoon baking powder
3 extra-large eggs, at room
    temperature
5 teaspoons whole milk

FOR THE PUDDING

½ star anise
1 teaspoon black peppercorns
4 cloves
½ long pepper, smashed
2 green cardamom pods
3 cups (1¼lb/600g) demerara or
    other sugar
3½ tablespoons coarsely
    chopped fresh ginger
6 cups (2lb/900g) fresh or
    thawed frozen black currants
    or blueberries
5 teaspoons crème de cassis,
    black currant syrup, or
    raspberry liqueur

1. Preheat the oven to 350°F (180°C). Grease and flour two 7-inch (18-cm) cake pans. Scrape out the seeds from the vanilla bean. In a large mixing bowl, cream the butter and sugar together, then add the vanilla seeds and mix well. Sift the flour and baking powder into a second bowl. Whisking all the time, add an egg to the butter mixture, then add a spoonful of flour and whisk lightly. Repeat until all the flour and eggs are combined, then add the milk and mix to incorporate. Divide the batter evenly between the two pans, leaving a slight indent in the center of each. Put on the middle shelf of the oven and bake for 20 minutes or until a toothpick pushed into the center comes out clean. Cool on a wire rack. Remove the cakes from the pans and slice each into ¾-inch (2-cm)-thick lengths, then cover with a dish towel and set aside.

2. Lightly crush the spices, using a mortar and pestle. Put the sugar, ginger, 3 cups (26fl oz/750ml) water, and the spices into a large saucepan, then stir and put over medium heat. Cook until the sugar has dissolved, then let it simmer for 3 minutes. Let cool, then strain through a fine strainer into a small bowl. Discard the spices. Set the syrup aside. Put the berries into a large saucepan over medium heat. As soon as the berries begin to burst, add the spiced sugar syrup, stir well, and bring to a gentle bubble. Add the cassis, syrup, or liqueur, stir, and take off the heat.

3. Line the bottom and sides of a deep 1¾-quart (3 pint/1.8 liter) ovenproof dish, or two 1-quart (1½-pint/900-ml) ovenproof dishes, with the cake slices, cutting the lengths to fit. Reserve some cake to form a lid. Drizzle the sponge with the warm syrup, then fill the lined dishes with the berries to about 1¼ inches (3cm) from the top. Add more syrup to cover the fruit, then cover with one even layer of cake slices. Drizzle with syrup.

4. Put a small plate on top and weigh it down with something heavy. Let cool. Put it in the refrigerator for 24 hours before carefully turning out onto a serving plate. Serve with chilled cream.

RASPBERRY CLAFOUTIS

Here's a beautiful light yet rich version of this popular dessert. My recipe tends to be a little more full-on than the traditional, but the spices help to lessen the richness and anyway, desserts are supposed to be indulgent! You can serve the clafoutis with chilled cream, but I like it with my lightly scented Tejpatta Ice Cream (see page 234).

SERVES 6

FOR THE FRUIT
½ teaspoon black peppercorns
½ star anise
Seeds of 2 green cardamom pods
2 cloves
⅓ cup (2¾oz/75g) superfine or
    granulated sugar
4 gratings nutmeg
4 cups (1lb 2oz/500g)
    raspberries
2 tablespoons Grand Marnier
    or Cointreau

FOR THE BATTER
⅔ cup (2¾oz/75g)
    all-purpose flour
3½ tablespoons ground almonds
    (almond meal)
3½ tablespoons superfine or
    granulated sugar
1 pinch sea salt
3 extra-large eggs, plus 1 yolk,
    lightly beaten
1 cup (7fl oz/200ml) whole milk
⅓ cup (2½fl oz/75ml)
    heavy cream
2 tablespoons (1oz/30g) unsalted
    butter, melted, plus extra for
    greasing

1. Preheat the oven to 400°F (200°C). Lightly grease a 1-quart (1¾ pint/1-liter) or 9-inch (23-cm) pie dish. Finely grind the spices, using a mortar and pestle.

2. Mix the sugar and all the spices together, then take 1 teaspoon of the mix and set it aside for later. Put some of the remaining spiced sugar into the buttered pie dish and roll it around to coat the bottom and sides as evenly as possible. Set aside.

3. Pour the raspberries, the remaining spiced sugar, and the liqueur into a small bowl, toss around gently to combine, then cover and set aside for 30–40 minutes.

4. Meanwhile, make the batter. Put the flour and almonds into a large mixing bowl, add the sugar and salt, then the eggs and yolk, and whisk lightly. Add the milk, cream, and melted butter, then whisk lightly to a smooth batter.

5. Add the raspberries and their macerating liquid, give them a quick but gentle stir, then pour everything into the pie dish and bake in the center of the oven for 25–30 minutes, until the mix is just set with a little comforting wobble.

6. Remove from the oven, sprinkle with the reserved spiced sugar, then put under a hot broielr to caramelize if you'd prefer a little extra texture. Let cool slightly before serving warm with Tejpatta Ice Cream.

Apple Sorbet & Peach Gazpacho

This recipe is full of refreshing, fruity flavors. Use the ripest peaches and melon you can find; it will make a surprising difference. It's best to make the sorbet the day before you want to serve the gazpacho. You can forego the garnish if you can't get your hands on fresh currants.

SERVES 4

FOR THE APPLE SORBET
¾ cup plus 2 tablespoons (6oz/175g) superfine sugar
5 green cooking apples, such as Granny Smith
Juice of 2 lemons
½ cup (4fl oz/125ml) apple cider or apple juice
2 teaspoons apple brandy (optional)

FOR THE GARNISH
2 tablespoons superfine sugar
2 cloves, finely ground
4 small sprigs red currants or white currants
1 large egg white, lightly whipped and foamy

FOR THE GAZPACHO
1 small handful blanched almonds
6 ripe white peaches, pitted, halved, and chilled
⅔ cup (5fl oz/150ml) Prosecco, chilled
2 teaspoons confectioners' sugar
3 cloves, finely ground
1 ripe Charentais melon or cantaloupe, halved and seeded
5 pitted green olives, dried with paper towels, finely chopped

1. To make the sorbet, put the sugar and ½ cup (4fl oz/125ml) water into a small saucepan over medium heat and simmer for 1 minute, then remove from the heat and let cool. Cut the apples into quarters, core them, leaving the skin on, then put them into a food processor or blender with the lemon juice and briefly process. Add the cooled sugar syrup, the apple cider or juice, and brandy, if using, and process to a smooth puree.

2. Line a baking pan with parchment paper, pour in the puree, and put it in the freezer for at least 3 hours or until semifrozen. Remove from the freezer and put the mixture back into the food processor, then process again. Pour and scrape the mix back into the lined pan, smoothing it down with the back of a metal spoon. Put back into the freezer for at least 1 hour, then shape into golf ball-size balls and return to the freezer.

3. To make the garnish, mix the sugar and cloves. Dip a sprig of red currants into the whipped egg white, then into the spiced sugar, and gently lay it on a wire rack. Repeat with the other sprigs, then let dry.

4. Put four soup bowls into the refrigerator. Put the almonds for the gazpacho into a small saucepan over medium heat and dry-toast until golden. Coarsely chop them and set aside.

5. Put the peach halves, Prosecco, confectioners' sugar, and clove powder into your food processor or blender and process to a smooth paste. Pass the paste through a strainer into a small bowl, pushing the pulp through with the back of a ladle. Put in the refrigerator.

6. Cut out little balls from the melon, using a melon baller; you should get about 20. Set aside.

7. Take the bowls from the refrigerator, rub them dry with a dish towel, then put a ball of apple sorbet in the middle of each. Pour in the peach and Prosecco mixture (it may first need to be quickly blender), add five melon balls, a sprinkle of nuts, and then the olives. Put the candied berries on the side and serve immediately.

223

BLACKBERRY-PEPPER FROZEN YOGURT & LEMON SHORTBREAD

This is based on my recipe for kulfi (see page 244), an Indian style of ice cream. It's a really easy way to make a creamy, textured frozen dessert. And the great news is that this frozen yogurt contains 50–60 percent less fat than commercial ice creams and up to 80 percent less fat than homemade ones.

SERVES 6

½ cup (3½oz/100g) superfine or granulated sugar

3½ cups (1lb 2oz/500g) fresh or thawed frozen blackberries

1 teaspoon black pepper, finely ground

1 tablespoon vodka (optional)

1 (14-oz/400-g) can condensed milk

1¼ cups (10½oz/300g) whole plain yogurt

2 extra-large egg whites

1. Put the sugar and ⅓ cup (2½fl oz/75ml) water into a saucepan, stir, and put over medium heat. Once the sugar has dissolved, add the blackberries and black pepper, and let simmer gently for 5–8 minutes, until the blackberries are just softened.

2. Take off the heat, add the vodka, if using, then pour all the ingredients into a food processor and process to a smooth puree. (Alternatively, use a wire whisk to beat the fruits and vodka together throughly.) Pass the puree through a strainer into a bowl, pushing the pulp through with the back of a ladle. Discard the seeds. Let the puree cool completely, but don't chill.

3. Put the blackberry puree, condensed milk, and yogurt into a large mixing bowl. Whisk the ingredients together throughly, using an immersion blender, if you desire.

4. In a clean, grease-free bowl, whisk the egg whites until stiff. Carefully fold the egg whites through the creamy, fruity mixture until all the ingredients are mixed well and you have a thick, sticky mousse.

5. Pour the mousse into a plastic container, put it into your freezer, and let set for at least 6 hours or overnight.

FOR THE SHORTBREAD

1 vanilla bean, split lengthwise

²⁄₃ cup (2¼oz/60g) superfine or granulated sugar

1 stick plus 1 tablespoon (4½oz/125g) salted butter, at room temperature, cubed

1²⁄₃ cups (6oz/175g) all-purpose flour

Zest of ¼ lemon

Confectioners' sugar, for dusting

1. Preheat the oven to 350°F (180°C). Line a baking sheet with parchment paper. Scrape out the seeds from the vanilla bean. Put the vanilla seeds and the remaining ingredients, except the confectioners' sugar, into a big mixing bowl and use your fingertips to rub the butter through the dry ingredients until the mixture looks like coarse bread crumbs. Bring all the ingredients together into a ball.

2. Sift the confectioners' sugar over a work surface and use to dust the rolling pin. Roll out the dough to ¼ inch (5mm) thick. Cut out shapes, using a cookie cutter, and space apart on the baking sheet. Bake for 10–15 minutes or until they're a pale beige. Use a spatula to gently lift onto a wire rack to cool. Serve with the Blackberry-Pepper Frozen Yogurt.

PEACH CARDINAL

This simple, summery dessert is light yet indulgent enough to satisfy. Poached peaches, Angostura, raspberry sauce, vanilla ice cream, almonds—and a touch of spice. Foodie heaven!

SERVES 4

1¼ cups (9oz/250g) demerara or other raw sugar

1 vanilla bean, split lengthwise

1 teaspoon black peppercorns

¾-inch (2-cm) piece fresh ginger (about 1oz/30g), peeled

½ red finger chile

1 tablespoon rose water

4 large, ripe peaches, peeled if you prefer (see page 193)

A few splashes Angostura bitters

½ cup (3½fl oz/100ml) heavy cream, lightly whipped

2 tablespoons toasted slivered almonds

4 scoops vanilla ice cream

FOR THE RASPBERRY SAUCE

1²⁄₃ cups (7oz/200g) fresh raspberries

¾ cup (3½oz/100g) confectioners' sugar

Juice of ½ fresh lime

1. Put the demerara sugar and 3 cups (26fl oz/750ml) water into a saucepan, stir well, and put over medium heat. Once the sugar has dissolved, let simmer gently for 1 minute. Add the spices, fresh ginger, chile, and rose water, and continue to simmer gently for another 3 minutes.

2. Turn up the heat, add the whole peaches, and bring to a gentle boil, then turn the heat down and gently poach for 10 minutes.

3. Remove the peaches, set aside, and let cool, then put in the refrigerator to chill. Strain the syrup into sterilized bottles (see page 255) and reserve for another time you'd like to poach fruit.

4. To make the sauce, put the raspberries, confectioners' sugar, and lime juice into a food processor or blender and process to a smooth puree. Push through a fine strainer into a small bowl or small bowl, pushing the pulp through with the back of a ladle. Discard the seeds.

5. To serve, put a peach into each serving bowl. Splash with a couple of drops of Angostura, lightly coat with a spoonful or two of raspberry sauce, and top with a little whipped cream and some slivered almonds. Add a neat ball of ice cream to the side and serve immediately.

BLUEBERRY & LYCHEE SORBET

I love the color and texture of this sorbet; I prefer sorbets not to be too jagged and icy. The flecks of blueberry skin simply add to its appeal. I've used nutmeg to add a fragrant, bitter note as well as black pepper for background heat and to cut through sweetness. The clove backs up the fruity notes while the vanilla provides a complementary perfume.

SERVES 4–6

⅔ cup (4½oz/125g) superfine or granulated sugar
1 clove, smashed
2¾ cups (14oz/400g) blueberries
1 cup (7oz/200g) drained, canned pitted lychees
1 tablespoon lemon juice
1 tablespoon vodka
1 small pinch sea salt
4 gratings of nutmeg
¾ teaspoon black peppercorns, finely ground
1 teaspoon vanilla extract
Fresh mint leaves, torn, to decorate

1. Line a baking pan with parchment paper. Put the sugar, ¼ cup (2fl oz/50ml) water and the clove in a saucepan over medium heat. Swirl the pan around gently as the water starts to bubble; this helps to dissolve the sugar.

2. Once the sugar has completely dissolved, pour the mixture through a strainer into a small bowl, then set aside and let cool.

3. Put all the remaining ingredients—except the mint leaves—into a food processor or blender, add the cooled sugar syrup, and process to a smooth puree. Pour the puree into the lined pan and put it in the freezer for at least 3 hours or until semifrozen.

4. Remove from the freezer, put it back into your food processor, process again, then pour and scrape the semifrozen fruit mix back into the lined pan. Smooth it down with the back of a metal spoon, then put it back into the freezer for another 1 hour.

5. Serve generous scoops of the sorbet with torn leaves of fresh mint and Thyme & Pepper Lozenge Cookies (see page 229) for a refreshing treat.

THYME & PEPPER LOZENGE COOKIES

Simple cookies—the perfect crunchy partner to any fruit sorbet.

MAKES ABOUT 10

⅓ cup (1½oz/40g)
    all-purpose flour
⅓ cup (1½oz/40g)
    confectioners' sugar
2 large egg whites, lightly
    whipped with a fork
1–2 gratings orange zest
3 tablespoons (1½oz/40g) salted
    butter, melted and cooled
1 teaspoon black peppercorns,
    coarsely ground
½ teaspoon thyme leaves

1. Preheat the oven to 300°F (150°C). Lay a sheet of parchment paper or a silicone sheet on a baking sheet.

2. Sift the flour and sugar into a bowl, then steadily pour the egg whites into the flour, stirring all the time with a fork.

3. Add the orange zest to the melted butter, then pour this into the egg mixture and stir throughly to a smooth paste. Take a large tablespoon of the cookie paste and dollop it onto your lined baking sheet, then spread the paste with the back of a spoon into a lozenge shape, about 1¼ × 4½ inches (3 x 12cm). Don't worry too much about dimensions; let the paste take its own shape.

4. Repeat until you have used all the cookie paste, then bake in the oven for 4–6 minutes, until the cookies turn a light brown.

5. Immediately sprinkle the pepper and thyme across the cookies' surface. Let them rest on the baking sheet to cool completely, then carefully remove them, using a spatula.

6. There, done! Serve alongside the Blueberry & Lychee Sorbet (see page 226) for a little wow and crunch factor.

SWEET THINGS

MY FATHER IS INDIAN AND MY MOTHER FROM YORKSHIRE IN ENGLAND. I never stood a chance of not having a sweet tooth or being a dessert junkie. It's in my genes! As children, however, we were only allowed to buy candy once a week, there was the odd road trip. My mother and father would pack us all into the maroon Peugeot and we'd head down to London to visit relatives. We'd always make time to go to Drummond Street for a splurge on Indian confectionery. And when my father came back from his visits home to India, he'd bring a brightly colored, sticky box or two full of sweet treats.

This chapter offers a really intriguing number of possibilities when it comes to spice. Gorgeous, sweetly warming ginger, intoxicating nutmeg, the freshest of cloves to reinforce and heighten fruity intensity for a cozy, comfort-food factor. When balancing sugars, I look for intense, clean spices, sweetly aromatic with vibrant perfume. Fresh Mixed Spice (see page 266) is just such a blend; it's the ultimate mixed spice for Christmas cake and mincemeat.

Spice can be used to tone down sweetness in a dish. In Gingerbread Mess, I use cubeb and dried rose petals to offset the cake's deep sugary notes, green cardamom and powdered ginger to heighten flavor and highlight warmth, star anise for depth, and Sichuan pepper to twist and back up the citrus notes of the fresh ginger.

I've included a couple of traditional Indian confectioneries, Halwa and Kulfi, and I must say, I am pleased with the Knickerbocker Glory presentation of the kulfi. The Greek yogurt adds a little lactic bite, the black cardamom a subtle smoky balance to the honey brittle, and the touch of salt brings a little "weight" to its mid-notes.

My biggest projects were the Chocolate Pot, the Triple Chocolate Meringue Cream Pie, and my Christmas Cake. With the chocolate pot, I wanted to create more than just a pure chocolate hit and so added subtle salt butterscotch, then the merest hint of clove, black pepper, nutmeg, and whiskey to add different layers of defining depth. Nutmeg is traditionally used to bring out cacao notes in the spice world, and I have employed the same technique here. And for a real show-stopping dessert, try the triple chocolate pie. With its Garam Masala cookie crust, intense orange-chocolate filling, and the rose-meringue topping, it really is something special. The Christmas Cake looks a little daunting, but that's the nature of the beast—with the vanilla, black pepper, Mixed Spice, and Angostura bitters, juicy macerated fruits, and deep, sweet notes of dark brown sugar, I don't use any white fondant; that would just take it over the top.

Previous page: Cubeb, or Javanese pepper, is a spice I often use in place of allspice for its assertive flavor and "twisted" perfume.

TRINITY COLLEGE VANILLA CREAM

My twist on crème brûlée: the shiny caramel topping is made separately, flavored with green cardamom and freeze-dried raspberries. I make this in a large, shallow bowl about 1¼ inches (4cm) deep with a 1¼-quart (2-pint/1.2 liter) capacity, to really show off the caramel shards.

SERVES 6–8

2 vanilla beans, split lengthwise

3 cups (about 1¼ pints/750ml) heavy cream

8 extra-large egg yolks (use the egg whites to make meringues, see page 206)

⅓ cup (2¾oz/75g) superfine or granulated sugar

⅓ cup (2½fl oz/75ml) low-fat milk

1. Scrape out the seeds from the vanilla beans. Put the cream into a saucepan over low heat and add the vanilla beans and seeds. Heat until a few bubbles appear, then take off the heat.

2. In a bowl, beat together the egg yolks and the sugar, then stir in the milk.

3. Pour a small amount of the hot cream onto the yolk mixture, whisk, then put the yolk mixture back into the pan and cook over gentle heat until the mixture thickens, stirring almost constantly.

4. When the mixture coats the back of a wooden spoon, remove the vanilla beans and pour the mixture into a blender to process, or use an immersion blender. Pour into a wide, shallow heatproof bowl and let cool.

5. Cover with plastic wrap and chill in the refrigerator for up to 48 hours.

FOR THE CROQUANT CARAMEL

Sunflower oil, for greasing

⅓ cup (1¼oz/35g) almonds

1¼ cups (9oz/250g) superfine or granulated sugar

1 tablespoon honey

⅓ cup (1½oz/40g) skinned pistachio nuts, coarsely chopped

Seeds of 6 green cardamom pods, finely ground

2 tablespoons freeze-dried raspberries, coarsely broken

1. Oil a baking sheet. Put the almonds into small saucepan over medium heat and dry-toast them until golden. Chop them coarsely and set aside. Make a caramel by putting the sugar and honey into a saucepan over medium–high heat; once the sugar has dissolved, swirl the pan to keep the heat moving through the sugar, but do not stir. If sugar starts to catch on the sides of the pan, brush it down using a moistened pastry brush.

2. Once the sugar has browned to a dark golden caramel, quickly pour it onto your prepared baking sheet to form a ⅟₁₆-inch (2-mm)-thick layer. Immediately sprinkle over the nuts, then sprinkle on the ground cardamom and raspberry pieces and let cool.

3. To serve, gently smash the croquant with a rolling pin to achieve dramatic shards. Take the vanilla cream from the refrigerator, remove the plastic wrap, and sprinkle the sugar shards over the surface.

TEJPATTA ICE CREAM

This subtle, gently flavored ice cream goes perfectly well as an accompaniment to fruit pies and desserts—an alternative to the ubiquitous vanilla ice cream.

MAKES ABOUT 20 SCOOPS

2 cups (18fl oz/500ml)
   heavy cream
7 large Indian bay leaves
   (tejpatta), crushed in your
   hand
4 large egg yolks (use the egg
   whites to make meringues,
   see page 206)
⅔ cup (4½oz/125g) superfine
   or granulated sugar
1 large egg white

1. Pour ⅓ cup (2½fl oz/75ml) of the cream into a saucepan. Add the crushed bay leaves and put over medium heat. Bring to a gentle boil, turn down the heat, and let simmer for 2 minutes, then turn off the heat and set aside to steep and cool.

2. Put the egg yolks into a large mixing bowl. Whisk with an electric handheld mixer on high for 6–8 minutes or until they're pale, light, and fluffy and have doubled in volume. Set aside.

3. Put the sugar into a saucepan, add 2 tablespoons water, stir, then put the pan over medium heat. When the sugar starts bubbling and melting, cook for another 1 minute, then take a metal spoon, dip it into the molten sugar solution to catch some syrup, and lift it up; when you see a gloopy drop fall from the spoon like honey, leaving a thin, wispy thread behind, it's ready. (This is known as the soft ball stage.)

4. Remove the pan from the heat and pour the hot sugar syrup into the whisked egg yolks, whisking constantly for about 5 minutes, until the mixture is room-temperature cool.

5. Put the remaining cream into a large bowl, then pour the steeped cream through a strainer into the same bowl and whisk lightly to form soft peaks. Pour the cooled egg–sugar mixture into the whipped cream and throughly combine the two, folding gently with a metal spoon or large rubber spatula.

6. Put the egg white in a clean, grease-free bowl and whisk to stiff peaks. Add 1 tablespoon of the whisked egg white to the cream mixture and stir in gently. Add the rest of the egg white and gently fold through the mixture.

7. Pour into a plastic dish or lightly oiled gelatin mold and put it in the freezer. It will take at least 6 hours to set completely. To serve, scoop it into balls, or turn out of the mold, if using, and slice.

Trifle

This trifle doesn't use gelatin but it does use cake, poached berries, vanilla custard, almonds, and whipped cream. I generally make this from pantry and refrigerator staples—it's so easy! You can, of course, make all the different parts, use leftovers, or simply buy your favorites— preserves, cake, custard, and so on—and assemble the dish in a jiffy. Don't forget to use your favorite dessert bowl. My mother-in-law has her "special" trifle bowl she has used since my wife, Olive, was a young girl. Wonderful!

SERVES 6

Pound cake or ladyfingers
Raspberry or strawberry preserves, for spreading
A large slug of sherry
A large slug of Grand Marnier or Cointreau (optional)
3 cups (1lb/450g) fresh or thawed frozen blackberries
¾ cup (5½oz/150g) superfine or granulated sugar
1 teaspoon black peppercorns, finely ground
2 cloves, finely ground
2 vanilla beans
2½ cups (1 pint/600ml) heavy cream
2½ cups (1 pint/600ml) vanilla custard (see below) or store-bought vanilla pudding

FOR THE VANILLA CUSTARD
4 extra-large eggs, separated
⅓ cup (3oz/85g) sugar
⅔ cup (5fl oz/150ml) whole milk
⅔ cup (5fl oz/150ml) heavy cream
1 vanilla bean

TO DECORATE
1 handful toasted slivered almonds
1 small handful fresh cherries

1. First, make the custard. In a large heatproof bowl, whisk the egg yolks with the sugar until mousselike. Pour the milk and cream into a saucepan over medium heat. Scrape out the seeds from the vanilla bean, and put the seeds and the bean into the milk mixture. Bring to a gentle simmer and let simmer for 2–3 minutes. While whisking the eggs, slowly pour the milk through a strainer into the bowl. Set aside to cool.

2. Cut the pound cake into finger shapes, spread with preserves, and sandwich together in pairs. Wedge them into the bottom of your dessert bowl. Drizzle the cake with the alcohol until well moistened. Set aside.

3. Put the berries, 1½ cup (3½oz/100g) of the sugar, pepper, and cloves into a saucepan. Cut a vanilla bean in half and scrape out the seeds. Add to the pan and put over medium heat. Bring to a gentle simmer, then turn off the heat and let steep for 15 minutes. Strain the berries through a strainer over a heatproof bowl, then set aside. Put the strained juice and vanilla bean back into the pan and reduce over medium–high heat for 2–3 minutes, until the liquid thickens slightly. Remove the pan from the heat, take out the vanilla bean, then pour the juice back into its bowl and let cool.

4. Whip the cream to soft peaks. Cut the remaining vanilla bean in half and scrape out the seeds. Add to the whipped cream. Add the remaining sugar, and gently fold the ingredients together until just combined.

5. Sprinkle the poached berries over the cake fingers and cover with the cooled custard, followed by the whipped cream. Sprinkle the almonds over the top followed by the fresh cherries. Serve the reserved vanilla berry juices in a little small bowl, together with, perhaps, some heavy cream and, for real indulgence, a glass of Madeira or sherry.

GINGER & LIME DRIZZLE CAKE

This is the ultimate sponge cake. Light sponge, sweet, citrus sauce, and creamy coconut custard. I know it may look a little daunting, but you'll be pleased with the results.

SERVES 6–8

4 large eggs, separated

Zest and juice of 2 limes

⅓ cup (1½oz/40g) finely grated fresh ginger

¾ cup (6oz/175g) firmly packed light brown sugar

2 tablespoons white rum

1 teaspoon white peppercorns

1 teaspoon fennel seeds

1¾ cups (7½oz/215g) all-purpose flour

1¾ teaspoons baking powder

½ teaspoon sea salt

1 teaspoon powdered ginger

1 vanilla bean, split lengthwise

1¾ sticks plus 1 tablespoon (7½oz/215g) unsalted butter, plus extra for greasing

2 pieces preserved ginger, drained and finely diced

FOR THE DRIZZLE SAUCE

2 tablespoons (1oz/30g) butter

½ cup (3½oz/100g) firmly packed light brown sugar

¾ cup (7oz/200g) light corn syrup

¼ teaspoon sea salt

2 teaspoons powdered ginger

Zest and juice of 2 limes

FOR THE COCONUT CUSTARD

1⅔ cups (14fl oz/400ml) coconut milk

1 cup (8fl oz/225ml) light cream

4 large egg yolks

30g (1oz) golden superfine sugar

1 teaspoon cornstarch

1. Butter inside the bowl and lid of a deep 1¼-quart (2-pint/1.2-liter) overproof dish. Put the yolks, lime zest, fresh ginger, and sugar into a large mixing bowl and beat with an electric handheld mixer for 2–3 minutes. Set aside. Warm the lime juice and rum in a small saucepan over medium heat until hot to the touch but not scalding. Slowly pour the hot lime and rum into the bowl, whisking constantly, until the mixture is really fluffy, about three times its original volume, and has cooled completely.

2. Finely grind the peppercorns and fennel seeds. Sift the flour, baking powder, salt, pepper, fennel, and powdered ginger into the bowl and gently fold through to just combine. Set aside. Scrape out the seeds from the vanilla bean. Melt the butter in a small saucepan, then stir in the vanilla seeds and prserved ginger. Slowly trickle some of the butter mixture into the bowl, and fold gently to combine, then repeat with the remaining butter. Set aside.

3. In a clean, grease-free bowl, whisk the egg whites to form stiff peaks. Mix one-third of the egg whites through the batter, then gently fold in the remainder. Pour into the prepared dish and cover with the lid. Put the dish into a large saucepan and pour in boiling water to come up one-third of the side of the dish. Cover the pan and simmer gently for 2 hours. Rest for 5 minutes before lifting out.

4. Meanwhile, make the sauce. In a saucepan, gently heat the butter, sugar, syrup, salt, and ginger until the sugar has dissolved, then let simmer gently for 1 minute. Remove from the heat, and add the lime zest and juice. Set aside and keep warm.

5. To make the custard, heat the coconut milk and cream in a large saucepan over medium heat until the first bubble or two appear. In a small heatproof bowl, whisk together the yolks, sugar, and cornstarch. Whisk in one-third of the hot coconut milk, then pour it back into the pan. Stir with a wooden spoon over low heat until the custard thickens and lightly coats the back of the spoon. Turn the cake out onto a warmed serving plate, pour the sauce over, and serve with the coconut custard.

GINGERBREAD MESS

This is a really amazing dessert, rich, indulgent, and wonderful as a treat or celebratory dessert.
The cherries, spice, and textures will dazzle your palate and delight your friends!

SERVES 4–6

**Spice blend: 1 tablespoon dried
rose petals, 1 teaspoon white
peppercorns, ½ star anise,
¼ teaspoon cubebs, seeds of
2 green cardamom pods,
½ teaspoon Sichuan pepper,
5 teaspoons powdered ginger**

**½ Granny Smith apple, peeled,
cored, chopped**

**4 tablespoons (2oz/55g) butter,
plus extra for greasing**

**¼ cup (2¼oz/65g) light
corn syrup**

¼ cup (2¼oz/65g) molasses

3 tablespoons dark brown sugar

**2 tablespoons finely grated
fresh ginger**

Zest of ¼ orange

½ teaspoon baking soda

¼ cup (2fl oz/50ml) whole milk

1 large egg, beaten

**¾ cup (3½oz/100g)
all-purpose flour**

¾ teaspoon baking powder

**1 piece preserved ginger, drained
and finely chopped**

FOR THE MERINGUE

3 extra-large egg whites

**¾ cup plus 2 tablespoons
(6oz/175g) superfine sugar**

FOR THE MESS

**2 cups (18fl oz/500ml) heavy
cream, whipped and chilled**

**3 tablespoons pitted brandy
cherries, drained**

1. Preheat the oven to 340°F (170°C). Butter a small ovenproof dish or a 9 x 5 x 3-inch (23 x10 x 7.5-cm) loaf pan, and line it with parchment paper. Finely grind the rose petals and whole spices for the spice blend, then add the powdered ginger. Put the apple and 1 tablespoon water into a small saucepan over medium–low heat and cook until pureed. Cool.

2. Put a heavy saucepan over fairly low heat and add the butter, syrup, molasses, sugar, fresh ginger, and orange zest. Add 1 heaping teaspoon of your spice blend and stir to combine. Cook gently until everything's dissolved and mixed together. Mix the baking soda in a small bowl with 1 tablespoon warm water. Take the pan off the heat, and add the milk, egg, and dissolved baking soda. Stir to only just combine.

3. Sift the flour and baking powder into a large mixing bowl, then gently pour in the contents of the pan, beating until it's completely combined. Fold in the apple puree and preserved ginger. Pour the batter into your prepared dish and bake for 25–35 minutes, until a toothpick inserted into the center comes out clean. Put the dish on a wire rack and set aside to cool completely, then cover the dish with plastic wrap and put it into the refrigerator.

4. To make the meringue, preheat the oven to 275°F (140°C). In a clean, grease-free bowl, whisk the egg whites to soft peaks, then continue whisking while adding 1 tablespoon of the sugar at a time until all the sugar is incorporated and the egg whites form glossy stiff peaks.

5. Line a baking sheet with parchment paper. Put tablespoonfuls of the meringue onto the sheet, evenly spaced. Bake in the center of the oven for 1 hour, then turn off the oven, leaving the meringue inside until the oven is completely cooled. Break up the meringues into small nuggets.

6. Add the meringue to the whipped cream and gently fold through. Break off small nuggets of the chilled ginger sponge and add to the bowl. Add the cherries and give the mix one final, gentle stir before pouring the mixture into your favorite serving bowl to serve immediately.

CARROT HALWA

The texture of this beautiful dessert could be described as a curiously decadent combination of marshmallow, soft fudge, and squishy brownie rolled into one. Divine for Diwali, the Hindu Festival of Lights, which is celebrated in October, it's a real treat. I love to eat halwa whenever I can! It reminds me of my father's return home from trips away, opening up garishly colored cardboard boxes and diving into the sticky, sweet delights wrapped within. This version is really easy to make and goes well with chai tea or coffee, family and friends.

MAKES ABOUT 6 THICK, CHUNKY PIECES

1 (14-oz/400-g) can condensed milk

Seeds of 2 green cardamom pods, finely ground

2 teaspoons rose water

2 tablespoons ghee (or a combination of unsalted butter and a little sunflower oil)

16 carrots (about 2¼lb/1kg), shredded

8 pistachio nuts, finely chopped

1. Line an 8½ x 4½ x 2½-inch (22 x 11.5 x 6-cm) loaf pan with parchment paper. Combine the condensed milk, cardamom, and rose water in a bowl, then set aside.

2. Put a wide, heavy saucepan over medium heat. Add the ghee and let it melt, then add the shredded carrots. Immediately turn the heat down to low and carefully stir the mixture, leting the carrot simmer gently for 20 minutes or until the raw aroma disappears, the color darkens, and the volume has reduced by about two-thirds. Add the condensed milk mixture, scraping the bowl with a rubber spatula to get every last drop.

3. Turn up the heat up slightly, but continue to stir the sticky mixture gently and constantly to combine all the flavors and prevent it from catching. After about 10 minutes, the mixture will have thickened, come away from the sides of the pan, and formed a gloopy mass. It'll look a little like soft-set scrambled egg when it's ready.

4. Sprinkle in the pistachio nuts. Mix them through, then carefully spoon the hot mixture into the prepared loaf pan, using a wetted spatula to spread the mixture level.

5. Let it to cool slightly, then cut the mixture into chunky diamonds or squares and put the pan into the refrigerator to let it set completely. Serve the halwa chilled.

Tip

Why not try a handful of chopped almonds and the seeds of 1 vanilla bean instead of the pistachio nuts and green cardamom? Experiment and enjoy your cooking.

CHOCOLATE POT AEVAL

This is a beautiful recipe. It took some time to get right, but I'm pleased with it. I wanted to add a touch of perfume, some butterscotch, and a hint of uisce beatha (that's whiskey in Gaelic), backed up with the warmth of pepper, to a smooth, rich chocolate pot. And here it is—you have to try it. Aeval is a reference to a Celtic fairy queen with similar associations to those of chocolate (look her up). She hails from Munster, my adopted home, so this seemed the perfect way to honor her!

SERVES 4–6

2 cups (16fl oz/450ml)
   heavy cream
½ cup (3½fl oz/100ml)
   whole milk
20 black peppercorns
3 cloves, finely ground
5 gratings nutmeg
3½oz (100g) bittersweet
   chocolate, coarsely chopped
   to gravel-size chips
5½oz (150g) milk chocolate,
   coarsely chopped to
   gravel-size chips
2 tablespoons (1oz/30g)
   salted butter
¼ cup (1¾oz/50g) firmly
   packed light brown sugar
¼ cup (2½oz/70g) golden syrup
   or light corn syrup
1 small pinch sea salt
4 extra-large egg yolks (use
   the egg whites to make
   meringues, see page 206)
2 teaspoons Irish whiskey
2 teaspoons vanilla extract

1. Preheat the oven to 275°F (140°C). Pour the cream and milk into a saucepan. Add the spices and cook over low heat until bubbles just appear around the edges of the pan. Remove the pan from the heat and let steep for 4–5 minutes.

2. Add the bittersweet and milk chocolate and let stand for 1 minute, then use a wire whisk to gently combine until it's all smooth. Set aside.

3. Put the butter, sugar, syrup, and salt into a small saucepan and heat gently over low heat to just dissolve them together. Stir well, then let simmer for 30 seconds before turning off the heat.

4. Add this butterscotch mixture to the creamy warm chocolate and whisk gently but throughly to combine.

5. Put the egg yolks, whiskey, and vanilla into a small mixing bowl and whisk together. Add the chocolate-cream mixture and whisk gently to combine.

6. Pour the mixture through a strainer into a small bowl, then into individual serving dishes, ramekins, or espresso cups. Discard the spices.

7. Put the ramekins into a baking dish or roasting pan and pour in warm water to come two-thirds of the way up sides of the dishes. Bake in the oven for 35–40 minutes, until set. Let cool slightly, then serve with a little crème fraîche or Greek yogurt.

TRIPLE CHOCOLATE MERINGUE CREAM PIE

Spiced cookie crust, oozingly rich chocolaty middle, and delightfully soft-crunch pistachio meringue. Be sure to let it cool completely in the pan or the pie will collapse and you'll end up covering your table in a lake of molten chocolate; I speak from experience!

SERVES 12

FOR THE COOKIE CRUST

1¼ sticks plus 1 tablespoon (5½oz/150g) salted butter
½ cup (3½oz/100g) superfine or granulated sugar
⅔ cup (2½oz/70g) all-purpose flour
2 cups (6oz/175g) rolled oats
1 pinch baking powder
2 teaspoons Garam Masala blend (see page 267)

FOR THE FILLING

7oz (200g) milk chocolate, broken into chunks
10½oz (300g) bittersweet chocolate, broken into chunks
1¾ sticks (7oz/200g) unsalted butter
½ cup (3½fl oz/100ml) heavy cream
Finely grated zest of ½ orange
1 teaspoon black peppercorns, finely ground
4 gratings nutmeg
1 small pinch sea salt
1¼ cups (5½oz/150g) all-purpose flour

1. Preheat the oven to 220°C (gas mark 7). Put the butter and sugar into a food processor and cream together at high speed for a few minutes, until pale.

2. In a separate bowl, mix together the flour, oats, baking powder, and Garam Masala.

3. Turn the food processor to a slow speed and add the dry ingredients, a handful at a time, to avoid clouds of flour engulfing you and your kitchen.

4. As soon as the dough has come together, turn off the food processor. Turn the bottom of a 9-inch (23-cm) springform cake pan upside down and place it back in the pan. Close the spring, then spread the cookie dough over the bottom of the pan, keeping the edges nice and thin. Bake for 25–30 minutes, until lightly golden.

5. Let cool, then put the pan into the freezer while you make the filling

6. Preheat the oven to 300° (150°C). Process the milk and bittersweet chocolate in a food processor.

7. Put the butter and cream into a large saucepan over medium heat and let the butter melt, stirring frequently. Remove from the heat, add the chocolate, then let stand for 1 minute. Gently stir to combine.

8. Add the orange zest, ground pepper, nutmeg, and salt, then stir gently to combine. Set aside to cool.

9. Sift in the flour and cocoa powder, and stir gently and briefly.

10. In a large bowl, lightly beat the eggs to only just combine the yolks and whites. Add the sugar and molasses and stir gently to just combine, then add the chocolate mix and lightly stir to just combine.

½ cup (1¾oz/50g) unsweetened
   cocoa powder
6 large eggs
1 cup (225g/8oz) firmly packed
   light brown sugar
1 tablespoon molasses

FOR THE MERINGUE

4 large egg whites
½ teaspoon cream of tartar or
   white wine vinegar
½ cup (3½oz/100g) superfine
   sugar, plus 1 tablespoon
1 vanilla bean, split lengthwise
¾ cup (3½oz/100g) pistachio
   nuts, coarsely chopped
1 teaspoon dried rose petals,
   finely chopped

11. Pour the mixture onto your chilled cookie crust, then bake for 40 minutes, until just set, with a little wobble. Remove, then turn the oven up to 350°F (180°C).

12. To make the meringue, put the egg whites into a clean, grease-free bowl and whisk until they form soft peaks. Add the cream of tartar, then continue whisking while adding 1 tablespoon of the sugar at a time until all the sugar is incorporated and the egg whites form glossy stiff peaks.

13. Scrape out the seeds from the vanilla bean and add them to the meringue with the pistachio nuts, then fold them through using a spatula. In a separate bowl, mix the remaining sugar with the rose petals and set aside.

14. Top the warm pie generously with the meringue, then sprinkle with the rose sugar and put it into the oven for 25 minutes, until the meringue has just started to brown.

15. Remove from the oven and let cool completely in the pan for at least 10 hours. Run a spatula around the inside of the pan and release the spring, then serve.

MANGO & CARDAMOM KULFI

Kulfi is an Indian style of ice cream and something dear to my heart—I'm such a dessert junkie! My father bought me my first kulfi cone from a street vendor in Connaught Circus, Delhi, back in the late seventies and I was hooked.

SERVES 4

FOR THE KULFI
2 fresh mangoes, peeled and pitted
2 teaspoons granulated sugar
Seeds of 1 black cardamom pod, finely ground
1 (14-oz/400-g) can condensed milk
1 cup (9fl oz/250ml) heavy cream
1 extra-large egg white
½ level teaspoon fine sea salt

1. First, make the kulfi. Put the mango flesh into a food processor or blender with the sugar and process to a puree. Put the mango puree into a large mixing bowl and add the cardamom and condensed milk. Using an electric handheld mixer, beat for 3–4 minutes, until you see ribbons in the mixture. Add the cream and continue to beat until you can see the mixer making ribbons again.

2. In a clean, grease-free bowl, whisk the egg white to stiff peaks. Fold the egg white and salt gently through the creamy mango mixture, using a spatula, until all ingredients are combined and you have a thick, sticky mousse. Pour the mixture into a bowl, cover with a dish towel, and put it into your freezer. Let it set for at least 6 hours or preferably overnight.

FOR THE HONEY BRITTLE
Sunflower oil, for greasing
1 cup (3½oz/100g) slivered almonds
2 tablespoons dried mango, cut into long, thin slivers
¾ cup (5½oz/150g) superfine sugar (or the same amount granulated sugar blended in a food processor for 1 minute), plus extra for dredging
1 teaspoon honey
Seeds of 4 green cardamom pods

TO SERVE
1 fresh mango, diced
1 cup (9fl oz/250ml) mango coulis or puree
1 cup (9fl oz/250ml) Greek yogurt

1. Generously oil a large square of parchment paper or aluminum foil. Toast the slivered almonds in a dry, nonstick saucepan over medium heat until golden. Set aside. Dredge the mango slivers in sugar, then put them into a strainer and gently shake off the excess sugar.

2. Put a saucepan over medium–low heat, add the sugar, and let it melt, without stirring, to make a light, golden caramel. Carefully, add the honey. It will spit, so be careful not to let the molten sugar hit you.

3. Continue to cook until the mixture thickens slightly, then take it off the heat. Work quickly now, before the caramel gets too viscous. Add the toasted almonds and mango slivers and quickly mix them together. Carefully but quickly, pour the sugary mixture onto the parchment in a thin layer—the madder the shape, the better! Sprinkle with the cardamom seeds and let cool completely, then crack into shards and set aside.

4. To serve, put a little of the fresh mango dice into four sundae dishes or tall glasses, then add a spoonful of coulis, a dollop of yogurt, and the kulfi. Repeat and finish with brittle shards towering out of the top.

COFFEE EGG FROTH

Stefano is a friend from Umbria, whom I met when I first moved to London, when we were working in a restaurant together. He made this for me after a particularly hard week and the odd night out or two. He promised it would pick me up. It worked its magic and I got through the shift. I often have this coffee with its added spice—although less for its "medicinal" qualities, and more for the simple enjoyment these days.

SERVES 4

4 large egg yolks
4 teaspoons sugar
**Seeds of 2 green cardamom
    pods, finely ground**
**4 double shots hot espresso or
    strong coffee**

1. In a small bowl, beat the yolks and sugar really well together, either with a wire whisk or an electric handheld mixer, until they're light, voluminous, and mousselike—at least 5 minutes with an electric mixer.

2. Add the ground cardamom and mix well.

3. Pour even amounts into four espresso cups, top up with hot strong coffee, stir well, and serve immediately. Simple but "rock-on" effective!

Variation

If you serve this coffee in the afternoon, add 2 tablespoons grappa to the mousse mixture while whisking, then add the cardamom and coffee, as above. Superb!

FAT-FREE MINCEMEAT

This recipe uses no butter or suet; it just relies on the freshest of flavors. You'll really notice the difference. It will keep for up to six months, so don't just reserve it for Christmas mince pies: try spreading it thick on toasted brioche, or use it as a topping for winter-warming oatmeal, or to fill baked apples.

MAKES 6 X 12-OZ (350-G) JARS

½ cup (1¾oz/50g) almonds
½ cup (3½oz/100g) firmly
    packed light brown sugar
2 crisp sweet apples, such as
    Braeburn, cored, peeled, and
    chopped
2½ cups (1 pint/600ml) sweet
    hard cider or apple juice
1 vanilla bean, split lengthwise
1¼ cups (6oz/175g) raisins
¾ cup (4½oz/125g) dried
    currants
1½ cups (8oz/225g)
    golden raisins
⅓ cup (3oz/85g) candied peel
15 dried figs, coarsely chopped
1 cup (4½oz/125g) dried
    apricots, coarsely chopped
12 pitted prunes (dried plums),
    coarsely chopped
3 cooking apples, such as
    Granny Smith, peeled,
    cored, and grated
1 teaspoon Mixed Spice blend
    (page 266)
½ teaspoon finely ground
    black pepper
Finely grated zest of 1 orange
Finely grated zest of 1 lemon
2 tablespoons apple brandy

1. Put the almonds into a small saucepan and dry-toast them over medium heat until golden. Coarsely chop and set aside.

2. Put the sugar and 1 tablespoon water in a large, heavy saucepan. Stir to combine, then heat until the sugar dissolves and starts to simmer. Slide the chopped apples into the hot sugar, being careful not to splash yourself. Stir with a metal spoon until the apple pieces are evenly coated, then let to cook until they've softened slightly. This will take only a couple of minutes.

3. Again, being careful not to cause too much splashing, pour the cider or juice into the pan, stirring all the time you're pouring. It'll sizzle and spit, so be careful of the steam.

4. Scrape out the seeds from the vanilla bean. Slide all the dried fruit into the pan, followed by the grated cooking apple, Mixed Spice, vanilla bean and seeds, and the black pepper.

5. Simmer, partly covered, for 15 minutes or until the fruit has turned slightly pulpy and most of the liquid has evaporated.

6. Remove from the heat and take out the vanilla bean. Let the mixture cool slightly, then stir in the lemon and orange zests, almonds, and brandy.

7. Spoon into sterilized jars (see page 255) and seal. Store in the refrigerator and use within six months.

CHRISTMAS CAKE

This festive recipe is based on my mother's Christmas cake and a Caribbean fruitcake made by a friend. Don't be put off by the amount of alcohol or the length of time the fruit is steeped in it; it's really easy to make and you'll have all the bottles ready for next year; do use the best-quality ingredients. Instead of icing the cake, I prefer to toast the almond paste, which gives a natural look. I might decorate the serving plate with holly and Christmas ornaments. Anyway, this is really fun to make, but remember to give yourself enough time and try not to rush things. You need to start the first step at least one week before you want to bake the cake; once baked, it will keep for at least three months in an airtight container. Good luck and enjoy!

MAKES 1 CAKE, OR ABOUT 24 SERVINGS

TO STEEP

¼ cup (2fl oz/50ml) apple cider or apple juice

4 teaspoons espresso or strong black coffee

A dash Angostura bitters

½ cup (1¾oz/50g) blanched almonds

2 vanilla beans, split lengthwise

1⅔ cups (9oz/250g) each raisins, golden raisins, dried currants

¾ cup (4½oz/125g) sour cherries

⅔ cup (4oz/115g) natural candied cherries, halved

⅔ cup (4½oz/125g) candied orange and lemon, finely chopped

2 teaspoons Mixed Spice blend (see page 266)

½ teaspoon black peppercorns, finely ground

1 pinch sea salt

2½ tablespoons molasses

¼ cup (2fl oz/50ml) each brandy and Grand Marnier

2 tablespoons kirsch

2 tablespoons Madeira or sherry

1. One week before you're going to bake the cake, put the apple cider, coffee, and bitters into a large saucepan. Put the almonds into a small saucepan and dry-toast over medium heat until golden. Coarsely chop, then add to the pan. Scrape out the seeds from the vanilla beans. Add the beans and seeds to the pan. Add the remaining steeping ingredients, but NOT any of the alcohol, checking off each item on the list as you add it.

2. Stir everything to combine, then put the pan over low heat and cover. Stirring frequently, let cook gently for 10 minutes.

3. Remove from the heat, give everything another quick stir, then set the pan aside and let the fruit cool slightly for 1–2 minutes. Pour in the brandy, Grand Marnier, kirsch, and Madeira, and stir once again.

4. Pour the mixture into a large sterilized jar (see page 255) with a lid, or an airtight plastic container. Put the jar in the refrigerator and let rest for seven days, shaking or stirring it from time to time.

5. When you're ready to bake the cake, grease an 8-inch (20-cm) square cake pan, or 9-inch (23-cm) round cake pan, and line it with a doubled sheet of parchment paper, cut so that it comes ¾ inch (2cm) above the top of the pan. Then, measure and cut some brown paper (package paper is perfect) so that it wraps nicely around the outside of the pan. This should be much taller than the parchment paper, about 3¼ inches (8cm) above the top of the pan. Tie in place with kitchen string, and you're ready to start baking.

[Continued]

FOR THE CAKE

- 2½ sticks plus 1 tablespoon (10½oz/300g) unsalted butter, softened, plus extra for greasing
- 1¼ cups (9oz/250g) firmly packed dark brown sugar
- 5 extra-large eggs, at room temperature
- 2 cups (9oz/250g) all-purpose flour
- 2 teaspoons baking powder
- 1 small cooking apple, such as Granny Smith, peeled, cored, and grated
- Finely grated zest of ½ orange
- Finely grated zest of ½ lemon
- 2–3 tablespoons Grand Marnier

1. Preheat the oven to 275°F (140°C). Put the butter and sugar into a large mixing bowl and cream them, together using a handheld electric mixer, until they're really well combined, fluffy, and pale.

2. Add 1 egg to the bowl and beat it into the mixture, then sift in 1 tablespoon of the flour and mix that in.

3. Now simply add the eggs, one at a time, beating each one in really well before adding the next. Sift in the remaining flour and the baking powder, and gently fold it through the batter, using a metal spoon.

4. Put the steeped fruit into a large bowl and remove the vanilla beans. Add the grated apples, and orange and lemon zests. Stir well. Pour the fruit into the cake batter, scraping out every last syrupy scrap, and carefully fold together until everything is evenly mixed. Be sure to use a gentle touch and don't overwork it.

5. Spoon the batter into your prepared pan and smooth the surface with the back of the spoon or with a spatula. Make a slight hollow in the center of the cake, then wet one of your hands and gently, briefly, lightly pat the cake's surface all over. This will help to maintain a smooth surface while it's cooking. Cover the cake with a doubled sheet of parchment paper, laying it gently on the surface.

6. Put the cake pan on the center shelf of the oven and bake for 3½ hours without opening the door. Remove the parchment paper from the surface and continue to bake for an additional 30 minutes or until the center feels springy when you touch it lightly.

7. Remove the cake from the oven and put the pan onto a wire rack. Let it to cool for 1 hour.

8. Prick the top of the cake all over with a toothpick, and "feed" it with Grand Marnier, carefully spooning the alcohol into the tiny holes. Let the cake cool in the pan overnight.

9. The next morning, remove the cake from the pan, leaving the parchment paper around it. Wrap it completely in more parchment paper, then in aluminum foil, and store in an airtight container until you need it. The cake will keep nicely for three or four months or so, all wrapped up.

ALMOND PASTE

2¼ cups (1lb/450g) superfine
    sugar (or the same amount
    granulated sugar blended in a
    food processor for 1 minute)
4½ cups (1lb/450g) ground
    almonds (almond meal),
    plus extra if needed
2 medium eggs
2 tablespoons Grand Marnier
2–3 drops bitter almond extract
1 vanilla bean, split lengthwise
Confectioners' sugar, for dusting
1 large egg white
1 tiny pinch fine sea salt
2 large egg yolks

1. Mix the sugar and almonds together in a bowl. In another bowl, beat the eggs, Grand Marnier, and almond extract, and scrape in the seeds from the vanilla bean. Pour this mix into the almond mixture and stir to a stiff paste. The paste should be really stiff, like marzipan, so add an extra sprinkling of ground almonds, if necessary.

2. Lay a sheet of wax paper on a work surface and dust it with confectioners' sugar. Roll out half the paste on the wax paper, rubbing your rolling pin with confectioners' sugar as you work, to about ½ inch (1cm) thick.

3. Lightly mix the egg white with the salt and use to brush the top of your cake, then turn the cake over and put it on the rolled paste, sticky side down. Gently press the cake down onto the paste. Cut around the cake, leaving a thin border of paste around the edge. Reserve the leftover paste for cutting into shapes later. Set aside.

4. Lift and turn the cake back over and remove the wax paper if it's still sticking to the paste. Use a little of the leftover paste to patch any gaps between the cake and paste, and to make sure the surface is level.

5. Put a piece of string around the outside of the cake to measure its circumference (mark the length with a pen). On another sheet of wax paper, roll out the remaining paste into a strip the same length as your measured string and ½ inch (1cm) thick. Cut it into two equal lengths.

6. Brush the sides of the cake and one side of the two strips of paste with the egg white. Carefully put the two strips around the sides of the cake, sticky side to sticky side. Roll a straight glass against the cake side to smooth it. Tidy up the cake's appearance with your hands, molding it gently until you're happy with it.

7. Preheat the oven to 425°F (220°C). Mix the egg yolks with 1 tablespoon water. Roll out the remaining almond paste to ¼ inch (4mm) thick and cut out some festive shapes with a cookie cutter. Brush the cake all over with the egg yolk mix, arrange your cutout shapes on the cake, then brush them with a little more egg. Carefully lift the cake onto a baking sheet.

8. Put the cake into the oven for 15 minutes or until the paste turns a light nutty brown. Take it out of the oven and put it onto your cake board. Let cool, then decorate the plate with a little holly and maybe a few ornaments. That's it. One beautiful, totally yummy Christmas cake!

Relishes, Chutneys, Preserves & Jellies

THIS CHAPTER IS MADE UP OF SOME FAVORITE RECIPES I'VE MADE OVER THE LAST LITTLE WHILE. If you're wondering which to try first, then I'd recommend the Strawberry, Tequila, and Pepper Preserves; the Clementine, Date, and Chile Chutney; and the Chile, Cilantro, and Lime Relish. That way you'll have something for toast, something for lunch, and something for when you want a fiery kick for your taste buds!

When making preserves or chutney, the trick lies in gauging the setting point. This will come with practice, although I know there's nothing more frustrating than someone telling you, "it just takes practice." You could watch videos of making preserves online, ask an experienced family member or friend, or just try it on your own. It really is simple and even your first experiments will yield good, if not necessarily perfect, results. All the preserves, relishes, chutneys, and jellies can be stored in the refrigerator for the specified time. Look online for advice on preserving procedures as timings can vary depending on the size of your jars and the altitude where you live (see pages 255 and 257).

For my Strawberry, Tequila, and Pepper Preserves, I wanted a hit of perfume to match the fragrant fruit, plus a touch of bite and heat to enliven the sugary sweetness. It is often said that black pepper enhances the flavor of strawberries. While I agree to a point, I don't think black pepper is the way to go. I always prefer long pepper with fruit. I find the sweet acidity of the fruit makes a great match with the subtle perfume and increased heat of long pepper. The additional pepperiness of tequila brings the two flavors together and orange adds a zesty top note.

I use fresh chile in my Clementine, Date, and Chile Chutney to cut across the richness of dates and heavy brown sugar, and the perfumed "ping" of green cardamom to pick up the orange notes. My wonderfully simple Chile, Cilantro, and Lime Relish is all about fresh zing and citrus bite, with an uncompromising hit of fragrant heat. Cumin and mint are an excellent pairing: the cumin works to both "ground" the relish and add twisted citrus flavors to the fresh mint. This relish is wonderful with meat and fish of all types and is particularly good with my Vada Pav potato rolls (see page 183).

Previous page: Lush, pliable vanilla beans, tiny purses full of precious heady aromas. I use vanilla for its creamy sweetness: mellowing the sharpness of rhubarb, emphasizing the sweetness of strawberries.

RELISHES, CHUTNEYS, PRESERVES & JELLIES

Rhubarb Four-Spice Relish

This is great with rich meats, goose, and the like. Freeze some rhubarb from the summer's sweet abundance and bring it out in the depths of winter to make this richly rewarding, simple relish.

MAKES 2LB (900G)

1¾ cups (14oz/400g) firmly
    packed light brown sugar
½ star anise
3 cloves
1 small piece blade mace
1 vanilla bean, split lengthwise
14 rhubarb stalks (about 14oz/
    400g), cut into 1¼-inch
    (3-cm) batons
1 teaspoon Quatre Épices blend
    (see page 266)
4–5 gratings nutmeg
1 long pepper spike, grated
1 teaspoon rose water

1. Put the sugar into a heavy saucepan with 2 tablespoons water. Give it a quick stir to dampen, then put over medium heat and let dissolve gently.

2. Finely grind the star anise, cloves, and mace, using a mortar and pestle. Scrape out the seeds from the vanilla bean. When the sugar has dissolved, add the rhubarb, all the spices, vanilla seeds, and rose water, then stir and cook for 2 minutes. Remove from the heat.

3. Pour into sterilized jars (see below) and secure with the lids. Pasteurize for 20 minutes (see page 257), then remove from the pan and let cool. Store in the refrigerator for three weeks unopened. Once open, keep in the refrigerator and use within one week.

Preserving Basics

It's important to use fresh, good-quality fruit and vegetables that are in season for your chutneys, relishes, and preserves. It's also vital to make sure that your storage jars are properly prepared, sterilized and pasteurized.

For essential advice and detailed instructions on all aspects of home canning, please visit www.usda.gov/.

Preparing
If you're recycling jars (though preserving jars are a better choice), remove the labels, wash the jars and lids in hot water with detergent and thoroughly rinse by hand or in a dishwasher. Don't use any jars with chips or cracks.

Sterilizing
Put the prepared jars, right side up, on a rack in the bottom of a large saucepan. Fill the pan with hot (not boiling) water until the jars are submerged, then boil the jars for 10 minutes. Turn off the heat and remove the jars from the pan with stainless steel tongs. Let dry upside down on clean kitchen cloths. Boil the lids in water according to the manufacturer's instructions. [*Continued*]

Chile, Cilantro & Lime Relish

This zingy, hot, salty, and sour relish is a perfect accompaniment to any broiled, fried, or curried meat or vegetable dish. Keep a jar in your refrigerator to liven up any meal.

MAKES ABOUT 1LB (450G)

⅓ cup (1oz/30g) green Thai chiles
½ bunch (1½oz/40g) cilantro, leaves and thin stems
⅓ cup (½oz/15g) mint leaves
2½ tablespoons cumin seeds, finely ground
20 garlic cloves
Juice of 1½ lemons
Juice of 6 limes
1 teaspoon sea salt
1 teaspoon sugar

1. Put everything into a food processor or blender and process to a paste, or pulp all the ingredients using a mortar and pestle.

2. Pour into sterilized jars (see page 255) and secure with the lids. Pasteurize for 20 minutes (see below), then remove from the pan and let cool. Store for up to ten days. Keep in the refrigerator both before and after opening.

[*Continued from page 255*]

Pasteurizing

Fill the sterilized jars while they're warm; putting hot food into cold jars can cause them to crack—a process known as "thermal shock." Pour the chutney, relish or preserve into the jars, leaving a gap of around ¼in/5mm at the top of each one. Remove any air bubbles by stirring a plastic utensil through the mixture, then wipe the rims of the jars clean. Tightly seal using hermetically sealed lids. Wrap each jar in a kitchen cloth (this prevents them from breaking during boiling), and then line a large pan with another cloth. Place the wrapped jars in the lined pan and add enough cold water to cover them by 1in/3cm. Bring the water to the boil, then reduce the heat to medium and boil for the time stated in the recipe. Turn off the heat, but leave the jars in the water until it is cold. Remove the jars and unwrap, then dry with a clean cloth and label.

CLEMENTINE, DATE & CHILE CHUTNEY

I came up with this chutney recipe to go with rich winter meats, especially fowl and game. The combination of orange and cardamom and the soft texture and depth of flavor from dates and brown sugar make this one of my favorite chutneys.

3–4 clementines
⅔ cup (5fl oz/150ml) best-
   quality cider vinegar
½ cup (4oz/115g) firmly packed
   dark brown sugar
10 plump soft dates, pitted and
   coarsely chopped
2½ tablespoons peeled and finely
   grated fresh ginger
1 red finger chile, seeded and
   finely chopped
Seeds of 1 large green
   cardamom pod, finely ground

1. Over a small plate, gently rub 3 clementines across a small grater to remove their zest, then chop them in half widthwise and squeeze out their juice into a measuring small bowl. You may need the fourth clementine to get the right amount of juice: you need ⅔ cup (5fl oz/150ml).

2. Put the vinegar, clementine juice, and sugar into a saucepan, put over medium heat, then stir and let simmer gently until the sugar has dissolved.

3. Add the dates, ginger, and chile. Stir and lightly squash the dates to combine. Cook for 3–4 minutes, until the dates have softened down and the mixture feels a bit oozy and not too stiff, like honey.

4. Remove from the heat, let cool for 2 minutes, then add the clementine zest and cardamom. Stir well.

5. Serve immediately or pour into sterilized jars (see page 255) and secure with the lids. Pasteurize for 25 minutes (see page 257), then remove from the pan and let cool. Store in the refrigerator and use within three months.

Fat Chile Pickle

This is a really simple pickle to prepare, but should be left in the refrigerator for a least a month before you use it to let the flavors marry and the chiles soften naturally. It makes a wonderfully fruity, salty hot pickle, great with red meats and vegetable dishes alike. In India we'd use Achar (pickling) or Moti (fat) chiles and call it Moti Mirch ka Achar, but I've been using jalapeños for convenience and calling it chile pickle.

MAKES 12OZ (350G)

10–12 large chiles, a mix of green and red, halved and seeded

1 tablespoon black mustard seeds

1 tablespoon fennel seeds, coarsely ground

½ teaspoon amchoor

1 tablespoon sea salt

4 teaspoons English mustard powder

⅔ cup (5fl oz/150ml) grapeseed oil

1. In a bowl, mix the chile halves with the mustard seeds, fennel seeds, amchoor, and salt.

2. In another bowl, whisk the mustard powder with the oil.

3. Pack the chiles snugly into a sterilized jar (see page 255), top with a layer of the mustard oil and secure with the lid. Pasteurize for 20 minutes (see page 257), then remove from the pan and let cool. Store in the refrigerator for a month or so, turning the jar over once or twice a day—whenever you remember.

4. After a month, it's ready to use. Keep in the refrigerator and use within six months.

Strawberry, Tequila & Pepper Preserves

This wonderful preserves is perfect for a twisted take on toast and jelly or preserves.

MAKES ABOUT 1½LB (700G)

1 vanilla bean, split lengthwise
2½ cups (14oz/400g) hulled
    fresh or thawed frozen
    strawberries
¼ cup (2fl oz/50ml) lemon juice
1½ cups (10½oz/300g)
    granulated sugar
Zest of ¼ orange
Butter, for greasing
4 teaspoons silver tequila
A little grating of long pepper

1. Scrape out the seeds from the vanilla bean. Put 2 cups (12oz/350g) of the strawberries into a large, stainless steel bowl, followed by the lemon juice, vanilla bean and seeds, sugar, and orange zest. Stir to combine and let rest overnight.

2. The next day, crush the strawberries with a potato masher, leaving a good few lumps. Put a saucer or small plate into your freezer. Cut the remaining strawberries into quarters. Set aside.

3. Lightly grease a large saucepan with butter, then pour the vanilla-strawberry mix into the pan and put it over high heat. Bring to a boil, then turn down the heat and, stirring frequently, cook until the sugar dissolves.

4. Turn up the heat and boil for 10 minutes, then remove the vanilla bean (scraping it clean) and test the set of the preserves by putting a small dab onto the cold saucer and pushing it with your finger. If it wrinkles, and the channel made with your finger remains fairly well parted, it's ready. If not, put the pan back on the heat for a few moments, then try again.

5. Skim any scum from the surface, then add the quartered strawberries, tequila, and long pepper, and stir through.

6. Decant into sterilized jars (see page 255) and secure with the lids. Pasteurize for 15 minutes (see page 257), then remove from the pan and let cool. Store for up to three months in the refrigerator.

CHILE PRESERVES

A simple recipe that produces a tart-sweet, hot preserves that's great with all kinds of savory dishes. I make it all the time and keep jars on hand for whenever it's needed. The apples provide pectin to help the preserves set. Just make sure no seeds go into the preserves.

MAKES ABOUT 2¼LB (1KG)

2 red bell peppers, seeded and
  coarsely chopped
⅔ cup (3½oz/100g) seeded and
  coarsely chopped red finger
  chiles
⅓ cup (1oz 30g) red Thai chiles,
  seeded and coarsely chopped
16 (1¾oz/50g) dried Kashmiri
  chiles, seeded and finely
  chopped
2 cups (18fl oz/500ml)
  cider vinegar
5 cups (2¼lb 1kg)
  granulated sugar
3 cooking apples
Juice of 2 limes

1. First, sterilize three jars (see page 255). Set aside. Put the red bell pepper pieces into a food processor or blender and process to a smooth paste. Add all the chiles and pulse to form a textured paste. (Alternatively, chop the bell peppers and chiles finely, then pulp them, using a mortar and pestle.)

2. Put the vinegar, sugar, and apples in a large saucepan over medium-high heat. Swirl the pan, but don't stir, and let the sugar to dissolve completely, then pour and scrape the pepper and chile mixture into it.

3. Turn up the heat, bring to a rolling boil, and cook for 12 minutes, boiling all the time, then remove from the heat. Remove and discard the apples.

4. Pour the lime juice through a fine strainer into the chile mixture and set aside to cool in the pan for 30 minutes. Pour or ladle into sterilized jars (see page 255) and secure with the lids. Pasteurize for 15 minutes (see page 257), then remove from the pan and let cool. Serve when cooled completely, or keep in the refrigerator and use within three months.

Mom's Crab Apple Jelly

I first remember discovering crab-apple jelly upon moving to Ireland, and I came across a recipe when I moved into the "sweet" section of the Ballymaloe House kitchens. "Mrs. A," known to everyone else as Myrtle Allen, showed me how to make it; she was great at taking the time with me. Then my mother piped up that she used to make it when my brothers and I were children. So, here's my version: perfect for biscuits, warm brioche, cake fillings, or dolloped on ice cream.

**MAKES ABOUT
3LB (1.3KG)**

2¾lb (1.2kg) crab apples, or
    8 slightly unripe cooking
    apples, such as Granny Smith
½ star anise
½ nutmeg
1 teaspoon coriander seeds
½ teaspoon white peppercorns
2 blackberries (they give the
    jelly a wonderful, warm
    pink color)
Granulated sugar, as needed,
    see method

1. Cut the apples coarsely into quarters, put them into a large saucepan, cover with water, then add the whole spices and blackberries and put over high heat. Let them boil for 20–30 minutes, until the apples have collapsed completely.

2. Remove the pan from the heat, give the pulp a quick stir, then pour and scrape into a jelly bag suspended above a large bowl. (Alternatively, use a large square of cheesecloth. Gather up the corners of the cloth and securely suspend it above the bowl.) Let drip for 8 hours, or overnight. Don't be tempted to squeeze the bag or you'll end up with a cloudy jelly.

3. Pour the juice into a measuring small bowl, note the total volume of liquid, then decant it into a preserving pan or heavy saucepan. Discard the pulp and spices.

4. Preheat the oven to 275°F (140°C). Put a saucer or small plate into the freezer. For every 2½ cups (1 pint/600ml) of juice, measure out 2¼ cups (1lb/450g) of sugar. Put the sugar in an ovenproof bowl and put it into the oven to warm through.

5. Put the preserving pan over medium-high heat, pour in the warm sugar, and stir to dissolve, then turn up the heat. Do not stir anymore, but simply let the jelly boil for 10 minutes. Test the set of the jelly by dropping a teaspoonful onto the cold saucer and pushing it with your finger. If it wrinkles, it's ready. If not, put the pan back on the heat for a few moments, then try again.

6. Take off the heat and pour through a funnel into sterilized jars (see page 255) and secure with the lids. Pasteurize for 15 minutes (see page 257), then remove from the pan and let cool. Store in the refrigerator and use within one month.

BASICS

SPICE BLENDS

It's difficult to be prescriptive with spicing; it's largely a question of trusting your senses, opening your mind, and getting to work. The recipes in this book will provide a good starting point to your own journey. The following recipes are for basic spice blends you'll need for some of the recipes in this book. Use whole spices and seeds, freshly ground. Make up only small amounts of these blends at a time, because they'll be past their best in three months. Keep the blends in an airtight jar in a dark, cool pantry. Each recipe yields varying volume amounts but by weight, 1½–1¾ oz (40–50g) of blend.

• Ras el hanout is a North African spice blend; the name means "top of the shop," implying that these are the spice merchant's best spices, and each merchant makes their own blend. My company's version includes dried lavender, rose, and orange. But it is always a complex mix of at least 20–30 spices and this is one spice blend I recommend you buy from a store.

MIXED SPICE

2 teaspoons allspice berries
1 teaspoon coriander seeds
1 teaspoon black peppercorns
1 teaspoon cloves
1½ teaspoon freshly ground cassia
½ teaspoon freshly ground mace
1 teaspoon freshly grated nutmeg
1 heaping teaspoon powdered ginger

Grind all the ingredients, using a mortar and pestle, or process them in a spice or coffee grinder.

QUATRE ÉPICES

4 teaspoons white peppercorns
1½ teaspoons cloves
1 teaspoon allspice berries
1½ teaspoon freshly ground cassia
½ teaspoon freshly ground mace
¼ teaspoon freshly grated nutmeg

Grind all the ingredients, using a mortar and pestle, or process them in a spice or coffee grinder.

TAGINE

1 heaping teaspoon sweet paprika
1 teaspoon powdered ginger
1 teaspoon powdered turmeric
1 teaspoon black peppercorns
1 teaspoon allspice berries
1 teaspoon coriander seeds
1 teaspoon freshly ground cassia
½ teaspoon green cardamom pods
¼ teaspoon freshly ground mace
4–5 gratings nutmeg

Grind all the ingredients, using a mortar and pestle, or process them in a spice or coffee grinder.

PANCH PHORON

2 teaspoons black mustard seeds
2 teaspoons black onion (nigella) seeds
2 teaspoons cumin seeds
2 teaspoons fennel seeds
2 teaspoons freshly ground fenugreek seeds

Mix the ingredients together in a small bowl.

GARAM MASALA

2 teaspoons black peppercorns
1½ teaspoons cumin seeds
1 teaspoon coriander seeds
1 teaspoon fennel seeds
1 teaspoon freshly ground cassia
1 star anise
1 teaspoon green cardamom pods
½ teaspoon cloves
¼ teaspoon freshly ground mace
12 gratings nutmeg
1 black cardamom pod
1 teaspoon dried rose petals

Grind all the ingredients, using a mortar and pestle, or process them in a spice or coffee grinder.

MOUCLADE

Used for the French mussel dish, mouclade (see page 126), this also serves as a curry powder.

2 heapinf teaspoons powdered turmeric
2 teaspoons coriander seeds
1½ teaspoons cumin seeds
1 teaspoon black peppercorns
1 teaspoon green cardamom pods
½ teaspoon superfine sugar
1 teaspoon cloves
1 teaspoon freshly ground cassia
¼ teaspoon freshly ground mace

Grind all the ingredients, using a mortar and pestle, or process them in a spice or coffee grinder.

Kitchen tips

• Always read a recipe through before you start to cook. Do you have all the ingredients? Do you need to marinate something overnight? However, once you've made it a few times why not adapt it to your own taste: a little more ginger here, a little less garlic there …

• Preparation is crucial: Grind your spices, and measure and chop ingredients so that everything's on hand as you work through the recipe.

• I've created my spice blends to get the balance exactly right, and my recipes often call for ¼, ½, or 1 teaspoon of a spice. Larger mixtures measure ingredients in tablespoons. These are not just rough, "by eye" spoonfuls but accurate measurements:
1 teaspoon = ¹/₆fl oz (5ml)
1 tablespoon = ½fl oz (15ml)
You will ideally need a set of standard measuring spoons—they're inexpensive and metal ones will last a lifetime.

• An electric spice grinder (or coffee mill) is the quickest way to grind spices; a mortar and pestle takes slightly longer, but you can improvise by putting spices in a heavy-duty plastic bag and banging them with a heavy saucepan or rolling pin.

• A food processor or blender is a kitchen essential for many home cooks, but there's usually a way to manage without; individual recipes explain how.

• For grating nutmeg and long pepper, lemon and orange zest, I recommend a Microplane grater: the holes are cut by etching instead of stamping through the metal, which means they don't clog.

INDEX